THE CRIMEAN WAR:
A DIPLOMATIC HISTORY

DAVID WETZEL

EAST EUROPEAN MONOGRAPHS, BOULDER
DISTRIBUTED BY COLUMBIA UNIVERSITY PRESS, NEW YORK

1985

EAST EUROPEAN MONOGRAPHS, NO. CXCIII

Copyright © 1985 by David Wetzel
ISBN 0-88033-086-4
Library of Congress Card Catalog Number 85-70781

Printed in the United States of America

TABLE OF CONTENTS

PREFACE: THE APPROACH

The Crimean war is of unusual interest to the diplomatic historian. It was the first large-scale experience of war by the belligerents since 1815; it was the only war of the nineteenth century that involved all the Great Powers of Europe, Prussia less than the rest; the only war that Great Britain fought in the hundred years between the battle of Waterloo in 1815 and the battle of Mons in 1914.

The results of the war were more decisive still. The war shattered the union of the three conservative courts—Prussia, Austria, Russia—to which the name Holy Alliance still clung; it led to the isolation of Austria; it eliminated Russia as a Great Power in Europe for a generation; it opened the road to the unification of Rumania, Italy, and Germany; it brought about a wholesale reform of the Ottoman and Russian empires. Indeed, as I looked into the Crimean war and the upheavals that it caused, I realized that in many ways it was the most important of all the wars fought in Europe in the century between the downfall of Napoleon and the outbreak of the First World War. Else how to explain the birth of Italy? the chain of events that gave Prussia mastery of Germany? or even the abolition of serfdom in Russia?

The importance should not, of course, be exaggerated. Historians have, under pressure from the dominant French school, come to show an increasing awareness of the economic and social forces that have shaped the destinies of humankind, "les forces profondes," as Pierre Renouvin has called them; and the historian who ascribes too much to one event runs the risk of being written off as hopelessly old-fashioned. Still, with this warning the generalization can stand; and this, I hope, justifies a diplomatic history of the Crimean war in which the attempt is made for the first time to take in all sides.

My aim is to summarize the diplomacy of the Crimean war, to tell a story and to tell it in chronological order. I want to strike a balance, not to attack a point of view; to be stimulating as well as scholarly, pleasant as well as authoritative. For that reason, I have kept to a minimum what is usually considered the sine qua non of historical scholarship: footnotes. Many of my references are explained in the text (for example, "as Palmerston wrote to Clarendon on 4 May 1855"). All the material I have used—archival, books, articles in the learned journals—is described in a considerable bibliographical essay that I have appended to my narrative. Anyone who wants to have a particular page or document number need only write to me in care of my publisher and I shall be happy to oblige by return mail.

I have received much help along the way. I welcome this opportunity of thanking my former colleagues at the University of Chicago and elsewhere for their untiring patience as well as for their criticisms and suggestions, most of which I endeavored to incorporate. William H. McNeill read my entire manuscript three times. He saved me from many errors, queried many of my conclusions, and watered down the dogmatism of my style. A.J.P. Taylor graciously read three of my chapters with critical care and helped me at many points. As a writer, he is my model, and my text is peppered with epigrams that seek to imitate his. In addition, my manuscript has benefited from criticism of one kind or another by Gordon A. Craig, Paul W. Schroeder, Lynn M. Case, and Ann Pottinger Saab; it has benefited from meticulous typing by Helen Bailey and Gloria Valentine and equally meticulous proofreading by Vivian Tow. Dr. Paul Mageli rendered me great assistance by smoothing some of my German translations. I am deeply grateful for all this help so generously given and hope that those who gave it will feel free to criticize the results.

How did the Crimean war begin? And, once begun, how did it end? What were the motives of the statesmen at the precise moment when they signed their respective declarations of war? How did these motives differ, if at all, from the temper of times? At what point, if any, did war become inevitable? At what point, if any did peace become inevitable? What were the implications of the war for the history of Europe and—more remotely—for the history of the world? These are questions of endless fascination, whether considered in terms of the personalities involved or as an exercise in diplomatic history.

The diplomacy of the Crimean war involved the five Great Powers of Europe: in alphabetical order, Austria, France, Great Britain, Prussia, and Russia; and one, Sardinia, a considerable power in the middle rank, which was later to take the lead in the unification of Italy, the sixth Great Power. The diplomacy of each of these Powers had a different character, and historians have often treated them in independent narratives, though the

French side has been rather slighted. I have tried to bind them together and to fill the one hole, to remember that France was the strongest Power to come out of the Crimean war and that Napoleon III was its chief beneficiary.

Otherwise I have written in a straightforward narrative, pausing every so often to replenish my intellectual capital. My book begins with a rough summary of the diplomacy of the great year of revolution, 1848. It looks at the changed relations of the Great Powers as a result of the revolutions and examines the significance of those changes. It then examines the attitudes of the statesmen of Europe on the eve of the Crimean war, attempting to answer the reader's question: how did those attitudes come about? It then shows how those attitudes interacted in the crisis that exploded over Turkey in 1853, how new solutions were unsuccessfully attempted as the crisis developed, and, finally, how war emerged as the tragic result of the collapse of those attempts. It then narrates the diplomatic history of the war start to finish, ending with the congress of Paris of 1856.

I have written in the belief that what is pleasant should also be useful. This book comes as close to accounting for all the diplomatic events in the history of the Crimean war as I could manage within the limits of space and organization. I have been gathering information off and on for the past five years and I have spent two years doing more intensive research in Europe. I express my gratitude to the directors and assistants of the Archive du Ministère des Affaires étrangères in Paris, of the Haus-, Hof-, und Staatsarchiv in Vienna, and of the Public Record Office in London. I have, through the help of Professor Hugh Trevor-Roper, made use of the invaluable papers of the British foreign secretary, Lord Clarendon, at the Bodleian Library at Oxford. And I have come across many important documents regarding French policy in the private papers of the political director of the foreign ministry, Edouard Thouvenel, at the Archives Nationales of Paris.

To be sure, my research has been far from exhaustive, for the quantity of surviving documents—in manuscript as well as in print—is such that even a team of scholars would have not been able to tackle more than a small part of them. But I have at least managed to read all the private papers, letters, memoires, and diaries—both published and unpublished—of the major characters of my book and many of their friends and associates. I have looked at what many of their contemporaries left in the form of printed books, journals and newspapers. And I have taken note of everything I could possibly find that has since been written about my subject by the more recent biographers and historians. I do not write as a partisan of any group or country, though I happen to think that Great Britain and France fought on the right side, and where I make a judgment of controversial topics it is after careful consideration of all the available evidence.

The Crimean war has long been fertile ground for historians. In some ways it had a long background or a long fuse or as that great practitioner of diplomatic history, Pierre Renouvin, would say, "profound causes." It has often been described as a clash of two world ideologies, each implacably hostile to the other. The economic rivalry of Great Britain and Russia has sometimes been cited. The overweening ambition of a single ruler—Tsar Nicholas in most accounts, Napoleon III in some of them—was often emphasized by historians who wrote contemporaneously on the basis of speeches, public documents, and newspaper accounts. The deceitful practices of the western Powers, especially Great Britain and France, have recently bulked large. Diplomats too have not escaped censure. The Crimean war was once widely attributed to the personal diplomacy of Stratford de Redcliff, the British representative at Constantinople, and to the Turkish intractability that was its outcome. On a slightly more academic level, the war was allegedly provoked or at least encouraged by public opinion inflamed by a warmongering press, which made it impossible for the British government to take a conciliatory line towards Russia. Sometimes the balance of power itself has been blamed. The ever-changing system of international relations, it is said, confused the statesmen charged with operating it, and led tragically, even inevitably to war.

All these explanations have some validity. But none alone is sufficient to provide the bird's eye view of the war's diplomacy that has hitherto been lacking. And this is what I have tried to do: to draw the general outline of the diplomacy of the Crimean war. I am a narrative historian. I believe that the chief function of the historian is to answer the question, "What happened next?" In my opinion a work of history misfires unless readers get from it the same pleasure they do from a novel. For that reason, I took it as a compliment when a critic told me: "You worried about your style as much as about your scholarship."

Chapter 1

1848: THE REVOLUTIONS AND THEIR LEGACY

A new era of history opened with the revolutions of 1848. The revolutionary cry, "All change!" thundered across Europe. Virtually every country in Europe, except Belgium, from the Pyrenees to the frontiers of Russia and Turkey was swept by revolution. Virtually every absolute monarchy was shaken or challenged. Virtually every state was given or promised some form of constitution. Virtually every revolutionary on the continent was unshakably convinced that he could bend the bow of Achilles, had hit on eternal truth. All had limitless confidence in the power of ideas. All were inspired by a deep-seated belief in the goodness of man. All imagined that universal happiness had arrived or was just around the corner. Civilization had once been the property of throne and altar; now it was claimed by new nations, new creeds, new visions and new classes.

II

The revolutions of 1848 occurred; they were not made. They were, moreover, universally expected. The rulers of Europe had tried elaborate panaceas and nostrums to stay the flood of discontent that followed the economic crisis of 1846 and the meager harvests of 1846 and 1847. None worked. Respect for traditional forms of authority had everywhere worn very thin, and the ruling circles of Europe had lost faith in themselves. It was easier to pick on superficial explanations of failure such as the vanity and snobbishness of Guizot and the civil servants of the July monarchy or the intrigues of the secret societies in Italy and Germany than to face the real difficulties. But new ideas were knocking at the door of authority and tradition. The rulers of Europe had failed to straighten out their own ideas: their systems of rule had become antiquated and rotten, though these dragged on a shadow existence until the economic misery of 1847 lit the spark that ended their sway.

Revolution erupted in Sicily in January 1848; it spread to France with the Paris revolution of 24 February. Louis Philippe, the king, was chased off his throne by riots; the next day the provisional government that had been set up in his place declared him deposed and France a republic. This was the signal for revolution everywhere. Eighteen days later the revolution reached central Europe. Metternich announced to his wife: "Yes, we are all dead," after resigning as chancellor of Austria on the afternoon of 13 March 1848. He thereupon vanished into the mists of history. His system vanished with him. On 18 March there was social upheaval in Berlin. Frederick William IV, the king of Prussia, was in a panic. He promised solemnly: "Prussia merges into Germany." Uproar followed. The lesser German princes were terrified. They all granted constitutions. Even more important, on 28 May 1848, an assembly of university professors and academics met at Frankfurt to determine the future of the German nation—its structure, its spirit, above all its geographic shape. All the same, this and other developments in Germany were predominantly domestic events. The three great areas of international concern were Italy, Denmark, and Poland; and these three drew the line on which the diplomacy of 1848 unfolded.

Italy exploded first. On 18 March insurrection broke out in Lombardy and Venetia. Revolutionary governments were established at Milan and Venice; and the Italian revolutionaries called on Charles Albert, the king of Sardinia. Charles Albert responded. He felt himself acutely menaced by "the revolution"; rather than become its victim, he determined to become its leader. For this reason Charles Albert declared: "Italy will do it herself"; and declared war on Austria on 24 March 1848. Diplomacy thereupon went into the background on the Italian peninsula.

The frontiers of the new Germany were inextricably connected with two other areas—the Elbe duchies of Schleswig-Holstein and the province of Posen, formerly a part of Poland, which had, since the end of the eighteenth century, belonged to Prussia. Both proved decisive in the outcome of the German revolution. Though under the suzerainty of the king of Denmark, a German sentiment had existed in both of them for a long time. Schleswig, though Danish in its northern districts, was overwhelmingly German in the south; Holstein was German in everything except its sovereign, and—a more ominous point for the future—a member of the German confederation. This situation was abhorrent to Danish national sentiment—also on the loose in this Springtime of Nations. With ingenious perversity, the Danes regarded the duchies as both weak and dangerous and proposed to incorporate both, or most, into Denmark. The estates of the two duchies retaliated in kind. On 24 March 1848 they declared their union with Denmark at an end and appealed to the German confederation for support. Here was the chance for the Prussian government. Frederick William IV determined to make something of it. Like Charles Albert he viewed a foreign war as an opportunity to advertise his conversion to "the revolution." On 10 April Prussian troops marched into the duchies; within a fortnight the Danes were thrown out; by the beginning of May, the Prussian army was poised on Jutland, and within striking distance of the heart of Denmark.

This prospect threw the Great Powers of Europe into high alarm. Ever since the time of Napoleon, ever since the French Revolution as a matter of fact, the Russians had regarded national principle as "the negation of history" since its application would lead to breaches of the international order. Now attempts at national unification seemed successful, and from that moment there was a feeling in the minds of the Russian government that the guns would go off nearer home unless these attempts were arrested. This calculation became vital after the March revolution in Berlin and with it the prospect that German national feeling would avenge the "crime of 1772" and launch a revolutionary war against Russia for the liberation of Poland. The specter of a revived Poland generously stirred the root and branch emotions of the Russian rulers. In the words of Nesselrode, the Russian chancellor: "To repulse an attack by the Poles is to everybody's taste. For that there would be a *levée en masse,* even if this attack were supported by the entire world. But any army sent abroad to restore fallen thrones or to support Germany against France would not be popular here." [1]

Yet Russia far from being provoked was deterred. Why? Because, as Sir Lewis Namier has said, the statesmen and radicals of the revolutionary year were alike convinced that the question of war or peace over Poland—indeed over Europe—lay not in Berlin but in Paris, in the lap of the French government: "How far would reverberations and memories carry France in the sphere of international action? How much of the drama would be restaged?" [2] France, after all, was the mother of revolutions. Everytime she sneezed Europe caught a cold. It had happened twice before—in 1830 and even more in 1789. In 1848 it happened for the last time. After 1848 France caught colds from others. In the revolutionary year the eyes of all revolutionaries were riveted on Paris—the mother of revolution. They were disappointed. For one thing, the French army was not equipped for a foreign campaign. As well, the members of the provisional government were too absorbed by domestic events to worry about revolutions elsewhere. Their main concern once in power was to stay there. This meant staving off more radical revolution at home. They tried to solve this problem by making empty radical noises. Of these the Lamartine Manifesto of 4 March was most important. Alphonse de Lamartine was a poet-historian who had taken over the foreign ministry after the February revolution. To appease radical sentiment in France he issued a circular that announced that the treaties of 1815 had ceased to exist in French eyes. To assuage the anxieties of the statesmen of Europe he announced that France would still be bound by them. The manifesto was primarily symbolic; even so, it was a political stroke of the first magnitude: it touched off revolutions everywhere, and boosted French prestige within radical circles at home.

This was not all. Ideological considerations stood in the way. The two great grievances of French revolutionary sentiment were Italy and Poland; both harked back to the days of Napoleon. In 1848 both proved impossible to aid. Italy was being liberated by Charles Albert of Sardinia: how could revolutionary France assist the aggrandizement of a monarchy? Besides, Charles Albert did not want French help; "Italy will do it herself" was directed as much against France as against Austria—a way of getting the one out without letting the other in. More than anyone Charles Albert knew that he would have to pay a price for any French help; his son had to pay Nice and Savoy twelve years later. Poland presented even greater problems. Italy was just over the Alps; Germany stood between France and Poland. Liberating Poland meant war with Russia; even the most extreme radicals were convinced that France could not fight the tsar alone. The only stroke of the provisional government was a grandiose announcement that the rulers of Russia and Germany should immediately liberate Poland and a solemn, though barren, warning to them that, if they failed to do so, France would launch a war against them—a curious resurrection of the spirit of 1792. Then something extraordinary happened. On 15 May the French chamber was cleared of radicals by the National Guard. Those who attempted to rescue the cause of Poland were pulled down in their turn. Many were arrested; still more vanished altogether. The great cause of Poland died.

All the same, war hung over Europe. Prussia had gone against Denmark; Sardinia against Austria. Neither could be considered merely a dispute between two rational parties. The question of the Elbe duchies, in particular, was disturbing. This question was of an international character. The Elbe duchies had been tied to the Danish crown since the end of the eighteenth century; and this arrangement had been guaranteed by Great Britain, France, and Russia. Surely, the Danes thought, the guarantors would honor their guarantee and, if they did so, would arrest Prussia's aggressive designs: they could not repudiate their pledged word without losing all credibility as Great Powers. There were other, more practical considerations. Prussia's presence in Jutland threatened to bring Denmark to her knees, to push the German

Zollverein up into the peninsula, to give a Great Power control over the entrance to the Baltic Sea. None of these was at all attractive from the British point of view. The British certainly shrank from war with Prussia over Schleswig-Holstein. As on other occasions they were content to threaten Prussia with war from others—from the French, from the Russians, from anyone except themselves.

The French took towards Denmark the same line they had taken towards Poland: they resolved not to be willfully lured into disaster by a foreign war. As well the June days in Paris and the destruction of the revolution by Cavaignac's government sealed the fate of agitated radical sentiment that had once clamored for a foreign war. The Russians too held back. Here again Poland was the decisive factor. Nesselrode raised the alarm that any intervention abroad was likely to incite revolutionary war there and bleed Russia white—not the last time he would lay his agile finger on this prospect. The British were thus landed in an awkward predicament. They did not wish to go to war against Prussia; they dared not leave Denmark in the lurch.

The British were rescued by an unexpected source. Frederick William IV was ashamed of his connection with the Frankfurt assembly; and as the summer of 1848 wore on, he became increasingly convinced that German liberalism would tumble down of its own weaknesses and divisions if it were not propped up by enthusiasm created by a foreign war. In August Frederick William reached a clear resolve: he could pursue the Danish war no longer. The Prussian commander in the duchies, acting on explicit instructions from the king, duly summoned a conference of Prussian and Danish officers at Malmö and worked out an armistice on 26 August. The fighting stopped. German liberalism was indignant. The national assembly protested strongly. This legislative protest failed. A majority of the delegates fell into line and, backed by the force of Prussian troops against the Frankfurt radicals, acquiesced in the armistice on 17 September 1848.

With Schleswig-Holstein out of the way, Italy returned to the center of the stage. For a while it looked as though Sardinia would profit from the chaos inside the Hapsburg empire and eat up the whole of northern Italy. The confused miscellany of septuagenarians who ran the monarchy after the fall of Metternich[3] had their hands full of domestic problems. They were, for all their efforts, at a loss how to forestall the revolution at home, equally at a loss what to do about Italy. They flickered towards concession. After some fumbling, they hit on the idea of granting independence to Lombardy. By this stroke they hoped to embed Great Britain as their ally; convinced as they were that a French attack on Austria lay on the horizon, they thought to escape disaster by offering to give up the bulk of their Italian lands on condition that they got British support for the rest.

The British government rejected this proposal. Their immediate motive was practical: they could not swallow any plan that might disturb their role as impartial mediator. More deeply, they dismissed as hopeless any Austrian case for remaining in control of the north of Italy. They took the view, often to be restated, that Austria could better resist Russia in the Near East and maintain her own existence if she abandoned her Italian possessions than if she continued to cling to them. The object of this policy was to extract from the Austrian government concessions that would satisfy the Sardinians before the French trespassed into Italy and imposed their own solution.

French policy, too, fought shy of Austria, but with a considerable difference. The members of the provisional government were no longer the revolutionary enthusiasts who had toppled the July monarchy. They lived in the present. They wished to settle immediate problems and did not much peer beyond. They dreaded as most of their countrymen did the consequences of Charles Albert's success—a great neighbor. There was estrangement in another way. Charles Albert held Nice and Savoy. These symbolized French humiliation in 1815. Some of the more idealistic republicans in Italy raged against the feebleness of French policy. The government remained unmoved. They resisted any rash step that might increase European tension. Their only practical stroke, hastily improvised in the confused days of May 1848, was to propose that Lombardy and Venetia should become independent and that the Austrians should get out.

This plan was stillborn. In the middle of June Austrian policy at last approached convalescence. Radetzky, the Austrian commander in Italy, defeated Charles Albert at Custoza. In Vienna the mood of the government changed. Victory in battle had done the trick. Resolution took the place of apprehension. The Austrian success virtually eliminated Italy as a storm center in the revolutionary year.

There was a brief epilogue. In December 1848 Louis Napoleon Bonaparte was elected President of the Second Republic. The Sardinian chamber welcomed this development; they expected Louis Napoleon to be more friendly towards Italy than his predecessors. This expectation was to be disappointed. Louis Napoleon's first concern was to establish himself with the rulers of Europe, not to embark on a foreign war; so far as he concerned himself with affairs in Italy, he was concerned and apprehensive over the republic at Rome which had been set up by Mazzini; and the disturbing implications that this presented for his claim to be guardian of order, defender of the faith. The Sardinian radicals did not appreciate this. There was a renewed stir for dramatic revolutionary activity. Charles Albert resumed the war. Once more he was defeated—at Novara in March 1849. This time he abdicated. Hopes for a united Italy crumbled away.

III

The last, longest, and most important phase of the revolutionary era took place in central Europe; and since its outcome is essential to the Crimean war, it is worth looking at closely. The issue was simple: which of the two Germanic Powers, Austria or Prussia, would dominate Germany? The events of 1848 had shattered the Germanic confederation of the Metternichian era. After 1848 Austria and Prussia, hitherto conservative Powers, were both "on the make" in Germany. In 1849 each presented a plan for German unification. The Austrian plan was the work of Felix von Schwarzenberg, the energetic minister who had arrived from Radetzky's lines in October 1848 to take over the chancellery and foreign ministry. Nagged at by Bruck, his minister of commerce, Schwarzenberg developed the "Empire of seventy millions" by which the whole Austrian empire would be embedded in the Germanic confederation. Greater Germany would stretch from France to Russia and thus extend Austria's influence in Europe as never before. Frederick William IV aired a rival project: a "narrower Germany" under Prussia from which Austria would be barred. The Prussian plan foreshadowed Bismarck, the Austrian Hitler. Both were revolutionary; both involved the destruction of the old Germany, yet both came from the rulers of Prussia and Austria. This set them apart from the liberal plans for German unification. German opinion was important only to Frederick William IV and still more to Schwarzenberg as a lever for expanding monarchical powers. For instance, the plan for a narrower Germany had first been suggested to Frederick William by the Frankfurt parliament (April 1849). He had scorned the idea: "I will not accept a crown from the gutter!"

This attitude did not last for long. No sooner had Frederick William repudiated the Frankfurt liberals than he got into his head the idea of uniting Germany by a union of princes—to unite Germany that is, by merging nationalism with the conservative order. In the first months of 1849 it looked as though Frederick William would get his way. The Prussian army had purged Berlin of radicals the previous November. Its victory seemed complete. What is more, Austria was still absorbed by war in Italy and, even worse, by revolution in Hungary, the last seat of discontent in the Hapsburg empire from which her forces had been expelled in April 1849. Here an independent state had come into existence; Kossuth was made governor. Frederick William IV resolved to seize this moment of destiny—resolved, that is, to win the lesser princes of Germany for Radowitz's plan. The rising tide of Frederick William's ambition produced a general reaction against Prussia. His aggressiveness brought down upon him the wrath of Austria and Russia. The old habit of conservative cooperation was indeed a broken reed.

IV

This was a time of great upheavals. Austria was struck down. Prussia dominated Germany. Russia and Great Britain sat tense, on the margin of events, observing and sometimes trying to manipulate them. As with nations, so with men. For some months past Schwarzenberg and his colleagues had wrangled over what had happened in Hungary. Others wrangled too, Frederick William IV most of all. In May 1849 Frederick William at last offered to assist Austria in Hungary; in return Austria would recognize Prussia as a partner—an equal partner—in the conduct of German affairs.

Schwarzenberg rejected the offer. He believed that it was, at bottom, bluff—an ingenious way of forcing Austria to abdicate the mastery in Germany that Schwarzenberg was bent on recovering. There was a more overriding consideration. Tsar Nicholas I finally shook himself free of the policy of restraint to which he earlier had been pinned. Ideological motives entered in: Nicholas I was concerned to preserve the conservative order and to smash the revolution—a danger obviously threatening when Polish volunteers were threatening in the Hungarian army. There were deeper motives as well. In France Louis Napoleon's government had just decided to intervene at Rome; and Nicholas's fear that intervention in Hungary would provoke a French assault on the Rhine could now be waived safely aside. There was fear for Russian economic interest in the valley of the Danube. There was fear for Russian interests in the principalities where Nicholas had sent troops on the first muttering of a disturbance in 1848. The Russian government had no love for Schwarzenberg or his Empire of seventy millions. Most Russian authorities or Germans—diplomats, army officers, journalists—inclined to neither the Austrian or Prussian side. They wished only to push Austria and Prussia back under the old confederation of Metternich's time. In this new world of competition between the two Great Powers of Germany, Russian policy remained what it had always been.

The Hungarian revolutionaries knew that sooner or later they would have to reckon with the tsar. Anticipating a confrontation, they thrashed about for support from Great Britain and France. They had, of course, no success: Louis Napoleon was too busy in Rome to risk war away from home. The same was true in London: the Hungarians supposed that by offering the British economic concessions—for example, the cession of ports on the Adriatic and on the Danube—they could induce the cabinet to intervene at Vienna and St. Petersburg in their behalf. They failed miserably. Throughout the revolution Great Britain never deviated from the position that Austria must be preserved as a Great Power. A triumph of the national principle in Hungary would mean the end of Hapsburg power not only in central Europe, but also in the Near East, where it was a vital barrier against Russia. The Hungarian rebels were thus deserted on all sides. When Schwarzenberg and Nicholas concluded an agreement against them in April 1849, the die was cast; on 13 August 1849 the Hungarian army surrendered to the tsar at Villágos.

Meanwhile revolutionary events had shaken Germany. Frederick William and Radowitz, seeking to profit from Austria's troubles, tried to push through "narrower Germany." In May 1849 Radowitz won the kings of Hanover and Saxony for the Prussian scheme (Alliance of the Three Kings). As soon as Austria had recovered from the trauma of Hungary, Prussia's allies parted company with her. Radowitz, seeing that "narrower Germany" was impossible, tried to salvage at least part of his dream: at Erfurt (January 1850) he developed a "limited union" between Prussia and the small states of central Germany. In May Schwarzenberg answered by summoning the old diet at Frankfurt. The larger German states concurred; Prussia and her allies refused to come. Germany was thus split into two armed camps. At stake was the issue of who would be dominant—Austria or Prussia? An incident in Hesse Cassel in September brought matters to a head: the issue was a trumpery quarrel between the cranky prince of Hesse and his subjects. The prince had originally joined the Erfurt union, but had since switched sides and now wished the confederate army to impose order on his recalcitrant subjects. This posed a considerable problem: part of Prussia's military road lay in Hesse. Great tension followed. The tension was heightened by personal differences. Radowitz had now become foreign minister of Prussia. In office, he resisted all attempts by the cabinet to water down the blunt hostility to Austria expressed in the Erfurt union for fear of losing his grip on Frederick William IV, and indeed argued that the only way to avoid making too many concessions was to make none at all. In October the Frankfurt diet, on Schwarzenberg's advice, mandated the Bavarian army to honor the elector's call for an ultimatum. The Prussian army was mobilized; Schwarzenberg issued an ultimatum. An emergency cabinet session was held in Berlin—

would Prussia go to war with Austria for "Erfurt"? They were set to fight as of 5 November. Frederick William changed their minds. At the decisive moment he came down for peace. Radowitz resigned; and Manteuffel, a man of tradition and conservatism, was given control of foreign policy. On 29 November Manteuffel signed the declaration of Olmütz: Prussia (1) rescinded the order of mobilization; (2) abandoned "Erfurt" and "narrower Germany"; (3) agreed to participate in conferences at Dresden; there the future of post-revolutionary Germany would be settled.

Of course the drama was not confined to Germany alone; like the Hungarian rebels Radowitz and his followers dragged themselves anxiously over Europe, hankering for help. They tried the British. Frederick William had by now thoroughly disgraced himself in British eyes. He had betrayed the German constitutional movement by rejecting "the crown from the gutter"; worse, he had betrayed his word in Schleswig-Holstein. In March 1849, Prussia had once again been taken up by events in Denmark. The Danes had destroyed the armistice, had launched a new war. The pattern of the previous summer was repeated. Great Britain and Russia once again expostulated; and Frederick William was again brought to heel: on 10 July 1849 the Prussians and Danes agreed once more to lay down their arms. This decision did nothing to enhance the standing of Frederick William IV in British eyes. When Radowitz called for help Palmerston shammed reluctance to act without a similar commitment from France. This proved impossible. Though Louis Napoleon welcomed the prospect of playing one German Power against the other, he was taken up with intervention in Rome, and in any case he made French help conditional upon the cession of territory on the Rhine. The Prussian cabinet rejected this proposal.

Radowitz's behavior did not meet with Russian approval. Nicholas I had hit on a device that would solve all problems: Austria and Prussia were to make up their differences and unite against "the revolution"; he would shift his weight on the side of the Power threatened with aggression. This policy might have worked. It broke down on a personal obstacle: Frederick William's romantic infatuation with Radowitz led him to underestimate the depth of the tsar's wish. This was not clear until Radowitz threatened war if federal troops set foot in Hesse. Now Nicholas grasped the simple truth. For Prussia to stop she had to be warned by Russia. On 28 October Nesselrode promised Austria moral support if Prussia resisted federal intervention in Hesse. This was too much for Frederick William IV. He abandoned Erfurt, repudiated Radowitz, signed the Olmütz declaration.

Olmütz was a complete defeat for the illusory schemes of Radowitz. No more and no less. Certainly it was not a victory for Austria, still less a victory for Schwarzenberg. As a matter of fact, Nicholas I was the only gainer at Olmütz. The Russian position was clear: the settlement of 1815 had set up a confederation in which neither Austria nor Prussia held unchecked sway; anything that deviated from this arrangement was unacceptable. Nicholas was fertile in negation. He was contemptuous of those who shaped Prussian policy, especially of Radowitz; he was equally skeptical about Schwarzenberg.

An incident the next year showed this. In the spring of 1851 a conference on German affairs convened at Dresden. Schwarzenberg again proposed that the Hapsburg empire be brought into the confederation. The Prussians set their faces against this scheme, and with them most of the lesser states—not to mention the British and the French. The tsar too was offended: he warned Schwarzenberg that in the event of war Austria would have to make do on her own and that Russia herself might not be able to stay neutral. This turned the trick: Schwarzenberg dropped his plan at once, and, to bury the episode, snatched at a compromise offered by Manteuffel, a secret alliance by which Prussia guaranteed the various lands of the Hapsburg empire. The alliance seemed to leave Prussia and Austria in much the same position as in 1815, tied to each other against "the revolution" and a barrier against France.

This appearance was misleading. The bulk of the Prussian rulers and their more resolute opponents in Vienna had little faith in the new order to which they committed themselves. What is more, though the Russians blessed their alliance, they refused to join it. The patterns of Russian policy were soon revealed. In the spring and summer of 1851 Nicholas I had a series of meetings with Francis Joseph and Frederick William IV. These were curious conjugations. Prolonged and characteristically intricate discussion failed to shake the resolve of Nicholas to meet the two rulers of eastern Europe separately, not together—ostensibly for fear of bustling the British and French into the arms of each other, really because Russia could now afford to evade commitment. The events of 1849-51 had convinced everyone, Nicholas I most strongly, that Russia could defend herself against "the revolution" without foreign assistance.

Chapter 2

THE SETTING

In the summer of 1851 there opened in London the first great international exhibition, intended in the words of the prince consort, its sponsor, to "provide a living picture of the point of development at which the whole of mankind has arrived." European civilization put on its show. There was a great display of mechanical achievements, those of the British most of all. The Great Exhibition sought to show Europe as a single, civilized community—which indeed it was. Reaction reached its high-water mark in 1851. In Germany, a federal execution restored order in Hesse. In Denmark, the petty squabble over succession was settled by Russian dictation in November. On 2 December Louis Napoleon tore up the constitution of France and became dictator. Austria and Russia made up their differences, and cooperated, however grudgingly, at the federal diet. In England, the Whig government fell early in 1852; a Tory one replaced it. Though the despots on the Continent still shook at the turnip-ghost of a new challenge from "the revolution," their thrones seemed safe and sturdy: "reaction seemed to have triumphed; peace to be more secure than it had been for many years."[1]

The happy security of Europe was threatened by some profound forces. The first and most important was nationalism, though it did not seem so at the time. The events of 1849 had sapped the strength of the nationalist movements in central Europe. Many of the militants had been killed; others had fled; still more were driven out. On their heels came large numbers of the lower classes—dissidents who could not stomach the conditions of life in the countries where reaction had triumphed. Even so, the fundamental problem remained, and was indeed exacerbated by the changes that the revolutions of 1848 had ushered in. The Hapsburg monarchy, in particular, was affected. The abolition of the *Robot,* the labor rent, snapped the last legal link between the peasant and the soil. The lives of fifty million inhabitants were forever transformed. The peasants left the countryside and flocked to the towns. This was a tremendous breach with tradition. Its immediate consequence was the increase in the size and number of towns—an upheaval that stunned contemporaries and forced profound changes in their lives and especially in their economic direction. No longer were urban inhabitants isolated from the Continent as they had been before 1848. The old inhabitants of the towns were German; the new inhabitants Czechs and Slovenes. Upstart capitalists and unskilled workers now competed with old-fashioned capitalists and skilled artisans. Social resentment mounted. This eased the path for political conflict. Or rather broadened it. The towns now began to absorb the nationality of the rural Continent. Mass emotions were stirred that the rulers could no longer soften, still less monopolize; and the nationalities began to fight for wealth and power, not for abstract academic doctrine.

As well, tension between the nationalities was sharpened by a new doctrine which appeared in Europe about the middle of the century. Previously theoreticians had invoked "language" or "collective conscience" as the basis of national claims. In the 1850s these fell increasingly by the wayside. "Race" took their place. Joseph Gobineau, a leading writer on national questions, proved, to his own satisfaction at any rate, the biological superiority of the Germans to all other races. In power and cultural prestige they were on the way up and everyone else was on the way down. The Germans seized on this idea and pushed it hard; more and more "race" lurched into the conflict between the nationalities; it deepened the shadow of crisis in those places where the Germans and the "inferior" populations lived side by side— Transylvania, the Tyrol, Bohemia, for instance.

The other force was economic or, more accurately, the outburst of agitation in favor of freedom of trade between nations. The free trade movement was strongest in Great Britain, perhaps because it worked in line with political tendencies. In 1846 free trade conquered the country: the corn laws were repealed, along with the duties on foreign grain. For free traders the campaign was not merely a means to raise British prosperity; it was part of a wider plan for the extension of free trade as an instrument of international peace. The free traders believed that nations, like individuals, served the community best by minding their own business. Though they disliked tyranny and oppression, they shrank from riding out on a crusade of liberation. Universal prosperity was for them a sure path to social and international peace. It was also next door to godliness, if not the same thing. Cobden, their leader, was fond of quoting from the shorter Catechism: "The Eighth Commandment forbiddith whatsoever doth or may unjustly hinder our own or our neighbor's wealth or outward estate." Cobden and his followers believed that free trade was the wave of the future and imagined that the other Powers would quickly switch on the new light. Men would grow rich; national conflicts would be forgotten; war would fall out of fashion, as duelling had done.

This calculation did not work—at any rate not as quickly as expected. Between 1853 and 1855 French duties on iron, coal, and steel were relaxed, though not by much. Elsewhere free trade failed. The British industrialists were taken aback. The golden key seemed to jam in the lock; protective tariffs remained the rule throughout Europe, and the manufacturers in England were left high and dry waiting for the other Powers to switch round.

This was not the case universally. There was one area where British trade had almost free run. This was the Near East. By the convention of Balta Liman of 1838, British commercial interests had wrung from the Turkish government widespread concessions—the right to trade freely in all parts of the Ottoman empire; a special rate on most of the raw materials they bought; and a host of privileges, grants, and acknowledgements that gave them a unique standing among the Powers in economic dealings with Turkey. Afterwards British exports to Turkey soared. Of course this special economic relationship grew quickly in political importance. More than ever it made the independence of Turkey a vital element of British policy. Turkey was a good customer, therefore a good friend. Nor was that all. Friendship with Turkey slipped easily into hostility towards Russia—a sentiment that was reinforced by Russia's rigid tariff policy. In 1850, for instance, the Russian rate on foreign textiles was three times that of Austria's, four times that of the Zollverein. This is a fact heavy with consequences for the origins of Anglo-Russian rivalry in the Near East. It is sometimes said that Great Britain's whole policy in the area is explained by the fact that Turkey had low, Russia high, tariff rates—a line Palmerston once adopted when he presented Turkey as a civilized, high-minded country, worthy of British support. This is a curious argument if only because Cobden, the greatest free-trader of his day, was always a Turkophobe and a Russophile. No doubt the British line in the Near East continued to be dictated by strategic needs—the need to safeguard British preponderance over the Mediteranean routes; to preserve the Ottoman empire as a barrier against Russian expansion; to keep Russian warships behind the Straits. All the same the grievances of British manufacturers against Russia provided an emotional atmosphere that henceforth clouded Anglo-Russian relations.

There were slower, less perceptible changes which were preparing the way for a fundamental upheaval in British policy—changes in journalistic practices, in population, in political structure. These drew the underlying

pattern in front of which policy moved. The press reached its highest point
of influence in England during the 1850s. F. Knight Hunt, a prominent
contemporary noted: "The press is the mistress of intelligence, and intelligence is the mistress of the world"; the newspaper "a positive necessity of
modern civilized existence."[2] This was, no doubt, an exaggeration. There
were as yet few public schools; most Englishmen could not read. Still the
middle of the nineteenth century witnessed a runaway boom in the
newspaper industry. The written word had gone hand in hand with
civilization from the beginning. Now, theoretically, the literate could be better
informed about the world than ever. The abolition of the stamp duty on the
anniversary of the Magna Carta in 1855 cheapened the price of newspapers
and increased circulation. The written, or rather the printed, word triumphed
as never before. Nearly all the major newspapers were identified with some
broad political circle. Great editors thundered out their convictions or
pronounced on public policy in the widest sense. The newspapers were
among the most materialistic elements of a materialistic age. They did not
yet reach the bulk of the population; still, they did much to make public
affairs the affairs of the public.

Apart from this, policy was directly affected by the changes in population
which took place during this period. The change in the British position was
the most startling in Europe. Between 1800 and 1850 the population of the
United Kingdom increased by 71 percent; Great Britain alone increased 92
percent. This increase counted psychologically. Men began to think statisti-
cally in the middle of the nineteenth century; and England's growing
manpower helped to swell national pride. Other factors pushed the same
way. In 1815 less than two thousand people left the British Isles; in 1830
the figure was over fifty thousand; by the late forties and early fifties more
than a quarter of a million emigrants were leaving every year. They went
mainly to the United States and Australia where new opportunities lay
tantalizingly on the horizon. They did not go there merely to learn and to
admire; they went there to lead and to create. The movement of men
transformed the picture of overseas development; as a result Great Britain
secured an emotional as well as an economic tie to distant parts of the world.

On the other hand, conflict was becoming more likely in a vaguer,
emotional way. Combativeness was penetrating political life. Men's nerves
seem to have been on edge in the last two or three years before the war in
a way they had not been before, as though they had become unconsciously
weary of peace and security. This culminated in the storm of indignation that
arose in England against Russia on the outbreak of the Crimean war—an
emotional upheaval with few parallels in modern British history, and none

in the history of Anglo-Russian relations before 1878. In a way almost impossible to define those who had warned against Russia were now listened to where they had been ignored before. Here was a turning point in British policy. What produced it? No doubt many factors: the clashes of ideology between East and West; the effect of economic rivalry; the rise of an anti-Russian press; accidents of personality; accidents of communication; muddled diplomacy; the balance of power—we could go on indefinitely.

There is perhaps one factor that has not been sufficiently explored. In 1850 half the population of England was under twenty-six, a decrease of six and a half years over the average age ten years before. The general effect of this decrease was to make the working population a considerably larger proportion of the whole and, more important, to quicken the national pulse. Nor is this all: in the preceding fifty years there had been an unprecedented growth in population and—more striking still—an equally unprecedented movement from the countryside to the cities. Movement to the city increased between 1841 and 1851 at a rate of 48.8 percent—unequalled before or since. The people who came to the cities did so to escape the tedium of rural life—or so we suppose in retrospect. The city was, above all, a promising Heaven on earth, a blessed avenue of entry upon a better world. Yet life in the city was also risky and uncertain. Competition over jobs, food, and clothing was intense. This added a new dimension to British life. The combative instincts of those who came to the cities were reinforced by the presence of aliens. Xenophobia was created, the more so when the high expectations of the new urban inhabitants were disappointed, or at least not immediately fulfilled.

Of course it would be wrong to exaggerate the importance of the changes in population. The majority of English people could still be described in terms hardly changed from an earlier period. The gentry still followed country patterns, still hunted and fished, still upheld social standards. Workingmen still went to the public house. Prostitution still flourished. The young men who moved to the cities were a new England, shapeless, unplanned; they left their mark on the national conscience all the same.

There is, of course, a factor of fundamental importance in the configuration of international politics. British policy in the Near East had not been consistently anti-Russian before 1853, though it became so afterwards and that as a result of the revolutions of 1848. The defeat of the revolutions with Russian aid had a profound effect on British public opinion. Russian intervention in central Europe at last enabled radicals to wage the fight against tsardom literally. Hitherto the opportunity had been wanting. The struggle against Russia had been popular among intellectuals ever since 1830 and particularly since the Polish insurrection of 1831. It had been little more.

The movement was out of touch with the great body of opinion. There was in England not much appreciation of the Russian menace. Not so after 1848. The revolutions in Hungary and Germany had been battered into defeat by the tsar; and the refugees who poured into England after 1848 identified his success with abject tyranny, an alien conspiracy to destroy civilization.

The agitation against Russia was strong meat for parliamentary debate. The old topics of election reform, income tax, and the ostensibly depressed areas were still alive. But foreign affairs kept breaking in as never before in peacetime. The scope of foreign policy was extending yearly; the business of the foreign office rising dramatically. Dispatches poured in and instructions poured out. In 1830 there were 11,546 dispatches; in 1850, 30,725. Newspapers and weekly periodicals were equally obsessed. More books and pamphlets flowed from the press than at any other time in English history. The arguments and acts of those who cried out against Russia were conducted as much in moral as in rationalistic terms. Most Englishmen tended to assume that Great Britain could lay down the law to Europe. Hence she was free to choose the moral course, and if she did so, this course would triumph.

One moral argument told strongly against Russia, the argument that had been preached by the radicals for the last two decades. Enslaved peoples, yearning for their own liberation, wished to break off the shackles of barbarism and drive Russia back into the steppes of Asia. These passions were now felt by the governing classes. Yet it would be wrong to exaggerate the strength of this sentiment or to blame the Crimean war on the British people. Preoccupation with foreign affairs still affected only the conscious nation: politicians, businessmen, writers and readers of sophisticated journals—" the Ins" as someone once called them. Ordinary men and women had little idea that a European war might be imminent until they were caught up in the crisis over Sinope at the end of 1853; and national participation in public affairs peaked only in the winter of 1854-55, when these affairs went disastrously wrong. Besides, except among radicals, fear of France continued to haunt the corridors of British diplomacy right down to the spring of 1853. Indeed, belief that Belgium, not Turkey, was uppermost in the calculations of British diplomats was the central factor that led Tsar Nicholas into the crisis of 1853, the crisis that led to the outbreak of the Crimean war.

There was, to be sure, apprehension of the disruption in the existing structure of Europe brought about by the revolutions of 1848. The stability that had been attacked in 1848 was a system of principle and design on which British security depended. The revolutions of 1848 had brought Austria to the point of collapse as a Great Power; they had shattered the Metternich system—the system that had been designed to ward off a twin danger: a French advance across the Alps and the Rhine on the one side; a Russian advance into the Near East on the other. This suited the British book, as Palmerston bore witness when he once spoke of Austria as Great Britain's "natural ally." Now this calculation had been broken down. On the one side, France had come out of the storm in the grip of a Bonaparte whose mind harked back to the time of Napoleon I when the French empire had stretched across Europe to the frontiers of Russia and Turkey. On the other, the revolutions in central Europe had been defeated only with Russian aid; this brought the menace of Russia starkly into light. There were deeper factors at work. The revolutions left the British with a sense of moral superiority to the rest of Europe. Most Englishmen believed that their political system was suitable for export and were ready to acknowledge, however vaguely, a mission to rescue Europe from its follies and its tyrants. British procedures and habits of mind would set a pattern for all the world—a curious, belated flicker of the assumption that England alone possessed the secret of civilization. This was not far removed from Cobden's doctrine that all would be well once free trade became universal.

II

For almost forty years after the downfall of Napoleon, France had remained quiet. The only exception was the Eastern crisis of 1840—the exception that proved the rule. The regime which derived from the July revolution of 1830 was roughly the counterpart of the British system following the passage of the Reform Bill of 1832. It is often said that this regime was made up of bankers and speculators. This overlooks its origin. It was a regime of notables, most of whom were property owners even though they may also have engaged in business—much the same arrangement, in fact, that existed under the Bourbons. These men recognized that the greatness of France lay in the past—a greatness to be preserved, not to be advanced. Devoted to property rights and therefore seeking security, they asked only to be left alone. Until the middle of the century they held the field. Then French policy abruptly reversed; and France, hitherto a guardian of the status quo, reverted once more to the revolutionary course.

Why the change? Several explanations impose themselves. In the preceding forty years there had been an unprecedented French advance in the methods of industry and of transport. Industrialists and financiers were on the hunt for new customers and, before the great development of German industry was launched in the middle of the nineteenth century, looked across the Rhine for profitable investments. It is a far cry from this to supposing that they were willing to go to war to secure them. Their object was to wring concessions from the Zollverein tariff union, not to launch France on the path to revolutionary war.

Similarly about Italy. The liberation of Italy appealed to Frenchmen of all classes—more so indeed than the recovery of the left bank of the Rhine. Yet how would the economic interests of France be served by the creation of a Great Power south of the Alps? Railwaymen perhaps thought of grants for new roads; all the same, such men were never a single bloc, a solid lump in foreign policy. They divided over the Italian war of 1859; held aloof over the Mexican adventure of 1867; unanimously opposed war over Poland in 1863. Perhaps the change in French policy sprang from the welling up of public opinion. There were, it is true, Frenchmen who wanted an active foreign policy: soldiers who had fought in the *Grand Armée*; trading-houses in Paris and Marseilles who wanted government backing for their overseas trade; pedantic diplomats who liked to picture themselves in the flattering posture as guardians of the national honor; all those who clung with romantic attachment to Napoleonic France, the great France of 1812. Yet few, if any, desired the destruction of the settlement of Vienna: even in 1848 the handful of radicals who wished to trespass into Italy and Germany were reined in by the masses whom they had just enfranchised. As well, the members of the provisional government knew that France could aid Germany and Poland only by resuming the mastery of Europe that Napoleon had won and then lost; this task was already too much. Hence anyone who seeks to explain the changes in French policy by changes in economic development, social climate, or political opinion does the wrong sum.

The change in French policy sprang from a single source, Louis Napoleon Bonaparte. During his rule as president, prince-president, and emperor of France the map of Europe would be redrawn; and the face of history would be changed.

Louis Napoleon was a remarkable man. His mind teemed with original, often dangerous ideas that were years ahead of their time. These ideas cut across national frontiers; they were European, or rather worldwide in scope. In home affairs his ideas were also new. He wanted free trade, public direction of industry, and a systematic use of credit to promote expansion and full employment. His intellect was enriched by great personal charm. He was maybe vain, moody, solitary, yet, as Queen Victoria once said, a prince among men. He was a beautiful speaker with a ravishing voice and fine turn of phrase. He bewitched Tsar Alexander II and Francis Joseph. Statesmen and monarchs alike succumbed to his magic. There were great political gifts behind the cloud of phrases. He was a skillful and successful negotiator. Though he appealed to the fears of the middle class, he was also a socialist: he did more for the French working class than any other French government before or since; and when he died he was, like Benjamin Franklin, working on an economical stove for the poor.

Louis Napoleon was elected president of France in December 1848. He had run on a ticket of "law and order"; and his election was certainly a defeat for radicals and republicans. All the same the lesser bourgeoisie and peasant proprietors who formed the bulk of his support dreaded a return to the *ancien régime*. Napoleon I had been in their eyes a democratic sovereign, attached inextricably to the principles of 1789; they saw in Louis Napoleon both order and progress. Bonapartism meant balance: no reaction, no revolution. In the final analysis, Louis Napoleon won because his inner complexities had reached a precarious balance that matched exactly the complexities of the national mind. This was but a rare moment. For Louis Napoleon's mind was a tangle of contradictions. Outwardly he was bold, self-confident—an all-wise Caesar of implacable will who was convinced that he would tame hostility between the classes in France and would redraw the map of Europe. In reality he was a deeply emotional man, often weighed down by doubt and much given to tears. He broke down sobbing after his first speech as president and again after the battle of Magenta. He wept when he became emperor and even more when he was overthrown. He was a constant mixture of idealist and conspirator, consistent in only one thing. Or rather two things. He could never resist the temptation to speculate; equally he could never resist the opportunity to manufacture plans—first plans for getting power, then plans for using it. "But he hated the action which threatened to follow these plans. For example, the coup d'état of 2 December 1851 had been planned months before and put off at least twice. When it came to the point, Louis Napoleon hesitated again and might have put it off once more, had not the politicians of the assembly forced his hands by beginning to make plots against him." [3]

There was a further contradiction. Though Louis Napoleon talked ceaselessly to witnesses of every political stripe, he was not given to revealing himself on paper. The correspondence of the great Napoleon runs to sixty-four volumes; that of Louis Napoleon, even if it could be brought together, would not take one. Nor was he more forthcoming in the practical considera-tion of running the country. It was a hard task to be one of Louis Napoleon's ministers. He never learnt to give precise instructions. Walewski, illegitimate son of Napoleon I and later foreign minister of Louis Napoleon, once complained: "The ambassadors see my door open, but they by-pass it; they prefer, in matters of great sensitivity, to deal with the Emperor alone."[4]

In December 1852 Louis Napoleon proclaimed the Second Empire and took the title Emperor Napoleon III. The first whiff of the French empire brought cries of alarm from the Great Powers. The British were first to expostulate: they protested over the "III" of Napoleon's title, then recognized the new emperor without reserves. They were followed by Frederick William IV of Prussia who was in turn followed by Francis Joseph of the Hapsburg empire. Only the Russians hesitated. They had been won by the Austrians for a scheme to greet Napoleon III as a "friend" not "brother"; and they refused to drop the idea even after the Austrians had pulled out. The tsar noted: "Brother! This relationship does not exist between us and Napoleon. The title of 'Brother' can only be addressed to one whose authority is received from Heaven." Some of Napoleon III's advisors were outraged at this offense, and urged him to break off relations with Russia. Louis Napoleon replied: "God gives us our brothers, we choose our friends"; and refrained.

Louis Napoleon had now attained the summit of his ambitions. His title made him the master of France. Yet this mastery was not achieved without cost. As emperor, Napoleon III was not a free agent. He was reined in by the institutions, customs, and legal practices that he inherited from his predecessors, and especially from his uncle. It was hard to distinguish between authentic and sham, between what was genuine and what was imitation; for this reason Napoleon III aroused more unmeasured slander from contemporaries than any political leader since the days of Louis XVI. The popular image of his rule can be expressed in three sentences of Taylor's: "The Second Empire claimed to be Wagner and turned out to be Offenbach—a frivolous echo of the past, not an inspiration for the future. It was the bastard of the great Napoleon in name, in policy, even in men. It was said at the time that, though Louis Napoleon was not the son of his father, everyone else at court was the son of his mother."[5] Yet, at the same time, Napoleon III undertook a vast program for the reform of French institutions in the hope of giving the French people a richer life than any previously known in the history of the world. More jobs, longer holidays, shorter hours, higher wages—these were things he advocated, and worked for. He made Paris what it is—as far as appearance is concerned—the Paris of the great boulevards and the Paris of the operas. He turned the geography of world power upside down by building the Suez canal. He used the plebiscite more skillfully than say, de Gaulle, the twentieth-century figure with whom he has recently been compared.

The contradictions of Napoleon III were shown especially in foreign affairs. He advocated, or claimed to advocate, an entirely new system of foreign policy. He attempted to display this system in various ways: sometimes through speeches—speeches which retain a high reputation for oratory largely because the twists of Louis Napoleon's utterance make it almost impossible to pin down his thought; sometimes through manipulation of the press: he would write an article in *Le Moniteur* anonymous, though signed in every line, advocating a policy and often by implication criticizing his subordinates. He had, however, one overpowering belief: his belief in the power of nationalism. This was indeed the panacea for Europe's ills. Antagonism among the nationalities of Europe was a canker at its heart; remove this antagonism and peace would follow. It was for France to take up the cause of nationalism and discharge her European mission. But how? "By promoting a United States of Europe." Everything in Europe called for unification. More uniform in climate than China, less diverse in religion than India, less diverse in race than the United States of America: a single culture and a common social structure. Self-determination ascertained through a plebiscite was Louis Napoleon's goal; then free nations could live as happy neighbors. Such at any rate were the views which he outlined in *Napoleonic Ideas*—a remarkable little book which was published in 1839.

Championing nationalism had for Louis Napoleon a second advantage: it would open the door to a general revision of the territorial settlement of Vienna. Here was another point from which he never deviated. He said in 1852: "Nations are not thrones and crowns but men; people have a right to assert themselves against masters not of their own choosing."[6] To the kings and dynasts of the Vienna system this sounded like the trumpet of doom. These men played out their lives in the shadow of the Napoleonic wars. They saw in Louis Napoleon's program no mere revision of grievances and defects. Europe which existed on the basis that France had lost the wars was to be rearranged on the basis that she had won. Nor were their fears groundless. In Sorel's words: "His name drove him to dazzle France."[7]

Louis Napoleon liked to suppose that the congress of Vienna had brought France down from her high estate in Europe; on the contrary, this settlement had given her a position of preeminence in Europe and had made her secure. If it were changed France was bound to suffer. Hence Louis Napoleon was constantly driven forward, and yet shrank from the results. Two objects alone he persistently and genuinely pursued throughout his rule: an alliance with Great Britain, and the destruction of the Holy Alliance. Despite his inaction, he could never support the conservative cause when it came to the point: hence his penchant for Italian and German nationalism. Everything else about him thwarts analysis: conspirator and statesman; dreamer and realist; despot and democrat; maker of war and man of peace; adventurer, procrastinator, prognosticator, in the end elusive—a sprite vanishing into the garden.

III

Louis Napoleon despised the conservative monarchies of eastern Europe. As a matter of fact, he was in many ways their kindred spirit, or rather they his. Indeed in home affairs Schwarzenberg and his colleagues were more revolutionary than Napoleon III for they had three hundred years of tradition to wipe away. Schwarzenberg had readily accepted Russian help in Hungary and, later, in Germany and yet determined from the first not to acknowledge the unwritten debt. Quite the reverse, he wished to repudiate it; and astounded the Russians with the confident prediction that Austria would soon amaze the world by the enormity of her ingratitude. Metternich had feared that any European conflict would tear Austria to pieces. Schwarzenberg was eager to escape from the attitude of dependence on Russia into which "the revolution" had driven him, and sought openings for a dynamic policy. Like Louis Napoleon, he despised the treaty system of Vienna and hoped for gains in Germany and the Near East.

Schwarzenberg symbolized the desire of a disgruntled Power to reassert itself. He tried one diplomatic expedient after another. None worked. Austria had been irreparably damaged and weakened by the revolutions of 1848. Schwarzenberg's strokes of policy, which swell the volume of foreign office papers, were belated attempts to salvage something from the wreck. Schwarzenberg carried Austrian policy on his shoulders. These shoulders were broad. But the burden was excessive. Schwarzenberg provided political leadership and inspiration. He never drew breath. In this turmoil of activity, he sought to shake himself free of the tsar. The Holy Alliance, Metternich's policy of conservative solidarity, to which the great aristocrats still clung, seemed a world away. Schwarzenberg had turned Austrian foreign policy upside down.

This revolution was not so fundamental as it seemed at first sight, or as some of Schwarzenberg's critics took it to be. No doubt Schwarzenberg was anxious to assert the prestige of the monarchy abroad. No doubt he thought Austria strong enough to go with a new Napoleon. These impulses soon flattened out. The old restraints flooded back into his mind. War seemed to him an unmitigated disaster. Austria would have nothing to gain by it and much to lose. Schwarzenberg could easily contemplate the harvest of destruction that war would invite. A war threatened to liquidate the system of absolutism which he and his colleagues had erected, to bring "the revolution" in its train, to snap the last link of continuity between the dynasty and its peoples. Schwarzenberg's mind continued to be dominated by the events of 1848 when the Hapsburg monarchy seemed tumbling in ruins. In the end he came away empty handed. Olmütz was his last success. When he died in 1852 Austria was as dependent on Russia as ever.

IV

Of course, Schwarzenberg's policy was more than a personal quirk; it was imposed upon him from without. The Holy Alliance of Metternich's day could not be restored. The old condition for that had been Russian restraint in the Near East. This certainly existed prior to 1848. The new obstacle was the ambition of Russia, or rather Austria's unshakeable suspicion of Russian designs in the Balkans. It had always been something of a conjuring trick to avert an Austro-Russian conflict. Metternich had done it by raising the spectre of "the revolution" before the eyes of the tsar. He had been able to tide over the differences between Russia and Austria for more than thirty years by playing on this fear. Alexander I, more in touch with liberalism and more receptive to new trends and ideas than his successor, believed that after 1815 the Ottoman empire was his for the taking; his ambitions were hamstrung by the revolutionary storms that blew up in Italy in 1821. These convinced him that above all the peace of Europe needed to be preserved, and the congress of Verona, convened in 1822 to take up the question of Greece, turned itself instead into a grandiose intervention against the revolutionaries of Spain. As well, Alexander was held back by a motive of political calculation. A war against Turkey would, in his view, be a war to defend rebels against their legitimate ruler. This calculation was, no doubt, strengthened by the fear of the European uproar that a forward Russian policy in the Near East would produce; still, the calculation was genuine, a triumph for Metternich and the conservatism he personified.

The sudden death of Alexander I in the south of Russia in 1825 brought to the throne one of the most fascinating figures in modern history. Twenty-nine years old at the time he became tsar, Nicholas I presented an appearance of titanic calm, a piece of human nature on a gigantic scale. In the words of his biographer: "With his height of more than six feet, his head always held high, a slightly aquiline nose, a firm and well-formed mouth under a light moustache, a square chin, an imposing domineering set face, noble rather than tender, monumental rather than human, he had something of Apollo and Jupiter . . . Nicholas was unquestionably the most handsome man in Europe."[8]

Nicholas was indeed Nicholas and no one else. Outwardly harsh, resolute, a fire-eater, he was in reality highly strung and apprehensive. Profoundly religious and deeply skeptical of human affairs, Nicholas I tried to solve all his problems by the same means: ever more activity. He was highly conscious of the enormous power that lay in his hands and no wonder. Russia was, at the time he succeeded to the throne, the strongest Power in Europe—the quintessence of the absolutist, bureaucrat state. Her population was half again that of France, almost double that of Austria, and more than double that of Great Britain. Nicholas appreciated his unique position. He piled one position of authority on the other. He tried to exercise that authority intelligently, though firmly. He expected his word to be law, recognized without qualm or question, even by members of his own family, and he would endure no derogation of it. A contemporary opponent of his reign said: "The Emperor Nicholas . . . desires to be obeyed where others desire to be loved."[9]

Nicholas I was, of course, a profound conservative who believed that the system of power he inherited was not to be strengthened by liberal concessions. Quite the contrary. He had been thrust into supreme power against a background of conspiracies culminating in the Decembrist revolts of 1825. The Decembrist revolts gave Nicholas a shock from which he never recovered; and he always supposed that fresh more violent revolutions were only a matter of time.

At home, the combination of terror and loyalty maintained Nicholas's supremacy. He was, after all, the boss, the center of everything. Therein lay his worst fault. Nicholas had, as Grunwald says, "no exact idea of the natural limits of his powers."[10] In the words of a contemporary: "He sincerely thinks himself capable of seeing everything with his own eyes, of hearing all with his own ears, and regulating everything according to his own knowledge."[11]

In the field of religion too Nicholas showed some unique characteristics. He was fully Orthodox. He attended church service every day. He sang in the church choir. He had, nevertheless, a curious sensitivity to other forms of religion—to Lutheranism most of all, perhaps because many of his relatives were of German stock. His religious convictions were, to borrow a phrase from Professor Riasanovsky, "all pervasive, affecting every phase of his life in an important manner. They were consistently and thoroughly applied by the emperor to many complex personal and political problems."[12] Nicholas's religion had another effect. It gave his choleric disposition a settled purpose.

He said once: "I am firmly convinced of the divine protection which manifests itself in my case in too perceptive a manner for one not to be able to notice it in everything that happens to me and here is my strength, my consolation, my guiding light in all matters." [13] Nicholas believed that he was doing God's work in seeing to it that Russia remained strong. This belief he made heavy weather over; it sustained him and drove him on. God was on his side; therefore he could ignore the opposition of men. But this devotion to religion too had obvious dangers. Nicholas always sought for God's providence and he was only too ready to see God's hand in the victories of his own sword and the workings of his own will. God was for Nicholas what the general will had been for Rousseau and was to become for Lenin: the justification for anything he wished to do.

Nicholas I was, in the first years of his reign, anxious not to make any hasty changes in the foundations of foreign policy followed by his brother. All the same there were obvious differences. Like Alexander I, Nicholas recognized and accepted the tie to Austria that existed in the person of Metternich and more formally in the instrument of the Holy Alliance; but neither meant as much to him as to Alexander I. And when it was a question not of this personal tie but of Russia's interests as a cultural and religious phenomenon he was even more his own man. Nicholas I had, deep down, more sympathy than had his brother for Orthodox populations of Turkey and was, as the years passed, more tolerant of an ambitious and essentially expansionary policy in the Balkans and at the Straits. To cite Riasanovsky once more: "While Nicholas I recognized repeatedly the legitimate nature of the sultan's rule in his own domain, he remained uneasy about the sprawling Moslem state which believed in the Koran and oppressed its numerous Orthodox subjects. In a sense, Turkey simply did not belong to that Christian and traditional international order that the Russian emperor was determined to uphold." [14]

The basic theme of Nicholas' policies throughout his reign was always that he alone spoke for Russia, for the fatherland. Were the personal whims of Nicholas I, then, the only thing that determined Russian policy in the middle of the nineteenth century? By no means. There were, to be sure, fewer oscillations at St. Petersburg than, say, at London, but they were there. The professional diplomats were acutely aware of the dangers that a forward policy in the Eastern question would invite and believed, with few exceptions, that religious zeal outran Russian interests and Russian resources. Some of them occupied key positions in the bureaucracy; and it is important to note that Russia was, at the time Nicholas succeeded to the throne, already the most bureaucratized of the Powers with a foreign ministry of over three hundred, as against fifty-five for the French, twenty-eight for the the British. Nesselrode, the foreign minister, was a man of tradition, of restraint, concerned mainly that Russia not fritter away her position in Europe for the sake of the Eastern question. He sighed for the resolute authoritarian of the *ancien régime.* He agreed with his father who had written him in 1805: "Like you, my dear son, I cannot think without horror and without fear of the general development of European affairs in a moment of general crisis such has perhaps never existed before since the world." [15]

Nesselrode's background in diplomacy was elaborate and solid, and when he came to the foreground there was little else. One of the many foreigners in the tsar's service, he was by birth a Baltic German who never learnt to speak correct Russian. A member of the Anglican Church, Nesselrode did not concern himself with the problems of Orthodoxy. Generally regarded as colorless, routine, and unimaginative, he nevertheless became, by dint of hard work, chancellor of the Empire in 1841. Nesselrode looked with contempt upon activist elements in the tsar's entourage and they, in turn, looked with contempt upon him. His enemies—the partisans of war for Greece—blamed him for the vacillations of Alexander I and wrote him off as the puppet of Metternich.

For a while these enemies got their way. Nicholas indeed deserted Metternich and in 1829 Russian armies passed the Danube on the path towards Constantinople. This brought more trouble on Metternich's head than all his previous problems put together. He nerved himself to denounce Nicholas as a traitor to Emperor Francis I; he launched a plan for an Anglo-Austrian alliance, a hint and a shadow of events half a century later. His system was saved by the revolutions of 1830 in France, in Italy and, above all, in Poland. These were Metternich's lightning conductor; faced by them, Nicholas drew back. Besides, the Turks proved a tougher enemy than the Russians expected: even the Russian statesmen decided that Turkey was a European necessity for the time being. Vladimir Kochubei, a member of the foreign ministry, wrote a powerful memorandum towards the end of 1829 in which he argued that "the advantages of the preservation of the Ottoman empire exceed the inconveniences which it presents." [16] The memorandum became the keynote of Russian policy in regard to Turkey for more than a decade. In 1833 the two became full-fledged allies: the treaty of Unkiar Skelessi committed each to assist the other in case of war; a secret article exempted the Turks from furnishing armed support to Russia on condition that they closed the Straits to foreign warships. Sparks flew in western Europe as a result of the treaty. The Ottoman empire had, it was said, fallen unresistingly under Russian control. In liberal and radical segments of British opinion, it was counted great wickedness in Tsar Nicholas to have made the treaty. Later on, during the Eastern crisis of 1853, when the Russian menace seemed more awesome than ever, the moral degradation of Unkiar Skelessi was chalked up to Turkish weakness.

In fact, the treaty of Unkiar Skelessi was a status quo agreement. Nicholas was still looking over his shoulder: he wished to silence the last splutter of revolution which had erupted in the Near East with Mehemet Ali's rebellion in 1832. This, coming as it did on the heels of the European revolutions, led him to exaggerate the threat to "legitimacy," and drove him towards a new bargain with Austria that would consolidate monarchical strength as it had never been consolidated before. In 1833 Nicholas met Metternich at Münchengrätz, coming "as a pupil to a master." The alliance between Russia and Turkey was restored in a double sense: resistance to "the revolution" in Europe; no interference in Turkey. The Austro-Russian agreement operated with great effect during the Near Eastern crisis of 1839-40. Indeed this was in Metternich's eyes the ideal Near Eastern crisis since the threat to conservative stability was France, not Russia; and the seat of upheaval was on the Rhine as well as in the Levant. Insurrection in Turkey seemed linked inextricably to revolution in Europe, as Metternich had preached all along and certainly had Nicholas I not appreciated this connection, he would not have behaved so cautiously, admirably cooperating with England and Austria to prevent Turkey from falling to pieces.

This pattern did not last long. The weakness of Turkey was much in evidence during the crisis of 1839-40, as all observers of Turkish affairs recognized, Nicholas I, in particular, most strongly. All through the 1840s he developed new doubts as to the ability of Turkey to weather another storm, while his recollection of the problems faced by Russia in 1829 rapidly faded away. In the spring of 1844 Nicholas and Nesselrode were in England. They fell into talks with Peel, the prime minister, and Aberdeen, the foreign secretary, over the future of the Ottoman empire. The Nesselrode memorandum which summarized the talks bound both sides to maintain the status quo in Turkey as long as possible and to open discussions if her fall seemed imminent. The memorandum was strictly a personal agreement; it had no constitutional validity. Peel had readily authorized the conversations; but as, in his opinion, no question of policy was involved, he did not inform the cabinet. This did not trouble the Russians. Aberdeen and Nesselrode regarded the affair as a transaction among gentlemen whose word was as good as their bond. For their part, Peel and Aberdeen expected, absurdly enough, that the talks would wave aside all Russian doubts as to Turkey's capacity to survive. The object of their policy, so far as they had one, was to buy time—though without any clear idea what use to make of it. Their immediate object was to satisfy Nicholas's deep-seated love for speculation about the fate of Turkey. Aberdeen, in particular, supposed that he had accomplished this object, and that, as a result of the conversations, the tsar would turn his back on the Eastern question.

The reverse happened. The effect of the talks with Peel and Aberdeen was to convince Nicholas that the Near East could not be crossed off the agenda until the Ottoman empire had been pruned of its European lands—striking example of good intentions or, to be correct, good ingenuity gone wrong. Confusion resulted. As so often, men had negotiated with misleading phrases, had handled false coin. The underlying situation was real all the same—however much the Russians might talk of expanding in the Near East at Turkey's expense, the practical object of Russia's policy for the last ten years had been the preservation of Turkey. The Anglo-Russian exchange of 1844 showed that the Russians were now willing to tolerate, and perhaps even to encourage, Turkey's collapse—a vital shift of emphasis from the line they had taken earlier, and a subject of endless controversy. Some have seen in it simply a preconceived plan by the Russians to overrun the Near East. Others have found in it the ability to recognize the changes which by the middle of the nineteenth century had turned the Ottoman empire into an ossified carcass that was crumbling away overnight. Maybe it was neither. Nicholas I was as able intellectually as any other tsar of the nineteenth century—perhaps not a very high standard. He had played with the idea of partition before—and rejected it. It is possible that his change of mind sprang from the changes that had taken place inside Russia over, say, the preceding fifteen years. One was economic. Since 1830 Russia had been gradually moving her economic lifeline from the Sound to the Straits; the bulk of her exports had shifted from timber to wheat. Between 1832 and 1840 the amount of grain leaving Russian ports on the Black Sea had increased 56 percent. In 1844 Nicholas had ordered the creation of a special commission to consider new ways of securing national wealth. The commission recommended that the Russians thwart the export of grain from the principalities, since it competed with—and often undersold—their own. The recommendation seemed plausible to the government; and Nicholas accepted it without demur. The treaty of Adrianople of 1829 had given the Russians a protectorate over the principalities; and they had long regarded the treaty as an instrument for both political and economic domination. They now operated the latter instrument. However, the officials charged with implementing it were by and large incompetent. They surrendered to local outcry and local obstruction. The amount of reduction therefore fell far short of Nicholas's expectations; and by the middle of the nineteenth century Russia and Turkey were drifting towards overt economic hostility.

Religious changes pushed in the same direction. After all, Nicholas regarded himself as the divinely appointed defender of Orthodoxy. Orthodox sentiments had always counted for something in his view of the Eastern question. They were in evidence as early as 1827 when he cooperated with Great Britain and France to aid the rebels of Greece. During the 1830s they had been overshadowed by "legitimacy," or rather, by the fear of "the revolution." The forties were a different story. In 1843 the Ecclesiastical Academy of St. Petersburg persuaded Nicholas to dispatch several hundred missionaries to Damascus and Beirut. It nagged ceaselessly at him for all kinds of aid—a constant reminder of his role as protector of the church and the obligations which that role demanded. The Christian populations of the Balkans had long groaned under the sultan's oppressive rule, and Nicholas could not be indifferent to their fate. The Slavophile movement, a curious burst of pride in the originality and spontaneity of the Russian people, had swept Russian thought in the previous ten years; and Nicholas could not be indifferent to this either. The tsars of Russia, like all autocrats, were sensitive to the development of public opinion, however limited, within their empires, the more so when they felt at their back the threat of political assassination. They were, as well, seldom anxious that they might be opposed by their subjects if they followed a policy of aggrandizement; they sometimes feared the discontent which threatened to raise its head if they did not.

These are conjectures. No one knows why Nicholas took the line that he did; probably he did not know himself. He was committed to riding two horses: he wished to preserve legitimacy against "the revolution," and yet to champion Orthodoxy. He did not recognize the deep ambiguity between the two—or if he did, it was lost sight of thanks to the revolutions of 1848. The defeat of both national and dynastic revolution in Prussia and the Hapsburg empire boosted Nicholas's prestige as never before. The tsar's intentions in central Europe had been carried through without any difficulties from the western Powers. The abject collapse of the Polish insurrection freed his hands for action elsewhere—not the least of his victories. The Russians could congratulate themselves that they had defeated "the revolution" in Germany without provoking the intervention of the liberal powers. They had a deeper motive still. Russian policy in the Near East was, after twenty years of caution, moving forward once again, of which the occupation of the Danubian principalities in 1848, ostensibly to preserve order and prevent revolution, was only the most recent sign. Nicholas and his advisers realized the fundamental improvement in their position, though they had not

developed any plans for exploiting it. The same deduction was drawn by
Great Britain and France: they realized that Russia had single-handedly called
the tune in central Europe; this roused them against the prospect of a Russian
success in the Near East.

A crisis which erupted in 1849 announced a new direction in Anglo-
French policy. It was over the question of the Polish and Hungarian refugees
who had escaped to Turkey after the collapse of the Magyar revolution. The
presence of Polish generals in Turkey stirred the tsar's invective; he regarded
this as an affront to his prestige and sought to redeem it by demanding their
immediate extradition. Austria, not to be outdone, demanded the extradition
of the Hungarians. The British, alarmed at this splutter of the Holy Alliance,
insisted to the Turks that they resist any interference in their internal affairs.
In part this sprang from genuine liberal sympathy for the refugees, few of
whom wished to disappear into the artificial Hapsburg amalgam. In part, it
sprang from apprehension over the independence of Turkey, that Russia's
occupation of the principalities seemed to infringe. Stratford indeed appre-
hended a bolder line of policy from Nicholas than from Francis Joseph and
urged Reschid, the foreign minister, to stand firm. He was supported by
General Aupick, the French ambassador, and this pressure paid off. On 30
August the Turkish government rejected out of hand the demand for the
extradition of the refugees. Russia and Austria broke off diplomatic relations
in protest. The tsar sent Prince Radziwill on a special mission to Constantinople to warn the Turks that non-compliance might mean war. On 7
October Radziwill had an audience with the sultan and presented a letter
from Nicholas. The meeting of the two put Stratford and Aupick in a panic.
In the usual way of men on the spot, they exaggerated the surrounding
dangers and were convinced that Turkey would give way to the first Russian
threat unless assured of Anglo-French support.

They were too late. The Turks had already pulled out of the affair by
secretly dispatching Fuad Effendi, a master of duplicity, to appeal to the tsar.
Nicholas received Fuad on 16 October. He was genuinely moved by the
sultan's letter which spoke of "your regard for my dignity and your sincere
friendship." [17] He dropped the demand for extradition and thereby solved the
difficulty. Instead he was infuriated by Austria's execution of thirteen
Hungarian generals on 6 October; and readily brushed aside his pro-
Hapsburg feelings. He regarded the wrangling over extradition as a gigantic
red herring, which indeed it was. Fuad and Nicholas worked out a plan by
which over three thousand refugees should be returned to Austria under the
offer of amnesty. Austria, deserted by Russia, had no choice but to accept.

Meanwhile both Great Britain and France had been forced to respond. On 29 September a desperate appeal from Stratford reached London. On 6 October Palmerston won the cabinet for action: the Mediterranean fleet was ordered to the neighborhood of the Dardanelles. More important still was the reaction of France. Though the new foreign minister, Alexis de Tocqueville, urged caution, Louis Napoleon waved his doubts aside. He saw a chance to get on a good footing with the British and instructed the French fleet to follow theirs. On 27 October Admiral Parker, commanding the British squadron, arrived at Besika Bay, outside the Dardanelles. It was at this moment that an impulsive action by Stratford threatened to explode the crisis. Nagged at by Calvert, the British consul at the Dardanelles, he acquiesced in a scheme to bolster Turkish resistance. The convention of 1841 had closed the Straits to foreign warships in peacetime. Calvert hit on the idea of moving the fleet into the Dardanelles. This was, he insisted, compatible with the terms of the convention; besides, it would anticipate any actions by the Russians should Turkey and Russia fall out over the question of the refugees. On 1 November Parker, "finding the wind very strong," entered the Dardanelles up to the so-called Narrows Point. Though he did not pass the Straits, this was clearly a forced interpretation of the convention of 1841. Strong protests were aired in London. Nesselrode warned Palmerston that the Russians regarded the move as a precedent by which the Russian fleet might enter the Bosphorus. This was strong meat. Palmerston knew that the Russian fleet was always close at hand in the Black Sea, the British usually far away in the Mediterranean. He immediately apologized; and Nesselrode regarded this sealing of the Dardanelles as one of the greatest achievements of his diplomacy.

By this time the emotional stir which had blown up over the question of the refugees had quietened down. In fact the question was settled before the British and French had moved. Still the British presence in the Dardanelles had an unmistakable impact on the Turks. They slipped into believing that British resolution, not Turkish duplicity, had caused Nicholas to yield; and as usual events were shaped by what men thought, not by what happened. Reschid was anxious to emulate the Anglo-French cooperation, or rather to outdo it. In November he proposed a defensive alliance to the British. This would, he supposed, arrest Russian ambitions in the Near East. The alliance would commit Great Britain to defend Turkey against "unprovoked aggression"; in return the Turks would promise to reform. Stratford urged acceptance. He said to Palmerston: "Are not the motives for making an exception to the general rule of British policy as strongly now in favor of Turkey as formerly of Portugal?" [18]

Palmerston was unconvinced. He resolved not to allow confused events to bustle the government into a guarantee "either of territory or internal institutions." Turkey must, he believed, reform on her own; this would bring foreign aid in its train. It was perhaps an additional score for the Russians that Palmerston jibbed at exacerbating the tension that Parker had caused by his move into the Dardanelles. Rumor went further. According to this, Reschid's scheme was destroyed by Russian expostulations at Constantinople. This was Stratford's view. Titov, the Russian ambassador, had discovered its existence by the end of the year; and Stratford was convinced that Reschid had been forced by his colleagues to break off once Titov had set his face against it. At any rate, 1849 ended with England and Russia on good terms. Both shrank from stirring up the Near East; both were convinced that they would quarrel if it exploded. The only Russian anxiety was the shadow of the Anglo-French alliance.

The Russian fears were exaggerated. In England there was much distrust of Louis Napoleon; and this distrust was not diminished by the grievances against Belgium which the Bonapartist press was unfolding. In France the decision of October 1849 was not planned policy, only hasty improvisation. Louis Napoleon had tried to make out that it was in the French interest to make an alliance with the British; he was reined in by a hostile assembly, and especially by the men of the Right for whom this project was a sort of "pie in the sky," a delusion. At any rate in 1850 a crisis over Greece blew the Anglo-French alliance sky-high. The Greek question had haunted the corridors of European diplomacy since Great Britain, France and Russia had guaranteed its independence in 1832. The guarantors did not see eye to eye and grappled endlessly with each other to secure the whiphand at Athens. During the 1840s the revolutionary convulsions in Europe washed over into Greece. This was a hint of things to come, a foreshadow of the nationalist revolt of the 1870s when the spirit which had brought Italy and Germany into being would be translated into Balkan terms. The first muttering of the storm had been the attack on the home of a wealthy Jew, Don Pacifico, in 1847. This touched on a sensitive point, for Don Pacifico, though of Portuguese extraction, was born in Gibraltar and was therefore a British subject. Don Pacifico, supported half-heartedly by the British government, put in for compensations. Negotiations dragged out tiresomely. The British were too absorbed by events in Germany and Italy to risk intervention for a cause both remote and unknown. By 1850 they had recovered their nerve. On 11 January Sir Edward Wyse was dispatched to Athens with a ten-day ultimatum that the claims of Don Pacifico be met. When this was refused, Wyse ostentatiously summoned the fleet from Salamis Bay to Athens.

Wyse's move infuriated the Greeks. They at once protested that their independence had been infringed and appealed to France and Russia. The Russian representative, Persiany, was a routine diplomat, incapable of any flight of policy. Thouvenel, the French ambassador, was a man of different stuff—a match for Stratford in diplomatic skill, the equal of Palmerston in high-minded aspiration, and master of all in romantic utterance. Resolute, self-confident, and with great powers of physical endurance, he was determined to redeem the prestige which had eluded France in 1848. Though he began his career as an Orleanist, he quickly became a sincere executant of Louis Napoleon's policy—friendly to Italian nationalism, ready to support Prussia in Germany. Thouvenel had real weight to throw into the scales. He had gained the confidence of the Greek government during his three years as undersecretary and sought to win them for negotiation not resistance. But he did this by the persistent pressure of events, not by threats. He believed with the Greeks that Don Pacifico's claims had been fantastically exaggerated; all the same, he did not believe that the affair was worth a breach with England. On 17 January he proposed to settle the question by Franco-Russian mediation.

The British sheered off at once. Wyse answered with a demand that the Greeks satisfy the claims against them within twenty-four hours. They refused. On 18 January Wyse ordered the seizure of several Greek warships and—more ominous still—instructed the fleet to blockade the southern coast of Greece. This was too much for Thouvenel. He at once sounded Persiany and the two of them demanded that the British abandon their aggressive pretensions. Wyse blustered and presented himself as the victim of a Franco-Russian persecution. This accusation was wide of the mark. Though Thouvenel resented Wyse's bullheaded obstinacy neither he nor, for that matter, Persiany wished to prolong the sordid business any further. On the contrary, they urged caution and delay, hoping that threats would dwindle and inducements would take their place. The bottom fell out of this hope. The effect of Wyse's expostulations was to complete the severance between England and France which Thouvenel thought that the British had begun by their ultimatum of 11 January.

The trouble in Greece took the British and French governments unawares. In France revolutionary policy had not begun. Still Louis Napoleon shrank from antagonizing the British to whom he pinned his hopes for an alliance. This was in keeping with his character. The other Powers had little to offer him. Schwarzenberg might talk of their common interest in restoring order; Nicholas of his sympathy for the republic. Louis Napoleon was unmoved by these words. Great Britain alone offered action, as the events of October 1849

bore witness. Though the British interest in action had been confined to the
Near East, Louis Napoleon viewed this as a prelude to intimacy elsewhere:
an Anglo-French alliance, once cemented, would open the door to treaty
revision in Europe. Palmerston, on the other hand, was afraid that the
"Broadbrims of the Cabinet" would restrain him as they had during his
Italian experiences; but for once the cabinet agreed on a resolute line—the
Don Pacifico affair had become an affront, a challenge to British greatness.
On 3 February, Palmerston diagnosed the situation with Drouyn de Lhuys,
the French ambassador. He denounced Thouvenel as the cause of all their
troubles and unfolded the British grievances against the Greeks. The Greek
rulers were incompetent, corrupt, empty; the ability and policy of Otto, the
king, was fraudulent; his ministers vain, blustering boasters who ruled in a
state of illegality. How could anyone believe in the sincerity of France when
her ambassador was treating them as the equal of England?

Palmerston was delighted with his work. The French agreed to settle the
affair to the exclusion of Thouvenel. A special mediator, Baron Gros, came
racing down to Athens in the middle of February to sort the tangle out. The
French government accepted the principle of compensations; their amount
was to be settled by Gros's mediation. The French had meant to make
reconciliation with England easier; instead they made it almost impossible.
For the divergence between the British and French views, which had been
covered over in February, again rose to the surface as soon as they tried to
fix a figure: the British still trying to push it up; the French impatiently scaling
it down. For six weeks there was a deadlock, nothing. On 19 April Wyse
and Gros conferred again—more wrangling, more accusations, more demands, more evasions. On 24 April Wyse offered to reduce the British claims
by a small amount. This was as far as he would go. He meant to settle things
for good and all and once more screwed up the tension by ordering the
bombardment of the southern coast of Greece if matters were not settled by
noon the next day. On the same day the Greek cabinet met in a state of high
indignation. Far from coercing the Greeks, Wyse's threats fixed them in an
attitude of implacable obstinacy. They refused any compensation for Don
Pacifico until the British paid for the damages they had caused by their
blockade. The negotiations between the British and Greeks became a
competition in blackmail, sensational episodes in a gangster film. The British,
or Wyse at least, threatened to choke Greece to death; the Greeks threatened
to die. The French were, for their part, exhausted. During the negotiations
Gros had been increasingly driven into dependence on Thouvenel, who had
been ordered to keep out of the way. Thouvenel had no new card to play.
On 25 April he advised the Greek government to give way. The Greeks

acquiesced in sulky silence. The affair had ended with a ringing assertion of British prestige.

But there was more to it. While Wyse and Gros had been at each other's throats in Athens, Drouyn had been busy in England. On 3 April he made secret contact with Brunnow, the Russian ambassador, and won him for a deal. The Russians were delighted to play the British off against the French; more, they saw a chance to drive a wedge into the Anglo-French alliance over the Near East that had checked them the year before. The pattern of January was repeated. On 6 April Drouyn brought a solid offer to Palmerston: France and Russia would extract from the Greeks a promise to pay the bill which the British had presented; in return, the British would pay for the damages caused by their blockade. Franco-Russian solidarity cut the ground from under Palmerston's feet; faced by it, he beat a retreat. On 24 April he accepted Drouyn's offer. The French had squared the circle. Drouyn had secured the reciprocity which the Greeks had demanded.

But Palmerston was not yet ready to concede defeat. As on other occasions, he found it impossible to rein in his irrepressible high spirits and groped for a way to pull out of the affair with his prestige intact. He had not yet learnt of the outcome of the negotiations at Athens and in his instructions to Wyse stuck in a rider to cancel the agreement of 24 April if more favorable terms had been obtained on the spot. Wyse jumped at this opportunity. This put the affair on a different footing. What had been an attempt at Anglo-Greek reconciliation turned into an Anglo-French conflict with the Greeks trailing along behind. On 14 May Drouyn was withdrawn from London. Palmerston at once saw that he had overreached himself and drew back. A second convention, modelled on the first, was agreed to in Paris. The Greeks, prompted by the French, accepted it on 21 June.[19]

The immediate crisis was over; the underlying tension remained. The Anglo-French alliance of October 1849 seemed irrevocably dissolved. The British resented the French behavior, especially their collaboration with the Russians that had snatched victory out of their hands. Memories of Tilsit flooded back into their minds. The hardened cynics who staffed the foreign office now talked in terms of security, the need for armaments, and resistance to aggression. The French, on their side, were frightened out of their senses by the militaristic blustering of the British. Only the Russians came away satisfied. The Anglo-French alliance of 1849 had alarmed them; this alarm blew over once the Don Pacifico affair had emptied it of meaning. There was another, more decisive result. Nicholas assumed that he could not achieve his objects in the Near East alone; he would have to bargain with France or Great Britain. The affair over Greece convinced him that he could do business with France, for as Alan Palmer rightly observes: "there was nothing wrong with Louis Napoleon as head of state provided he forgot to be a Bonaparte." [20] But Nicholas assumed that he would be bargaining from strength, the more so because relations between England and France had run downhill. Once more things had worked out to his advantage.

Chapter 3

THE EASTERN CRISIS OF 1853

The Anglo-French alliance was dead. The Russians rejoiced for what took its place was the old apprehension of Louis Napoleon in which they themselves most deeply believed. The shadow of the Second Empire lay across European political life—the system that Louis Napoleon had personally designed, the system that the majority of Frenchmen had voluntarily approved and that all of the Powers except Russia had just voluntarily accepted. Apart from this there were few general worries or pressing alarms. Eighteen fifty-two was the first orderly year which Europe had known in four years. Though the troubles which had caused the storms of 1848 were by no means over, there began a new stability which would, or so it seemed, set the pattern for years to come. Revolutionary disturbances diminished sharply. There were no wars between the Great Powers and—more remarkable still—no coups d'état. For a few months there was an uproar over the independence of Belgium. Louis Napoleon had complained of unfair treatment in the Belgian press and was supposed to be on the march to conquering her. He was held back by the prospect of an anti-French coalition of Europe that an aggressive policy there would surely provoke. Still, the upshot of the crisis was a solidarity against France, a solidarity that the Russians rightly regarded as a score for themselves. The episode, though trivial, was another reminder that Louis Napoleon had real difficulties with the Powers, which he could not always overcome. At least the goodwill to improve relations with "Europe" was clear, though unsuccessful.

In the middle of 1852 there was another danger signal, again from the French side. Louis Napoleon, "in his endless search for prestige," [1] had in 1850 decided to champion the cause of the Latin Christians for control of the Holy Places. One motive for this concern and insistence on the rights of Roman Catholics at Jerusalem was, of course, that it permitted him to divert attention from trouble at home. The Second Republic was on the point of

ıld have liked to proclaim the empire. For that he needed
. ıne clericals who had opposed him in the presidential election
...rs before. Still this was not his overriding consideration. Nothing was
ueeper or more constant in Louis Napoleon than his wish to redeem French
prestige. His uncle had been the representative and culmination of the French
Revolution; when he passed from the scene in 1815 the greatness of France
passed with him. Revolutionary values lost much of their force. Traditional
values took their place. Imperial grandeur went out; monarchy and legitimacy came back. Resolution disappeared. Caution became the order of the
day. So it was until the time of Louis Napoleon. A few radicals dreamt of
restoring French greatness in 1848; the task was beyond them. As early as
1839, three years after the abortive coup d'état, Louis Napoleon had revealed
what a Napoleonic restoration would mean for France. He snatched at the
idea that France was entitled to a place in the Near East commensurate with
her greatness in population, economic resources, and civilization.

Louis Napoleon's attitude cut across forty years of tradition and threatened
to ruffle the calm of Europe; for that reason it ran against the solid opposition
of all conservatives of France. Peace and stability were, these conservatives
argued, the necessary conditions of French greatness. To reorder society
according to the afflatus of one man would be to shatter what gave France
security for the sake of a chilling nightmare—a clear path to democratic
despotism. Though in many ways well founded, these criticisms lost much
of their sting by being yoked to a reactionary ideology; and the argument in
behalf of moving slowly all too often took the form of an argument in behalf
of not moving at all. Still, Louis Napoleon could not ignore their objections.
He calculated rightly that he needed cast-iron support at home if he were to
destroy the treaties of 1815. The clericals had puzzled, since the election of
December 1848, what do to about Louis Napoleon. They had always
identified themselves with the reactionary trend of French politics, the trend
that had produced the French Revolution. In their eyes order came before
progress, and revolution was anathema; but Louis Napoleon, they supposed,
wore a less revolutionary look than many of his contemporaries. Louis
Napoleon, despite his personal ambitions, shared their concern over the
spread of radicalism and sought to show that he could break the drift towards
civil war. The clericals made no secret of their belief that radical teachers
were at the root of France's trouble, and who was Louis Napoleon to disagree
with them? Any fragment of opposition threatened to undermine his grip on
power: this is the reason why he supported the Falloux law of 15 March
1850—as great a happening as any in French history since the signing of the
Concordat between Napoleon I and the papacy half a century before.

Henceforth education fell into the hands of the church; no long\
influence restricted to preaching. The Holy Places offered an even ᴜᴇ\.\
opportunity to pose as defender of the faith.

All the same Louis Napoleon was concerned as much to lay the foundations for a revolutionary policy abroad as he was to drum up conservative support at home. As on other occasions, one hand washed the other. There were, in fact, two motives rolled into one, a combination, or rather a contradiction, of principle. All men harbor contradictions. Louis Napoleon was their embodiment and ultimate victim.

By backing the claims of the Latins, Louis Napoleon lit the time-fuse of a considerable bomb. Russian religious pride was at once outraged. Tsar Nicholas I had long believed himself to be the protector of the Greek Orthodox Church that had, during the last century, gained control of the Holy Places. He was genuinely interested in the future of the Church, to say nothing of the future of his own prestige; and he believed that this prestige would be in difficulties if Louis Napoleon made good. Louis Napoleon would not have launched the debate over the Holy Places but for his desire to put himself on a firmer political footing with the Catholics of France. All the same, he had a good case. Precedent was on his side. In 1690 a firman issued by the sultan had granted the Latins a dominant position in the Holy Places— that is, the churches in Jerusalem, Nazareth, and Bethlehem. Its execution was haphazard; but in 1740 a treaty signed by France and Turkey appeared to give the Latins a decisive advantage over their Greek antagonists. This theoretical gain was soon wiped out: during the last half of the eighteenth and the first half of the nineteenth century the influence of the Greeks mounted steadily. By the 1840s there were signs that both the French and Russian governments were increasingly inclined to side with their protegées.

In particular, Russia's pilgrims stirred: they poured into the Holy Land during the 1840s. The French at first showed little interest. For them the Holy Places were trivialities, interesting only from the standpoint of sentiment, not of pressing national need. Religious conviction was weakened in the France of Voltaire and Napoleon I; and the Restoration governments of Louis XVIII and Charles X were too meek to redress the situation. But the crisis of 1840 turned French eyes towards the Levant. In 1842 the French made their first claim under the treaty of 1740: they asserted their right to rebuild the Church of the Holy Sepulchre. In 1843 the first French consul came to Jerusalem and sought to take the Latins under his wing. The Ultramontane Party pushed Louis Philippe into sending French monks to the Latin monastery.

There was deeper cause for French anxiety. For many centuries the pope had routinely named a patriarch of Jerusalem. That was all. The patriarch was a trival religious functionary with little or nothing to do. He lived in Rome; he did not trouble himself over the affairs of his designated see. In 1847 things changed. Pius IX, elected pope the year before, transformed the office into a reality; the Latin patriarch was packed off to Jerusalem with his blessing. Two years before, Cyril, the newly elected Greek Orthodox patriarch of Jerusalem, decided to take up residence there. For a century the Latin monks had been worsted in the battle at Jerusalem. The presence of a patriarch in the city stiffened their backs. Skirmishes broke out between Latins and Greeks in 1847 and 1848. The Greeks won. The Latin silver star that commemorated the birthplace of Christ was pried loose from a rock and stolen. The French would have liked to intervene. Revolutionary upheaval at home held them back. In 1850, however, Aupick (the French ambassador) delivered the first formal French demand to the Turks: France had certain rights by the treaty of 1740; and these could not be abridged unilaterally even by the sultan's firmans issued since.

Nicholas responded. He at once grasped the full import of Louis Napoleon's demands—a challenge by "the revolution" to Orthodoxy and legitimacy. He liked to make conflicts sharper where his predecessors had sought to smooth them over. He took a resolute line in foreign policy as in everything else. He had long groaned under Turkish drift and delay. He was impatient with words or phrases, whether those of the Turks or all that structure of pacts and treaties on which the French had relied. He disliked equivocation and uncertainty. It was obvious to him as it was to everyone else that France would one day strike a blow against the settlement of 1815; the more so because she was again in the grip of a Bonaparte. Nicholas was buoyed up by the belief that, since he represented the forces of conservatism (or so he claimed), the decision of "Europe" would go his way—that is, the other Powers would join him in resisting Louis Napoleon. His advisers—Nesselrode for one—were content to wait until that happened, and they laid more emphasis on waiting than that it should happen.

The first flush of conflict between France and Russia produced a noisy but not decisive debate. In the eyes of the Turks, the adversaries had much in common; and their confrontation seemed not much more than a passing aberration. Their controversies were marginal, often muddled, and wholly inconclusive. Still the Turks disliked Franco-Russian hostility on their doorstep and sought to contract out of it. France had the advantage that her fleet could demonstrate against Tunis or Tripoli without difficulty. But Russia was closer; she had occupied the principalities until 1851. The Turks' immediate reaction was cautious: a commission appointed to examine the French claims admitted the force of the treaty of 1740, but cited several ancient firmans affecting the matter. Louis Napoleon did not wish to push matters too far: not yet emperor, he sat uneasily in the presidency. LaValette, Aupick's successor, was ordered to behave moderately. The Greeks held exclusive possession of four out of nine holy buildings at Jerusalem; there was joint possession of the others. LaValette proposed that all sacred buildings be held jointly by Latins and Greeks, and swung the bulk of the Turkish ministry behind his plan.

Uproar followed. Nicholas at once objected. He pronounced the French scheme "heinous" and sent a note to Constantinople that snatched the issue out of LaValette's hands. The Turks climbed down. After some fumbling, the sultan decided to appoint a commission to settle the question. Negotiations ran away to deadlock; each side feared that the other controlled the commission and jockeyed for position while the matter was being adjudicated. The commission reported early in February. On 9 February the Turks sent a note to France; a few days later the sultan issued a firman. One document contradicted the other. By the note the Turks granted the Latins two keys to the great door of the Church of Bethlehem; by the firman they gave a secret assurance to the Greeks that the Latins would not be allowed to get through. But the firman was suppressed and thus lacked force of law. The Latins had received keys that could not open a door and the Greeks had been granted a firman that was not legal. Later it was learnt that the firman was merely a draft which had been given to Titov, the Russian ambassador, for inspection and criticism. Titov also had a copy of the French note; and in his revision inserted into the draft firman passages which nullified all concessions that had been given the French. The new firman was proclaimed in the middle of March 1852.

LaValette rushed back to Paris. In early May he returned on the *Charlemagne,* "a ninety-gun screw-driven ship and insisted on its sailing through the Dardanelles."[2] Permission was granted; the convention of 1841 was thus violated. Strong protests were invoked in Paris by England, Austria, and Russia. This did not deter Louis Napoleon. Quite the reverse. In July he screwed up the tension. He demanded the dismissal of the military and civil governors of Epirus; compensation for injuries to French nationals in Antioch; and the surrender of two French deserters who had fled to Tripoli. On 29 July a French squadron appeared in the Bay of Tripoli and prepared to open fire. The squadron quickly deflated Turkish resistance: the Turkish pasha gave way and released the French deserters. The practical control over the Holy Places went to the Latins. The French success was complete.

Such was the situation at the end of 1852. The French victory was the turning point in the dispute over the Holy Places, and it put the Russians in a panic—at once a challenge to their prestige as well as to their policy. On the one side they saw Turkey falling unresistingly under foreign control; on the other the triumph of "the revolution" in the Eastern question. There was a deeper calculation still. Hitherto the Russians had put the European Powers first and the Eastern question second. In the winter of 1853 this pattern was reversed. Nicholas I determined that the status quo in the Near East was intolerable, could be endured no longer. Still, though he wanted Russia to have her way in the Near East, this must be in agreement with the Great Powers, England most of all. Nesselrode and the official diplomats now had a new task. Previously they had devised excuses for avoiding the Eastern question; now they had to arrange things so that Russia could intervene in Turkey without having all Europe against her.

II

Nicholas, looking back, supposed that this would be easy. The new European order that had been created after the downfall of the revolutions of 1848 seemed to work wholly to his advantage. The Austrians had withdrawn into anxiety over "the revolution;" their alliance with Prussia barred the door against France in Italy; the German question, which had threatened to explode into war in 1850, had been settled by Russian dictation at Olmütz and Dresden. By 1851 Russian influence at Vienna and Berlin had reached its high-water mark—more so even than in 1815 when Tsar Alexander's plan to get Poland had been wrecked by the opposition of Austria and the western Powers.

Events ran more strongly on Russia's side in 1852. A coalition ministry had come to power in England in December under Lord Aberdeen; "and he was not merely the man who had listened favorably to the tsar's plans for partitioning Turkey in 1844—much more important, he was terrified of French aggression and of French power."[3] Aberdeen had been terrified by the *Charlemagne* incident. Now Nicholas told him: "The situation has developed as expected. Louis Napoleon is a *parvenu,* anxious for war, eager to embroil Russia and Turkey."[4]

So it proved. Louis Napoleon had tried his method in foreign affairs and it had worked. He had waited until opposition to France was inwardly demoralized and then intervened with decisive effect. Aberdeen was alarmed. Nicholas shared his anxiety. Both were convinced that the peace of Europe would not long survive Louis Napoleon's coming. It was a measure of the mastery which Louis Napoleon had already attained over the opposition at home that on 4 December 1853 he took the title Napoleon III, Emperor of the French. The re-establishment of the Bonapartist dynasty seemed to involve a disintegration of the European unity that had been created at Vienna. There was, particularly in Russia and England, a widespread belief that Louis Napoleon was a gambler who would play for high stakes with inadequate resources; he would not remain content until he had marched to the domination of Europe. In the eyes of the tsar, the indifference felt by the Great Powers over "the III" of Napoleon's title would drive him on. Russia alone held back. Nicholas regarded Henry V, the exiled Bourbon, as the legitimate ruler of France—hence he addressed Louis Napoleon as "friend," not as "brother." No doubt his hatred of "the revolution" was genuine; no doubt, as the champion of legitimacy, he feared the implications of Napoleon III's success nearer home; no doubt he saw that a breach between Russia and the French empire would put up his stock as the defender of European civilization against "the revolution incarnate." His immediate motive was, however, one of practical calculation: he must undo the French success over the Holy Places. He merely wanted Russia to be secure and even to triumph in diplomatic encounters. But he had not yet changed his pattern of general behavior that had somehow kept the Near East at peace for more than thirty years past.

The revolutionary excesses against which Nicholas was guarding were imaginary—or at any rate exaggerated. The coronation of 4 December 1852 had greatly improved Napoleon III's freedom of maneuver. He was not yet ready to take advantage of it. The coup d'état of 2 December 1851 had been a giant step on the road to supreme power; now the journey was completed. Napoleon III had no longer the need for an adventurous foreign policy and would have liked to wash his hands of the Holy Places. For once the drift of events on which he relied turned against him. In December 1852 the Turks had decided in his favor; and his success urged him into public propaganda. He was being pulled hard also in this direction by his Bonapartist supporters for whom the struggle over the Holy Places was a cover for the far greater struggle between tsarist Russia and Napoleonic France. Napoleon III knew well that improved relations with England would bring greater advantages than good relations with the Latin subjects of the Ottoman empire. Already in *Napoleonic Ideas* he had pointed to England as the predestined ally against the Holy Alliance. Now he wished to consolidate his gains and present himself to the British as the savior of France from the atrocities of the radicals. Yet it was harder for Napoleon III to renounce the Latin Christians for England's sake than it was for him to postpone controversy over Belgium and the natural frontiers for the sake of "the legend." Harder for him as leader of the French people: he stood for the restoration of French prestige and dared not renounce his victory once he had got it; harder, too, for him as the man whose claim to a place in the family of European sovereigns had been denied by the tsar. There was also a more rational ground. Russian influence over the Orthodox Christians of the Ottoman empire had been steadily growing; and the tsar's support of the Greeks against the Latins was thought to be pretense for more ambitious aims—a judgment vindicated by events. In the 1820s and 1830s Metternich had pointed to the path of duty and had thwarted the tsar's attempts to stray from it. Now Metternich was gone. Russia abandoned her alliance with the status quo and washed her hands of European affairs. The Russians never contemplated the grandiose design, attributed to them by revolutionaries, of overruning Turkey and establishing an empire across the wide expanses of the Near East. This could not be appreciated at the time. The Near East was vital to France for reasons of tradition and prestige. It harkened back to the early days of Bonaparte; it reminded them of the crisis of 1840 when they had treated Egypt as their private preserve; it had since become an area heavy with French financial penetration. As late as 1853 France still had a priority in resistance to the British and Russians at Athens and in Egypt. When Napoleon III plunged into the controversy at Constantinople, he genuinely supposed that he was in keeping with the tradition of half a century, a tradition from which France could not shrink for the sake of her traditional interests, to say nothing of her national honor.

Of course these considerations did not weigh with the tsar. The dispute over the Holy Places stirred up his doubts as to the capacity of Turkey to survive. Independent Turkey was on her last legs. She had never found self-confidence, though she had not done badly from an economic point of view. Turkish Christians and Turkish Moslems were incurably hostile one to the other; nor were they drawn together even by the threat from "the revolution." The ostensible grievance against the Turks was that they were weak. Their real fault maybe was that they did not strive even harder against their weakness.

In any case the decay of Turkey pushed Nicholas forward. He had kept out of the Eastern question in 1848. Now, with the French triumph at Constantinople, "the revolution" which he had choked to death in central Europe threatened to resurrect more ominously than ever. He appealed to Great Britain for support, and took out of the lumber room the forgotten agreement of 1844. On 9 January 1853 he had with Seymour, the British ambassador, the most famous of his many rambling discussions over the Eastern question from which both the Russians and posterity found it difficult to deduce a settled policy. He insisted that Russia and Great Britain should cooperate in the Near East, and threw out the idea of a partition with Egypt as the British share. Seymour replied gently: "The British government are generally unwilling to enter upon engagements regarding uncertain contingencies."[5] The hardheaded directors of Russian policy did not sympathize with the tsar's speculations. Nesselrode minuted: "The Emperor is too disposed to see matters *en noire* . . . Nations have more vitality than is often allowed."[6] Such subtleties were beyond Nicholas's grasp. In his eyes foreign affairs were something that could be dealt with and then finished, a book to be closed. He supposed that his conversations with Seymour had blunted the edge of British suspicions over his intentions, and brushed aside Nesselrode's advice.

The British almost came up to this expectation. The cabinet were hardly surprised by Seymour's report. After all, it was pretty much what Aberdeen remembered of the tsar's views in 1844, which he had brought to the attention of Lord John Russell (acting foreign secretary) when Russell was prime minister in 1846. Nonetheless, Nesselrode had anticipated the stumbling-block: British interests passed contingencies by. Russell drove home the point in a dispatch of 9 February—a dispatch that defined the policy of the British government as it unwound over the next twelve months. The dispatch dismissed the collapse of Turkey as "a remote contingency"; it asserted that any two-Power arrangement on the subject was not likely to avert war, but bring it on. The last part of the dispatch moved away from the specifics of Nicholas's proposal. It assured him that Great Britain would enter "no agreement concerning Turkey without previous communication with the Emperor of Russia."[7] It also referred to "that exceptional protection which H.I.M. has found so burdensome and inconvenient which is prescribed and sanctioned by treaty."[8] The reference here was unmistaken—a reference to the treaty of Kutchuk Kainardji signed eighty years before.

This was the essence of the situation. Previously the British had avoided discussing the Near East with the Russians so as not to destroy the fragile understanding of 1844; now they had to state their terms. The Russians tried successfully to sound the British. The British tried unsuccessfully to put a brake on the Russians. Russell hoped that this message would bring matters to an end. It did not. In the early part of February, Nicholas called in Seymour; once more he speculated about the situation that would arise if Turkey collapsed: Russia, he said, would have to arm immediately on her Turkish border; this way she could prevent any other Power from gaining the whip hand and, in the event of a general war, get her blow in first. Seymour tried to pin the tsar down: England would be more forthcoming in practical proposals if she knew his intentions in the event Turkey broke to pieces. Nicholas rambled. Seymour marked down Nicholas's answer: no permanent occupation of Constantinople by Russia or by any other Power; no reconstruction of the Byzantine empire by resurrecting a great Greece; "no breaking up of Turkey into little republics—asylums for the Kossuths and Mazzinis so long as I have a man and musket left."[9] Negotiations lagged, then jammed. By March events in the Near East had taken a turn for the worse, and the British had to break off. A myth later grew up, encouraged by the British government, that the tsar was aiming at the destruction of Turkey and that decisive estrangement had followed their refusal to go along. The estrangement was less decisive than the government made out. The British were not aggrieved by Nicholas's conversations with Seymour, except in distant retrospect. Throughout the negotiations there was scarcely a breath of ill temper between England and Russia; and when Russell, in April, raised the first peep of doubt as to the tsar's intentions, he found the rest of the cabinet vociferously against him.

All the same, the Seymour conversations made a watershed in Russian policy towards Turkey. However much the tsar might spin the crystal and sigh for a general revision of the Near East, for the past twenty years he had done nothing to bring it about. Twice before, in 1833 and 1840, he had made plans to reorder the Near East; these were paper schemes, without any solid backing from any class or party; they soon turned to smoke. Nicholas now cast off from his old moorings, and for a reason that is not implausible to advance: he was overwhelmed by the ease and extent of his triumphs during the years of revolution. This, aside from advancing his prestige in Europe, switched his attention to the Near East. Another pull towards it came from developments at home. The Slavophile movement and the call of Orthodoxy weighed with him as they had not done before. The great issues of power and strategy remained; the new issues of nationalism and Slav sentiment, however vague and intangible, cut across them, tempted Nicholas forward. Of course, no one appreciated this at the time, not even the stoutest champions of resistance. Palmerston later made out that he had long been sounding the alarm against Russia; in fact he, like the rest of the cabinet, tugged himself into war with Aberdeen and the Peelites pulling at his coattails: the plans of both sides which appeared aggressive to the other were alike based on fear and had mainly a defensive motive—at any rate in the eyes of those who made them.

III

There is one strong argument against this more or less pacific interpretation of Near Eastern politics: no sooner had the Seymour conversations ended than tension began to mount in the Balkans. A Turkish army had marched to the borders of Montenegro. This at once raised a life and death question for Austria: it was clear to the Austrian rulers that the destiny of the Slavic speaking peoples now trying to break away from Turkish control would excite the attitudes and aspirations of the fellow Slavs who were inside the borders of the Austrian empire—a vital domestic question, that more and more shaped Hapsburg policy and baffled her statesmanship. Count Leningen was therefore dispatched to Constantinople with peremptory orders that the Turkish army withdraw from Montenegro and that the fighting at once cease. Leningen succeeded brilliantly. The Turks had by now run out of steam. They were being pulled in opposite directions by the French and the Russians over the Holy Places and shrank from the prospect of adding Austria to their list of enemies, which seemed, as it was, too long.

In the uneasy sequel to the Leningen mission—the British uncertain of Napoleon III; Austria holding aloof from the Holy Alliance; the question of the Holy Places in suspense—there came a new and infinitely more dangerous alarm. The Leningen mission fired Tsar Nicholas to emulation. He proposed to repeat Austria's success at Constantinople with a mission of his own. Prince Menshikov, "a pure Russian," was selected to redeem the prestige of Russian tsardom. The Menshikov mission was designed to stiffen the claims of the Russians over the Holy Places rather than to provoke a war with Turkey. The main concern of Nicholas was to browbeat the sultan over the Holy Places, as Napoleon III had done over Tripoli, as Leningen had done over Montenegro. The tsar and his advisers believed, with innocent simplicity, that the Menshikov mission would be recognized as a normal operation in European politics—and indeed it might have been had it not become entangled with the Crimean war. It was an accepted convention of the time that Great Powers bullied small ones. But what if the Turks resisted? Nicholas refused to answer, refused even to contemplate the question.

Perhaps a psychological block stood in the way. Others had trembled and cringed before him; and maybe he slipped into believing that he could get his way at Constantinople as he had got it at Vienna and Berlin. Probably there was no deep calculation in sending Menshikov to Turkey, only the recollection of Russia's past achievements and the failure to realize the suspicions which those achievements had encouraged elsewhere. Nicholas supposed that Great Britain would look on with favor if not support; that

Austria and Prussia were safely in his debt; and that France, isolated from Europe, would back down. He believed, deepest of all, that his good faith was on trial. The Holy Alliance had kept the Near East quiet for the last decade; and it suited Russia's interests to keep it so. But Nicholas itched for some dramatic success. It is impossible to tell whether, as he claimed, he was merely seeking to get back the Holy Places for the Orthodox Christians of Turkey, or whether he hoped to outdo the French in bluster and actually to tear down the existing pillars of power in the Near East. The intention did not matter; the consequence could not be escaped.

The psychology of Nicholas determined the shape of the Menshikov mission. It determined as well the instructions which Menshikov was given. These were arrived at hit and miss. For example, he was instructed to demand a protectorate over the Orthodox subjects of Turkey, a privilege allegedly based on the treaty of Kutchuk Kainardji of 1774. It did not become the tsar to read the treaty, despite the expostulations of several of his advisers that he was on weak ground. This did not matter. In the eyes of Nicholas, Napoleon III was the symbol of "the revolution" and he snatched at any chance to undo his success. At the first sign of French protest, Menshikov was to offer the Turks a defensive alliance against France—"an alternative equally unwelcome."[10] Of course, the idea of negotiating "with a sword in one hand and an olive branch in the other"[11] did not seem so inconsistent to the tsar as to his advisers. He never closed his mind to any possibility. He did not, however, regard alliance with Turkey as likely until the question of the Holy Places had been settled. It was perhaps another measure of his distrust of the Turks that Menshikov was instructed to wring from the sultan a *sened* or convention which would guarantee the privileges of the Greek Christians of Turkey. Originally the Russians had supposed that they could secure this by a firman. Now they swung round to the view that a firman would not be good enough. In October of the previous year the Turks had assured Titov that they would not alter the position of the Latins to the detriment of the Greeks. This was a rash transaction, a promise that had been notoriously broken; this is the reason why the Russians believed that a firman would not count for much in practice, the reason why it was struck off the list of Menshikov's demands. The *sened* would, on the other hand, allow the Turks no loophole; it would pin them down, would bind them to their promises. Here was Russia's opportunity. The tsar had made the treaty of Kutchuk Kainardji the basis for his demands on Turkey; he supposed that it, like the treaty of 1740 to which the French had appealed, gave his religious claims a political foundation. The *sened* would confirm this supposition by giving a formal registration to the success of his claims.

The analogy with the treaty of 1740 was not on all fours. The treaty of 1740 dealt with religious concerns; it had no political, nor even practical, validity. Nothing in it bore any resemblance to the protectorate which was supposed to be in the treaty of Kutchuk Kainardji. The demand for a religious protectorate cut across Turkish sovereignty; no matter how much the Russians, and not merely Menshikov, might argue to the contrary. Some ministers, Nesselrode most of all, had some inkling of this and would have liked to take a softer line but, as often happens with Russian ministers, these men ascertained that they were a minority before raising their voices. Orlov, the diplomatic big gun and Turkish expert in the foreign ministry, was called in. Orlov's attitude towards the Near East was clear and simple: he was opposed to any Russian designs there beyond a resolution of her differences with Turkey. He was no doubt the best diplomat in the Russia of his day— a man of high intelligence, vaguely sympathetic to the Turks; he knew something of western Europe, and was not bemused either by Slav sentiment or principles of monarchical solidarity. He was against thrusting Menshikov on the sultan. He pressed for withdrawal from the religious question. Until this moment he had been very much in the tsar's favor, principally because of Nesselrode, and had been trying to win Nicholas's support for moderation. He made no headway. Nicholas was confident that Russia would get her way and was in any case interested only in discussing the prospects of Austria's cooperation. Evidently, however, Orlov's view impressed Nesselrode. For no sooner did Orlov shut his mouth than Nesselrode asked Tsar Nicholas to remove Menshikov and to send Orlov in his place. He failed. There is a simple explanation. A petition, signed by the patriarch of Jersualem, was sent off to St. Petersburg from Constantinople. It pleaded for a "special mission" by a "true Russian" as a demonstration of the tsar's determination to put matters right over the Holy Places. Nicholas could not refuse this appeal for fear of public outcry. Nor did he want to. He was used to getting his way by force, or the threat of force, and was concerned to express, more ostentatiously than ever, his support for the cause of Orthodoxy. Orlov was therefore ruled out. Menshikov remained in. At bottom Orlov's pleas for caution were more than an expression of his personality. They reflected the genuine Russian desire to succeed at Constantinople without a war, and the contradiction between this desire and the demands that Russia proposed to make upon Turkey. Orlov might talk of the value of conciliation. The prestige of the Russian army and the psychology of the tsar's mind made this impossible. Nicholas assured Orlov that Menshikov's demands could be modified if the Turks rejected them, or if foreign reaction proved too strong; but he was confident that no resistance would follow.

In the first draft of his instructions, Nesselrode had suggested "a wide latitude by turns friendly and threatening as upon the nature of the terms possible to accept."[12] There was a curious contradiction in Nesselrode between aims and methods. His aim was change, to destroy the French success over the Holy Places; his method was patience. Unlike Nicholas, he was a master at the game of waiting. He never plunged into a controversy without carefully examining all of its aspects. He preferred to wait until all the forces opposing Russia had been sapped by their own confusion and themselves brought success unto her. He had successfully applied this method in dealing with the revolutions of 1848. Now he resolved to try it again. Apart from cautiousness there was perhaps most of all in Nesselrode a deep but unavowed belief that the Holy Places were not worth a war. In that case, why send Menshikov at all? Nesselrode seemed to be advocating a new Russian line towards Turkey and something more. As a Protestant, he was judged by the tsar to be an amateur in dispute over the Holy Places. If the Menshikov mission were called off or—a more likely prospect—if Russia's demands on Turkey were scaled down, the chances for a diplomatic solution to the crisis would correspondingly improve. In Nesselrode's opposition to rigidity and flamboyance, there was a deeper political purpose that rested on a clear-cut analysis of the Eastern question. In a sentence, he wanted to restore Russian prestige at Constantinople without a breach with Turkey. Obviously he wanted to restore the Orthodox Greeks to the position which they had held before the French entered the field. Equally, though less obviously, he wanted to preserve good relations with the Powers of Europe, especially with England, and this could be done only by purging the Russian demands of their political taint.

Menshikov would have none of this policy. He had been against moderation from the start and was not likely to change now. He rarely listened to Nesselrode, still less to the advice of ambassadors. He was convinced that he had taken the measure of all diplomats, Russian and foreign, and that their nerve would crumble before his did. He did not even suppose that he needed to present the Turks with a list of precise demands. He would make one dramatic appearance, announce that he was dissatisfied, and then wait for the concessions to pour into his lap, merely holding out his hand for more. Nesselrode, with his usual gift of seeing both sides, objected to this approach; it would, he argued, be a grave blow to the hope of settling the dispute without estranging "Europe." Orlov objected also. Nicholas himself said: "It would be unfortunate to act so as to give the foreign governments the impression that we are pushing Turkey to one side."[13] No steps were taken to remove this impression. None was thought necessary. In the eyes of the tsar, the sultan was an unscrupulous and savage dictator; his armies were in chaos; his political system likely to collapse at first strain. Turkey needed protection. This calculation was near enough to the truth to bring her within an ace of disaster.

Menshikov supposed that the Turks would give him no trouble: "there were rumors of mobilization in southern Russia and a flamboyant review of the Russian fleet at Sebastopol." [14] He arrived in Constantinople on 28 February 1853 on the *Thunderer,* a prize Russian warship, along with two personal adjutants of the tsar. His estimate of Turkish strength was, as usual, entirely unflattering. There was not much astuteness or mental agility in his condescending behavior. On 2 March he went to see Mehemet Ali, the grand vizier. He wore a frock coat instead of the customary uniform of lace and stars. This was a dramatic gesture. There was more to follow. According to ancient practice, ambassadors to the Porte were received in the apartment of the foreign minister and by him taken and presented to the grand vizier. But the present foreign minister was Fuad pasha who had got the sultan to break his word over the Holy Places. Fuad was a symbol of Turkish duplicity. Nicholas despised him. He determined that there could be no softening in the relations of Russia and Turkey while Fuad was in office. Menshikov therefore bypassed Fuad and went unannounced and unaccompanied to the office of Mehemet Ali. The incident was a showpiece of Menshikov's personality. He was impatient enough with the sultan's ministers for whom ceremony and protocol were stock-in-trade; but he shrugged this off as the ineradicable effect of Turkish backwardness. He resolved to push to the full his weapon of the personal approach. He said to the Dutch ambassador: "Against Orientals the best cards should be played immediately. A few hours always decide the fate of policy." [15]

Fuad resigned at once. This tempted Menshikov forward. He had fired the first shot against the sultan's ministry. Now he determined to finish it off. The Turks were in no position to resist. Apart from the crisis over the Holy Places, they were faced by other, seemingly insoluble questions—insurrection in Montenegro; a threatened coup d'état in Serbia. They could never forget that while Menshikov's stories of Russian military preparations made them tremble, their authority in the Balkans was threatening to collapse; and while they feared Russia much, the reformers of the Tanzimat era, who formed the bulk of the Grand Council, feared "the revolution" in Europe more. As well, they had been flattered to be Russia's ally in 1833; it was a very different matter to act merely as advance guard for a combine between Russia and their dissident subjects in the Balkans. Rifat pasha, Fuad's successor, always possessed complete self-confidence, though not much else. He had been a disciple of Metternich; and he supposed that he could play Russia off against Austria, the more so because of the peaceful resolution of the Leningen mission. This was to misread Menshikov's personality. A check, if not a humiliation of Turkey, was the essential aim of his mission. A tame ending to the crisis was unwelcome to him.

Political developments were now playing into Menshikov's hands. The Turkish ministry was rent asunder. Mehemet Ali was puzzled what to do. He turned to Fuad for advice. Fuad took his usual line. He had advocated resistance to Russia from the start. He did so now. The other ministers had to walk warily for their own sake. Fuad had been thrown on the scrap heap as a result of his temerity. No one wanted to share his fate. As to the Menshikov mission, which was the more dreaded—its success or its failure? Some members of the Grand Council—especially the governors of the provinces and the *ulema* who had just been added unto it—regarded a Russian victory as inevitable and waited impassively for the automatic solution to mature. Mehemet Ali was less resigned to this prospect—or perhaps sought to reap advantage from it. So far as it is possible to read his devious mind, it appears that he hoped to shift the burden of decision from his own shoulders to someone else's—Rifat's, Fuad's, Stratford's—he did not mind whose so long as his own record looked clean on paper. Never for one moment did either Mehemet Ali or Fuad contemplate taking the lead in the hope this would bring foreign assistance. Rather they looked plaintively to London and Paris for some twist that would enable them to escape from their impossible situation.

On 16 March Menshikov called at the Porte and said that he had misgivings over the sultan's treatment of his Orthodox subjects. He showed Rifat a letter from the tsar, stating that the grievances over the Holy Places must be redressed if Turkey and Russia were to remain on good terms. On 28 March he took a further step. He announced that he had hit on the idea of a "solemn engagement" between Russia and Turkey as a way of getting the Turks out of their difficulties. The Orthodox Christians of Turkey were national minorities: sometimes quiescent, sometimes discontented, never convinced adherents of the existing order. So long as Turkey was isolated from Russia she was under their "imminent menace." Once relations with Russia were secure, all the grievances of the Orthodox subjects would go away—they would become not so much wrong as unnecessary. Rifat objected that Menshikov's proposal was a plan for reducing Turkey to subordination without a war. Menshikov remained unshaken. He insisted that there could be no improvement in relations with Russia until the Turks had discharged their existing obligations under the treaty of Kutchuk Kainardji.

He now produced his scheme for a defensive alliance against France: Turkey would recite her moral obligations; Russia would provide the strength with which to sustain them. In addition to this, he demanded the election for life of the four Orthodox patriarchs of the Ottoman empire—striking example of how political preoccupations blended with, or rather submerged, religious concerns.

Menshikov's demands had an immediate impact on the Turks. Faced by them, responsible Turks fled back to antiquated prejudices and practices which they had been unwittingly abandoning in easier times. Whether these suspicions were justified or not they could not be easily eradicated once they had been formed; exactly the same had been true, for instance, of the designs which the French had been supposed in 1840 to harbor against Turkey. No French assurances could remove these suspicions in the one case; no Russian assurances could remove them in the other. A vital change of emphasis followed. Henceforth the Turks were concerned to assert their independence, not to resolve the dispute over the Holy Places. They appealed to the Great Powers for aid. The Near East hummed with diplomatic activity with Constantinople as its center. Rose, the British chargé d'affaires, sought to pull off a dramatic stroke and telegraphed directly to Malta with orders to bring up the fleet. Dundas, the admiral at Malta, did not care for Rose and passed the appeal to London. There it was considered on 20 March by the "Big 4" of the Aberdeen government. The ministers were the "old gang," slightly reshuffled: Russell, leader of the House of Commons; Palmerston, home secretary; Clarendon, foreign minister. Together with Aberdeen they became the "inner cabinet" of the Crimean war, the Ministry of all Talents, as one writer[16] has called them. Contemporaries from ambassadors and rulers abroad to Oxford academics and readers of *The Times* tried to penetrate their secrets. The Crimean war played itself out in the shadow of their personalities.

Chapter 4

THE BRITISH CABINET

Russell had been prime minister from 1846 to 1852—and a rather unsuccessful one. His government was a severe blow to the Whig party—never was it to form a government again. Russell's creaky government of 1865 was not much better—the first Liberal government that almost ruined the Liberal party as well. Russell was not a leader even in appearance. He was tiny, delicate, and shy. He spoke crisply with a dry academic voice and certainly was no orator. He was too thin-skinned to be a successful practitioner of politics, so stung by the reproaches on his record of diplomatic bungling during the Crimean war that he took to hoarding estates to work off the tension. Nor did he make any effort to win the affection of his followers. He had too much pride for that: "pride of the House of Russell, of being the son of the sixth Duke of Bedford, pride also of having a better intellect and a better education than most politicians."[1] Such were the qualities that marked Russell off from his contemporaries.

Russell was a thoroughly Victorian character. He came of impeccable Whig stock; no one was more earnest, more worthy, more sincere. He was a pioneer in political reform and in economic experiment. The Reform Bill of 1832, the most revolutionary political measure of the early nineteenth century, stood to his credit; the New Poor Law of 1834, the most revolutionary economic measure as well. He was deeply involved too in the cause of religious freedom by which he meant to keep down the influence of the churches in politics. Himself a Deist, he was uncomfortable with deep religious faith. He summed up his feelings when he wrote a famous letter to a Dean Hereford who had raised objections against consecrating as bishop a man whom Russell had selected: "Dear Sir: I have had the honour to receive your letter of the 22nd inst., in which you intimate to me your intention of violating the law."[2] It was therefore no accident that his government produced the Ecclesiastical Titles Bill of 1851, the bill which barred the use of Roman Catholic titles in England and struck the popular imagination as did no other act of his ministry.

Russell's personality was a puzzle to contemporaries and remains so to the present day. He commanded great devotion, inspired great respect. He also provoked considerable hostility, not least for his refusal to aid the Irish during the Famine of 1846 when he was prime minister. He had also a snobbery that provoked and almost justified dislike. "He never forgot that Lord William Russell, who was the founder of the family greatness and whose life he wrote, had died on the scaffold for conspiring against Charles II; for the sake of this ancestor, Russell too had to be on the side of the radicals and rebels."[3] This snobbery showed in his later record as foreign secretary. "Russell's stock in trade . . . was the hectoring lecture speech when he told foreign rulers the awful things that would happen to them if they did not follow the British constitutional pattern. He lectured the Tsar on how to govern Poland; he lectured Bismarck for daring to attack Denmark; he lectured the Emperor of Austria on the way to treat Hungary; he lectured the United States for having a civil war; he lectured the whole of Europe on the virtues of Italian Nationalism."[4] There was in him a genuine humanitarianism reinforced by a powerful intellect, and an even more powerful pride in his roots and background. His conscience never ceased to trouble him. "Russell never followed up his lectures with any kind of action; he thought it would be enough to threaten tsars and emperors with his displeasure, the displeasure of a member of the House of Russell."[5]

Lord John Russell was indifferent to the foreign record of his own government. Domestic affairs were what mattered to him. Nor is this surprising: Russell believed that he was the greatest force in contemporary British politics; he considered it his duty to get on with the process of electoral reform that he himself had helped inaugurate in 1832. This was not an attitude likely to commend itself to his cabinet colleagues.

Lord John Russell was a fascinating man. He was brave and stimulating. He could certainly raise a spark. But he was also the spoilt child of privilege. He grew more intellectual and culturally snobbish as he grew older. He became increasingly contentious, believing that others had stolen the credit for achievements that were his own. His biographer sums up firmly: "He lacked winning ways, temperate common sense and good judgment . . . This is what Jowett [master of Balliol College] meant when he said in 1861 that high rank had the opposite effect with Lord John from what it did with most people—it 'prevented his being a man of the world.'"[6]

When Russell resigned in February 1852, there was much talk of a Whig-Peelite coalition, but it was not until December that a coalition was formed.

There was at its head Aberdeen a Peelite leader; with him was a strong Peelite contingent in the cabinet. Palmerston moved to the home office, though he would have liked the foreign ministry. This was given only on an interim basis to Russell, after many discreditable compromises and much bickering by Russell as to the "effect likely to be produced on his political friends by his acceptance of the office."[7] Between Palmerston and Russell there was a deep-seated hostility. Russell was always the subtle dividing line between the old order and the new, "belonging to the old order by birth, carried over to the new by his ideas."[8] He was unshakably convinced that he was a man born to govern, never imagined that positions of power would cease to be a monopoly of the Russells and Cavendishes and Stanleys, never regarded Palmerston as more than a mere upstart. Though Palmerston had been foreign secretary in Russell's government, the two were yoke fellows forced upon each other by the party whips. Cooperation between them became and remained superficial.

Political differences cut deeper. Palmerston rose to the top mainly through a shaky family connection; he kept it up by his pen and his tongue. Unlike Russell, there was nothing in his background to suggest anything unusual. He was an Irish peer, rather well off, who understandably took up politics to make more money. Born in 1784 he came to the House of Commons at the young age of twenty-three with neither developed beliefs or settled political convictions—still another difference from Russell. Competent in mathematics, gifted in money matters, he chose, among the junior offices offered him, the office of secretary of war—an office he held for twenty-one years. Amusing, vain, cheeky, with ravishing good looks, and a jaunty, unassuming air, he quickly established himself as Lord Cupid—a name that gives away everything.

Yet Palmerston had also an inner insecurity and a craving for affection that he often turned into fits of jealous rage. He enjoyed making money and was captivating to women. He shared Lady Cowper with her husband and with other men after she became his wife; the two had a number of illegitimate children. Nor did his sexual adventures end with matrimony. His biographer notes tantalizingly: "[T]here were plenty of other women in Palmerston's life. For while no one ever quite displaced Lady Cowper, he was about as unfaithful to her as she was to him."[9] But the years at the war office did not use up his energies: he had a more rewarding apprenticeship than any of his contemporaries—a trait that he turned to advantage later on.

The study of Palmerston's rise to power is a record of ups and downs. The story has a clear beginning: Lord Grey, the prime minister in 1830, wanted to dominate British diplomacy and hit on Palmerston as an agreeable understudy who would carry out the government's work in the House of Commons without getting into trouble. Palmerston had begun as a Tory but had gradually gone over to the Whigs. He rose rapidly in stature at the foreign office, starting out with rather amateurish conduct during the Belgian crisis of 1830 and ending up with an adroit performance during the Eastern crisis of 1839–41. All the same Palmerston was by and large still unknown to contemporary English opinion. During the Crimean war he would come into his own. The transformation of Russell's destiny was not as startling. Russell would have left a considerable mark on British history even if he had died before 1853. Had Palmerston died before January 1855 he would have been almost forgotten, except as a diplomatic figure.

The five years between 1841 and 1846 were memorable as the most important in Palmerston's life. Peel was prime minister with a Conservative ministry and the leadership of the Whigs fell vacant with the demise of Melbourne. Russell assumed that the post would fall into his lap without fuss and for good; he was, after all, the undisputed living symbol of the great Whig political tradition and felt that the support of the party whips was all that was necessary.

Russell underestimated Palmerston's ingenuity. Palmerston was at a loss for high ancestral cards; and these would not have amounted to much against Russell's even if he had had them. He was not, however, at a loss for words. He took to writing on public affairs, and established himself as a leading authority on foreign policy. He would choose a theme, make up his mind about it, and write down his ideas fast, in time to catch the newspapers. His articles were propagandist pieces, deceptively adorned with political analysis. Every work and argument was designed to produce an effect. He became a first-rate writer, a master of the telling phrase, many of which displayed the flippancy and bounce that he himself exemplified. Yet Palmerston remained unpopular with many of the Whig professionals. For instance, in 1845, when Peel resigned, the third Earl Grey refused to serve under Russell because Palmerston's inclusion in the government was, in Grey's words, "notorious. . . . a prospect . . . regarded with considerable apprehension." [10] This refusal was the death-knell of Russell's coalition-building and a considerable comment on Palmerston as well. Palmerston was never a good party man. He was too individual, too full of life to be fitted into a party pattern.

In 1846 Russell took office with the last Whig government in British history and immediately created an awkward problem for himself when he made Palmerston foreign minister. Palmerston seized this opportunity. No doubt he wished to carry out his duties in a serious, straightforward fashion; but there was a cynical calculation of personal expediency as well: Palmerston was, apart from wanting to make his own policy clear, consciously playing for public support and meant to steal the limelight from Russell. This was not difficult. Palmerston was the one-eyed man in a government of the blind. By 1850 events were running undisputedly on his side. The Don Pacifico affair pitted him against the greatest speakers of the age—against Gladstone, Cobden, and Peel; it secured, though it did not perhaps complete, his reputation as an outstanding figure in the popular imagination. The triumph was of a special kind; certainly not a triumph of oratory. "Palmerston was always a bad speaker full of 'hums' and 'haws,' his voice trailing away before the end of the sentence, and the pause filled up by the flourish of his handkerchief. Rather it was a triumph of character. With his dyed whiskers and his red face, Palmerston exemplified British self-confidence and bounce." [11]

The Don Pacifico affair displayed one of Palmerston's deepest convictions: his faith in the value of the institutions of Great Britain. A phrase coined by him in 1850 still rings down the avenues of time: "We have no eternal allies and no permanent enemies. Our interests are eternal and those interests it is our duty to follow." [12] Yet Palmerston recognized that there were limitations to British claims of political pre-eminence. In the words of Kenneth Bourne, whose masterly pages of Palmerston's biography contain some vivid passages of characterization: "There was no question of imposing . . . regimes on others. Nor did Palmerston think the British model everywhere appropriate, acknowledging, as he had in 1832, that they 'must vary according to the social habits [and] existing institutions of each nation.' . . . Palmerston was an optimist, not an enthusiast; a pragmatist, not a moralist." [13]

Palmerston brought many advantages to the task of diplomacy. He had, for instance, little faith in the prospect of Turkish reform. But he certainly regarded the defense of the Ottoman empire as a British interest, and he beat down critics of sultan's rule with the question: what is the alternative? "His emphasis had all along been upon those limited measures by which Turkish defense might be strengthened and European hostility softened. On the one hand he expressed an anxiety not to undermine the sultan's authority (as had been done in Egypt); on the other to demolish the fallacies of those who 'from mistaking a metaphor for an argument and by comparing a community to a dead man's body and to an old tree' forecast the inevitable collapse of the Turkish empire." [14] He could not pretend to have any policy except to be himself; and this he did with conspicuous success. Outcome of his diplomacy was, for instance, the Straits Convention of 1841, negotiated with Tsar Nicholas. In a strictly technical sense this arrangement seemed to infringe the freedom of the sultan rather than enhance it: henceforth he was forbidden to open the Straits in peacetime. In reality, he now had an immeasurable new asset: he could call in "Europe" if his security were threatened by another Power. Behind the theoretical restriction lay the overriding fear with which the British had been wrestling for a decade—that the Russian fleet was strong enough to pass the Straits without anxiety as to the British presence in the Mediterranean. Now, thanks to Palmerston, this fear was checked.

The crisis of 1839–41 made Palmerston the undisputed authority on British foreign policy; his performance as Russell's foreign secretary from 1846 to 1851 the undisputed master of it. Yet more than mastery of foreign policy was involved. Palmerston gave the office of foreign secretary a touch all his own. He wrote all his dispatches in his own hand. He regularized the system of records. He "worked" public opinion. He reproduced his official dispatches in the newspapers. He was law unto himself. Yet, though increasingly popular with the general public, he remained unpopular with many of the Whigs. A minor incident showed it. In December 1851, Palmerston, without consulting his colleagues, spoke approvingly of Louis Napoleon's coup d'état. A considerable indiscretion. The queen was offended by this breach of the constitution and complained to Russell; Palmerston was dismissed, to Russell's delight. Russell's was a short-lived triumph. Many MPs were exasperated by Russell's record of frivolity and incompetence. Palmerston turned this sentiment to advantage. For instance, he and his allies sent up a chorus of doubts over the preparedness of the British militia, and he himself supported a bill to increase its size. Russell was too set in his ways to cope with this "tit for tat." His government fell.

Of course there was more to it than politics. The antipathy between Russell and Palmerston could be illustrated in a thousand ways. Unlike Russell, Palmerston did not represent a class, or even claim to, though he defended the Irish landlords late in his life. He was simply a formidable figure with a strong personality and a nimble intellect. "In all his acts he was impudent—cheeky in his speeches; daring in policy, Lord Cupid when he was young, Lord Pumicestone when he was old." [15] "He was not an Irish peer or an Irish landlord for nothing. He had the Irish jauntiness which always wins English hearts. He could never rein in his high spirits; and even his best speeches have, here and there, a touch of flippancy. He would rather make a good joke than win a debate. He was not, as is sometimes alleged, a survivor of the eighteenth century. Rather he had Regency written all over him—in his clothes, his morals, even in his way of talking and his metallic laugh. . . . Palmerston was certainly the most entertaining of Queen Victoria's prime ministers. Though there have been better prime ministers there has been none more genial and, for that matter, none so good looking." [16]

As foreign secretary, Palmerston was always too independent of the prime minister and the cabinet; as home secretary, he surrendered to obstruction; and wrapped up this obstruction in ethical phrases. The other ministers were respectful administrators; only Palmerston felt at home with the professional members of the foreign office. The others looked at diplomatists with distrust—an attitude especially strong perhaps with Russell, the former prime minister, who was written off as a failure. In return, the staff of the foreign office had little confidence in the government.

Clarendon, the foreign secretary, was set on papering over the differences. For example, he knew that Russell would have liked to settle Rose's request to Palmerston's exclusion. He saw in this "a great crisis" and, anticipating that the government would fall if Palmerston were so slighted, got Palmerston in. This was his special talent. He came from one of the few genuinely diplomatic families and one of the few too that went back beyond the Glorious Revolution, a family which had joined in the hunt for honor under the Stuarts. He counted among his ancestors Edward Hyde, statesman, legalist, historian of the Great Rebellion, who had negotiated the secret treaty of Dover with Louis XIV.

Clarendon had, however, a fatal weakness. He had no political following. He commanded no wide popularity in the House of Commons, where he had never sat, or, for that matter, in the country. He was the first of a type common in Europe during the next century: impotent to resist the drift towards war, deploring its consequences, yet going along with it. Apart from this, Clarendon was a period piece—a tall, spare, aristocratic man in skin-tight breeches and tight-fitting frock coat, his greying hair and whiskers jutting out from beneath his chimney-pot hat. The contradictions of his character are best shown by his delicate physique. Palmerston often teased him about not taking enough exercise; he himself knew this to be so. He therefore posed as a man of decision and lightning judgment. His carriage would come careening into Downing Street and stop at the foreign office; he would alight, breathlessly ascend the stairs and disappear into the labyrinth of its interior. Still in spirit, if not in years, he was the "doyen" of the foreign secretaries of Europe. At the age of twenty, he had been attaché in St. Petersburg. Later he was made ambassador to Spain; and had watched the decay of Anglo-French relations over the Spanish marriages. Now at fifty-three he found himself at the foreign office for the first of three times. This was an appropriate gesture, a deserved recognition of Clarendon's unique skill as a diplomatic negotiator, a recognition too of his achievements in home affairs: lord privy seal from 1839 to 1841; president of the board of trade in 1846; lord-lieutenant of Ireland from 1847 to 1852.

Someone has called Clarendon "the amateur strategist"; someone else, "the great bargain-driver." Perhaps they are the same thing. Clarendon was a meticulous housemaid, great at tidying up. Despite his aristocratic mien, he had the sensitivity of a woman, incredibly quick in responding to the moods of another or even in anticipating them. He had, moreover, an unrivalled power of narration. No one ever read a dispatch with as much humor and lightness of touch. This enhanced his popularity. His colleagues often groaned under the tedium of work; Clarendon provided amusing pauses for refreshment. He felt the excitement of the negotiations, knew afresh the drama of the great decisions. In Argyll's words: "His running comments were inimitable . . . The readings of the character of each diplomatist were often as good as a play." And he added, with more exaggeration: "They were a real help in enabling us to judge how far we could test each separate element of the situation at the separate Courts." [17]

A coalition seemed to be forming against the government. Inside the cabinet were the strong men, Palmerston and Russell, each explosive on the wings; outside it were the conservatives led by Derby and Disraeli. Yet Clarendon survived. He escaped Aberdeen's ignominy; he did not achieve Palmerston's fame. It was his doom that he was branded by contemporary opinion and branded in history as the "vanished Victorian."

An epoch in Clarendon's life ended with the outbreak of the Crimean war. Hitherto he had, like Palmerston, been on the margin of events observing and sometimes manipulating them. Now events thrust upon him the responsibility of directing the foreign office of a nation at war. In the new atmosphere, he remained what he had always been. He ran his ministry as a trained administrator or a politician would have done. He had none of Palmerston's penchant for sowing discord. Palmerston was an extraordinary character, irresistibly captivating to some, immeasurably wicked to others. As home secretary, he was no innocent civilian. He was himself an expert on war, or so he believed. He was convinced that the war could have been averted if the government had listened to his advice. Attempts were made to shake Palmerston's high-minded resolve. Clarendon returned to his old trade of conciliator. Russia had threatened Turkey; she had trespassed into the principalities. Surely this was no time to stir things up; the government must go on. Clarendon argued in vain. Palmerston would not be moved. At the end of 1854 Palmerston could cheerfully survey the country as the man of destiny.

The man who would be overthrown by him had arrived on the stage a year before. In December of 1852, Aberdeen had become prime minister. This was, of course, primarily an event in British domestic politics not in international affairs. Essentially, Aberdeen had been called in to satisfy the Peelites. They had refused to join any coalition in which they did not have the largest share of the cake. Aberdeen was the least glamorous of prime ministers: industrious, conscientious, unimaginative. The coolness between the ministers and the foreign office has promoted the belief that Aberdeen and his friends were irresponsible amateurs. On the contrary, in practical matters, few governments were better equipped to deal with foreign affairs or worked more closely with the professional diplomatists. Aberdeen himself had many admirable qualities. He had courage and industry. His intellect was clear and sharp. Few politicians in the nineteenth century had a better administrative brain or used this gift better. The queen spoke of him when Wellington died as almost the only man left to her upon whom she could call for advice.

Though Aberdeen had many gifts, he also had some fundamental limitations. M. E. Chamberlain, his latest biographer, passes a verdict that deserves to be quoted in full:

> Aberdeen was not a naive man. His private papers show him to be a very shrewd, as well as a very independent observer of the political scene . . . Perhaps the word 'observer,' or as Aberdeen himself would frequently have said, 'spectator,' gives the clue . . . Aberdeen entirely lacked the instinctive flair for politics which Disraeli or Palmerston, or even Gladstone, possessed. His fundamental shyness and inability to project himself to the public was an important factor, but it was not the whole of it. Perhaps he was too intellectual. His very ability to think for himself, to stand out against public clamour and excitement, however admirable, made him a poor politician. He seems to have had no gut reactions. What other Prime Minister would have stood up in the House of Lords and defended the Tsar of Russia a few weeks after the outbreak of the Crimean War?[18]

Aberdeen came to power with long experience in British politics. He had, as well, over forty years of training as a diplomat. Byron, ever old-fashioned, once referred to him as "the travelled thane, Athenian Aberdeen." This did not count for much in the eyes of public opinion—or, for that matter, of posterity. The blame for the Crimean war was loaded on his shoulders, and Aberdeen uncomplainingly accepted this himself. Like King David, he refused to build a church on his estates: "But the word of the Lord came to me, saying 'Thou hast shed blood abundantly and hast made great war: thou shalt not build a house unto my name'"[19]

Aberdeen's policy is, however, capable of rational explanation; and it is on these that history is built. He had been negotiator at Vienna during the

Napoleonic wars. He had visited the battlefield at Leipzig and had there seen the wasted bodies of thousands of human beings. This left a deep mark on his character. The price of victory, though high, was less than that paid by other countries; this did not make it less horrendous in Aberdeen's mind.

As negotiator in Vienna, Aberdeen was not a success. As on other occasions, the Austrians were irritated by Great Britain's policy of aloofness and threatened to pull out of the coalition against Napoleon. Aberdeen's exhortations to Metternich were of no use. Castlereagh regarded him as overly compliant and recalled him. For the next fourteen years he was at a loose end. Even his appearance showed it. He was a thin man, made thinner by his persistence in skipping meals and by a history of chronic stomach cramps. Despite his bland personality, he became friends with the most successful statesmen of the day and in 1828 was chosen by Wellington for the foreign office. He dealt, in chronological order, with the war between Russia and Turkey, the July revolution in France, and the insurrection in the Netherlands. In 1830 Wellington's government fell; and soon afterwards Aberdeen broke with the Tories over free trade. Yet he remained a Tory at heart—at any rate in foreign policy: on the one hand, he wished to see Russia consolidate her reactionary hold over the Near East; on the other, he believed that Turkey was too decayed to be preserved; and he regarded any suggestions of dramatic reform—like the one which the Turks conveniently produced out of the hat with the Gulhané decree of 1839—as conjuring tricks, not as genuine promises of regeneration. In his view, the disintegration of Turkey would give the statesmen of Europe the tonic of relief, for Turkey was a ridiculous imitation of a Great Power, impressive only to professional diplomats and chroniclers of Islam.

This attitude was much in evidence when he served in Peel's cabinet as foreign secretary from 1841 to 1846. His patient negotiating skill produced first an entente with France and later the resolution of the Oregon question with the United States. The peculiar British mission, *chef d'oeuvre* of his work, was security in the Near East. This, he supposed, he had accomplished by his agreement with Nesselrode of 1844. His confidence in Russian good faith remained unshaken by the Eastern crisis of 1853. In his own words: "There is nothing whatever to justify . . . the reproach of [Russia's] territorial aggression or hostile ambition." Menshikov "could command himself sufficiently to wait for the arrival of Lord Stratford." The crisis should "be settled without coming to extremities." [20] Whatever misgivings Aberdeen might have felt, he had no faith in radical rantings against Russia. He continued to believe that Tsar Nicholas was a reasonable man and that this reasonable man would come to the surface if the British government did not lose confidence in him.

In his view the real threat to the peace of Europe was France—or rather Louis Napoleon. He mourned the departure of Louis Philippe and regarded Louis Napoleon as an upstart who would engulf Europe in "the revolution." The coup d'état of 2 December 1851 seemed to bear out this suspicion. He believed that Napoleon III was pushing Europe into a great war, lasting for many years and tearing Europe to pieces. Such a war he and nearly all Englishmen wished to avoid. Those such as Russell who thought that the tsar was out to destroy Turkey could be answered by the assurances that the tsar had made to Seymour or, for that matter, to Aberdeen himself. Nor did Aberdeen regret the decline of British influence in eastern Europe. This is precisely what British radicals such as Cobden had been advocating for decades. Two questions concerned him: first: should Menshikov's bluff, if it were bluff, be called? Later: is the infringement by Russia of Turkey's independence a reason to take up arms? In practice, the two questions were mixed up. It was absurd, in Aberdeen's view, to suggest that all the trouble had been caused by Russia. The civilization of Turkey was inherently unstable—both in Europe and the Near East. Here, as in some parts of Europe, two peoples, Moslems and Christians, were living together in the same community; and their mutual hostility could not be assuaged by the rational inquiries of a detached mediator. Weakness and disunion had sapped old loyalties. Those in power, whether Rifat or Mehemet Ali, had lost faith in themselves, existed on sufferance, and were grateful if they were allowed to survive. Not that Aberdeen approved of Menshikov's bluster. He declared the fall of Fuad "disgusting." But he blamed Turkish feebleness rather than Russian bullying; and he drew the moral that Turkey was useless as a partner, not that Russia should be resisted. In any case, Russia was merely seeking redress of her grievance and would then settle down to a happy partnership in prosperity with Great Britain.

It is possible to speculate whether Aberdeen ever envisaged an alliance with Russia against France. It is certain that he abhorred alliance with France against Russia. This was the favorite idea of one group of radicals—of writers such as Dickens and Browning, of MPs such as Roebuck and Morley, and of those revolutionary exiles who had fought against Russia in 1830 and 1848. The bulk of the cabinet shuffled towards it more reluctantly. It is a reasonable surmise that most English people came to regard Napoleonic France as less wicked than tsarist Russia only late in the day, perhaps not until the "massacre" of Sinope. Besides, there were in 1853 and the years immediately preceding it political and ideological objections. France was in the midst of a Bonapartist takeover and it was difficult to take seriously the work of a *parvenu* who had destroyed the republican constitution which he had been elected to uphold. The British service chiefs feared an invasion across the channel, and their opinion carried weight even if it sprang as much from political prejudice as from knowledge. Again, France would not be effective against Russia even if she had the power so long as Napoleon III alienated the rulers of eastern Europe, and the scheme to deny him the title of "Brother" was Austrian in origin, if not in implementation. The settlement of Europe was bound to be revised one way or the other. It was plausible to argue that a revision to suit Russia would be less drastic than one to suit France, and the outcome less painful. France would, in his view, want to take on all Europe, to tear up the treaties of Vienna and to put "the revolution" in their place. Russia was a different matter. Russian ambitions were confined to the Near East, the result of historic antagonisms, and therefore more legitimate—certainly easier for Aberdeen to skate over.

These were the more or less rational calculations which Aberdeen made to himself. The great debate over British foreign policy did not revolve around them. It was determined by domestic policies. At the end of 1852 Aberdeen for once stirred himself to action. The Conservative government under Derby had broken up. In a personal sense, the era of Anglo-Russian cooperation ended during the government of the man who had inaugurated it. Aberdeen at last reached the supreme position for which the Peelites felt he was uniquely qualified. He himself claimed to have combined Peelite economics with Whig politics and, though this is true in a technical sense, it would be truer still to say that he rode two separate horses and never got them teamed together. In any case political developments bounced back on him to his considerable discomfiture. After the election of 1852, Graham wrote to Gladstone: "It will be an impossible Parliament. Parties will be found too nicely balanced to render a new line of policy practicable without a first appeal to the electorate." [21]

This was not the only reason why Aberdeen found it difficult to hold his coalition together. Russell still supposed that he was the giant of English politics, despite his defeat in 1852. Isolated and resentful, he thought to drive Aberdeen from office. Little came of his efforts except a spate of words. Most of the Peelites wanted a quiet life and were won by Aberdeen's policy of accommodation and moderation. Besides, they distrusted Russell as they had always done—too clever, too quixotic, too Whiggish in the narrow sense. Russell estranged the Peelites and also deepened the profound hostility which practically all Conservatives felt towards him. When at this time Aberdeen and Clarendon thought of strengthening themselves against Parliament, they dangled a fly towards Palmerston, Russell's old enemy. Russell had not forgotten his humiliation from 1846 to 1852 and insisted to Aberdeen that if Palmerston entered the government he would go out. Russell stayed. Though he now had few followers and no friends, he was always inclined to believe that his family connections could work miracles. He tried to woo the Whig conscience. To no good purpose. The Whigs existed no longer and could not be rallied as a political force. Russell acknowledged defeat. Aberdeen offered Palmerston the home office; and Palmerston, for reasons that need not be gone into, accepted the offer on 23 December 1852. The coalition was made.

II

Such was the system into which British policy tried to be fitted and the personalities who sought to shape it. In practice, the British were more pushed along by events and less in control of them than they liked to think or than they later made out. Immediately after Fuad's fall Russell suspected, or so he alleged, Russian moves elsewhere. His ears were tuned to fresh alarms. Since Russell had resented Palmerston's bellicosity when Palmerston was foreign secretary in Russell's government and since he and his followers resented the way in which foreign affairs distracted the country from projects of electoral reform, this seemed a surprising suggestion. Its meaning became clear when he told Graham that the government would fall unless his advice was taken. As a matter of fact, he was once again attempting to wield his old power, if only for destruction. Though he now had few friends in the government, he thought a firm line against Russia would carry the day for himself in the competition that he was waging with Palmerston for public favor. Neither Aberdeen nor the Peelites believed that the Ottoman empire could be preserved in its existing form, though many shrank from admitting it. Russell and later Palmerston tended to talk as though Great Britain should lay down the law to Russia. Some members of the foreign office thought that the tsar should be "hit on the head." Sooner or later, they believed, he would come begging for forgiveness if the British wagged their finger at Menshikov. Aberdeen disliked this attitude. The pattern of his policy was clearly revealed. He stressed the Russian commitment to Great Britain under the agreement of 1844. Men usually believe what they want to believe; and Aberdeen was ready to believe that Nicholas would be satisfied if the claims of Menshikov were met. Therefore if the British pressed the Turks to yield, all would be well.

III

These were the calculations that weighed with the British government when they considered Rose's request. There was as well a more immediate concern. Sending the fleet to the Straits would encourage the Turks to resist Menshikov. Moreover, there was the case that relations with Russia were more important than relations with Turkey. This had been the case against making an alliance with Turkey in 1850; and Aberdeen, supported by Palmerston, made it now. Russell's demand was rejected. Thereafter tension relaxed. It bubbled up with indignation against Menshikov and lacked positive content. Resistance to Russia seemed pointless; and the concern of the British government was to satisfy Menshikov's demands, not to prepare for a war over the Eastern question—a remote peril for most English people.

Chapter 5

THE OUTBREAK OF WAR
IN THE NEAR EAST

On 19 March 1853 Napoleon III had a busy morning. In the afternoon he and his advisers received an appeal for aid from the Turks. This was the counterpart of the appeal which they had made to the British. But with this difference. Benedetti, the *chargé d'affaires* at Constantinople, was less headstrong than Rose and did not allow confused events to rush him into precipitous action. His elaborate report met with a curious response. The council of ministers speculated in the void. Persigny, the minister of the interior, tense for the Armageddon with Russia which he supposed "the legend" had foretold, demanded action. The foreign minister, Drouyn de Lhuys, coached by Thouvenel, now political director of the foreign office, tackled him. The council divided. Persigny continued to insist on a hard line: the fleet should go to Salamis. How soon? How many ships? Merely to Salamis? Drouyn cut in. He explained that such a move was premature and that, in any case, they should wait for England.

Drouyn de Lhuys deserves to be written about. He was the oddest great man in the history of the Second Empire by a long chalk. Nothing connected him with Napoleon III's dream for a reconstruction of Europe along the lines of nationality—nothing except perhaps his calculation that he could prevent its happening. He was not Bonapartist by blood; he had done nothing to spread "the legend"; he was lucky even to have been a national guardsman during the February revolution. In temperament he was even less suited to be Napoleon III's foreign minister than he was in origin. He always concentrated on the task at hand and when following a trail would reject every scent that led away from it. He despised revolutionaries even more than he disliked monarchists. His long experience as a diplomat, his clerical convictions, above all his years as director of commercial affairs of the July monarchy were demonstrations of conservatism in thin disguise. Yet in appearance he was least Bonapartist of all. Sloping shoulders, prominent cheekbones, wide, thin-lipped mouth, tufts of sideburns greying on the cheeks were not the marks of a Bonaparte or of any man of action, and his ambiguous twists of expression and halting, lethargic manner completed the foreign impression.

The political creed to which he belonged had been hammered out by generations of Frenchmen who distrusted convulsions in politics. He hated instability and political inexperience; he was impatient with proponents of nationalism like Persigny; the party to which he was aligned wished to preserve the social order and valued hereditary claims. These features give Drouyn's character its special fascination. Drouyn was more than a symbol. He was an individual capturing a cause for its own purpose and giving it a twist all his own.

He came from an ancient Soissonais family—one that went back to the time of Henry IV. The very geography of Soissons shaped his character and political outlook. Soissons was unmistakably in the north of France in a district largely inhabited by Catholics. Drouyn never came to sympathize with Protestants in the south and disliked for instance, Napoleon III's Italian policy. Yet Soissons was also west of the Seine; its inhabitants looked to Paris as the cultural metropolis. It had retained its aristocratic trappings during the storms of the Revolution and the Napoleonic wars. The date of Drouyn's birth, 1805, was also significant. The Napoleonic empire was at the height of its power. Drouyn was, despite his conservative outlook, always aware of the majestic splendor that was imperial France. His great regret was that it had been achieved by violence and by the destruction of the existing order of society. He often feared that the same fate might come again. Hence he welcomed the results of the presidential election of December 1848 as the dawn of a new age. Like many of his contemporaries, he viewed Louis Napoleon as the redeemer of French prestige, the man who would get French policy out of the mess into which it had been landed by the conflict between the pacifism of the provisional government and the erratic, unpredictable bellicosity of the radical republicans.

His expectation was soon met. A crisis of muddle that no one properly understood, led to Louis Napoleon's selection of Drouyn as foreign minister. A new government that had been elected to preserve order had to preserve it, presented itself as the savior of the country, and had its claim accepted by a heavy majority of Frenchmen. This claim was soon threatened. The elections of 1849 went badly for the government; and Louis Napoleon hit on the idea of increasing his freedom of maneuver by replacing Drouyn whose party had won the elections, with Alexis de Tocqueville, a sincere republican, whose party had lost them. At the beginning of 1852 Drouyn was again made foreign minister, after a stretch at the embassy in London. He was called in to deal with the recognition crisis—the cries of protest by the Great Powers over Napoleon's decision to place the "III" against his name. The efficient handling of foreign affairs was supposed to be his special talent; it needed a vivid imagination to get his master out of the tangle that was threatening to isolate him from the rest of "Europe."

Drouyn did his work well. His careful diplomacy disarmed the hostility of all the Powers save Russia. He had willed himself into a line of policy several years before and this gave a special foundation to his conduct of foreign affairs. In 1849 he had written: "French superiority rests on her national unity. . . . Everything that promotes the division of the great races is useful to us."[1] Promoting the division of the nationalities was the object of Drouyn's policy; alliance with Austria was the way to achieve it.

This was the bee in his bonnet. It harked back to the last days of the July monarchy when Guizot had cooperated with Metternich over Italy. Drouyn de Lhuys hoped to stretch this cooperation to Europe. An alliance with Austria would maintain the division of the Germanies; would, if supplemented by close relations with England, bar the door against Russia in the Near East.

Such were the calculations on which Drouyn based his policy. Their principal object was to damp down Napoleon III's restless ambition and make him more eager to accept things as they were. Any stroke that echoed "the revolution" was bound to excite the rulers of the Hapsburg monarchy whose favor he so earnestly wished to court. This is why he opposed Persigny's call for action. For Drouyn de Lhuys, the Austrian alliance, unlike any other, was an affair of the heart as well as of the head. The emotional stress that he laid on it caused him difficulties later. This is not surprising. For the policy of Drouyn and the other conservatives was singularly impractical. Drouyn de Lhuys was a negotiator of skill and stood in the first rank among French makers of diplomacy during the Second Empire. But he could not accomplish miracles, though he came near to it. Napoleon III was not equipped by temperament for alliance with Austria, and Drouyn frequently lost his hold on policy over his *idée fixe*. Relations between Drouyn and Napoleon III, though correct, were never intimate, frequently wore rather thin.

At any rate this was how things worked out now. Drouyn de Lhuys was pushed aside by the men of action; his opponents saw in the Turkish request for aid a way of throwing down the gauntlet and launching the war of liberation against the despotisms of Europe. This was not their only argument. As minister of the interior, Persigny ascertained opinion and did so by methods not unlike those of the political pollsters of the present day. Maybe he stacked the evidence against Drouyn; in any case he argued that French opinion would not tolerate inaction. Persigny's warning, not Drouyn's pleas, weighed with Napoleon III and shaped his decision. Opponents of aid were silenced. On 19 March a decision was reached: the entire fleet to Salamis.

On the following day Drouyn insisted to Cowley, the British ambassador, that the order could be stopped on conditions. Meanwhile Walewski, the French minister in London, had taken soundings for an alliance. His object was disappointed: in Cowley's words: "The restless ambition and energy of France have caused the trouble."[2] Napoleon III quickly realized that he could not make an alliance with the British. Instead he proposed to slide into one by turning the Straits convention of 1841 into a European guarantee of Turkey. He would, in this way, not merely drive Great Britain onto the French side; what is more, he would cement the ties with Austria as Drouyn had preached. Therein lay the difficulty. The British were on bad terms with Austria over the refugee question; they did not welcome the prospect of cooperating with her in the Near East. Besides, the circumstances did not warrant it. The affair over the Turks' request was, in Palmerston's words, "a concoction of street rumors, Russian gossip, Turkish alarm, and diplomatic zeal."[3] Napoleon III's hope for an alliance with England was in vain.

Meanwhile, developments in Turkey reached their most acute stage. On 5 April Stratford Canning, now Lord Stratford de Redcliff, returned to his post as ambassador: "he came with the mission of settling the dispute over the Holy Places in a sense favorable to Russia; this was attained, thanks largely to Stratford's advice, early in May."[4] Then a crisis exploded. On 5 May 1853 Menshikov handed the Turkish ministers a long memorandum. It demanded a protectorate over the Orthodox subjects of the Ottoman empire; no longer could the tsar be content with barren and unsatisfactory promises which could be broken at the sultan's will. The sultan's word must now be recorded in a treaty—a solid guarantee which would attest to his sincerity.

It is sometimes said that Menshikov's demands went back to arrangements that the Turks had before—to their treaty of 1740 with France; to their treaty of Kutchuk Kainardji of 1774 with Russia.[5] This is not so. The treaty of 1740 pertained to the Latin clergy and to the Latin clergy alone. Menshikov's treaty was something more: a demand to protect all Orthodox subjects of the Porte, laity as well as clergy. The French had, it is true, once advanced such a claim in connection with the Catholic subjects of Turkey; the claim had long since been abandoned; the French were now concerned only to protect the Latin monks and clergy. Besides, a French claim over the Catholic laity would affect only about 300,000 people; the Russian claim affect close to twelve million.

Similarly about the treaty of 1774. The Russians, or some of them, were trying to find in the treaty of 1774 what was not there. There were, to be sure, articles in the treaty that dealt with religion. In Article VII the Porte "promises at all times to protect the Christian religion and its churches" and also allows "the Russian ministers to make representations in regard to the new church at Constantinople." In Article XIV—the article dealing with the return of Moldavia and Wallachia to Turkey—the Porte promised "the completely free profession of the Christian faith as well as the building of churches new as well as old."[6] There was nothing in either of these articles that supported the Russian claim to a general protectorate over the Orthodox Christians of Turkey, though one of a sort was advanced as the years went by. For example, in 1849 Palmerston wrote that the Russian government could, under the treaty of 1774, make objections to the Turks; but that the Turks could, under the same treaty, choose to ignore them. This argument was, in the judgment of Brunnow, the ambassador at London, correct, a plain description of fact. According to him, the foundation of the Russian position "consists of deeds, not of words. Russia is strong, Turkey is weak—that is the preamble of all our treaties."[7]

This made no difference to Menshikov. He would hear no objections. He threatened to raise the Orthodox subjects of the Balkans if his demands were not met. His real aim was, of course, not religious but political: "Russia's honor, Russia's self-love, Russia's prestige is at stake. It cannot allow the preponderance of England to continue here to our detriment."[8] "Preponderance of England" meant Stratford de Redcliff. The demand for the protectorate was aimed at him. Nicholas was determined to destory his "infernal dictatorship" at Constantinople. This the treaty would accomplish. It would secure guarantees for the future—always a risky business in international relations. The demand for the treaty created a sensation among the ambassadors at Constantinople. Stratford declared it to be "wholly unacceptable";[9] he was bound to take this line as long as the independence of Turkey was the main spring of British policy in regard to the Near East. Yet, in the words of A.J.P. Taylor, "once it was admitted that Turkey was not truly independent (and every event of the Crimean War showed it) the Russians were justified in their demands for the sake of their own security: Turkey was tolerable as a buffer state only as long as she feared Russia more than any other Power. In seeking to maintain Turkish independence, Great

Britain and France were fighting for a pretence which they knew to be such; but it was a pretence which had to be kept up for lack of an alternative." [10] Menshikov's blustering turned British policy upside down. Even Aberdeen throught it "utterly unreasonable in its latest form." [11] Russell believed that his earlier suspicions had been vindicated and was in full cry for resistance. Now Palmerston joined him. He lamented the tsar's betrayal of the Seymour conversations and insisted that the government could not acquiesce in Menshikov's demands without danger to peace or to British interests—the same belief which he had held about the French in 1840. Clarendon, for once resolute, urged a strong line to prop up support among the backbenchers.

The British lion now roared. Stratford called upon the Turks to hold out against Menshikov. This was uphill work. Menshikov was a strong charac-ter—self-confident and resourceful, a military man who despised diplomats and diplomatic formalities. He claimed rightly that he represented the "purest and simplest" impulses of the tsar. Statesmen, in his view, had no place in a proceeding where Russia's honor was on trial. He therefore bypassed normal channels and went straight to the top. On 10 May he warned the sultan of impending disaster unless there were a change of government. In particular, he accused Rifat pasha and Mehemet Ali of intriguing with officials of the Russian embassy to have him recalled, and demanded that both of them resign at once. The accusation was altogether false. In the hugger-mugger of accusations and reproaches, it was believed for the nonce. Menshikov made a clean sweep. Rifat went—to be succeeded by Reschid, Menshikov's own nominee. Mehemet Ali went. Not only that, all the subordinates in the foreign ministry who had argued against the treaty were cleared out as well. Namyk, the minister of finance, was out: he had refused to deliver a personal message from Menshikov to the sultan. Even the sultan's interpreter was dismissed. Having thus changed the personnel, Menshikov tried to change the policies. He implored the sultan not to regard the treaty as a "European question." Belgium, Greece, and Switzerland had, by Europeanizing, lost their independence. So would Turkey. He insisted on the absolute necessity of a guarantee between Russia and Turkey. Menshikov came within an ace of winning the sultan for the treaty then and there. But the sultan demurred.

On 14 May Reschid, the new foreign minister, saw Stratford. Stratford made the most of the opportunity. He helped Reschid draft an evasive reply that asked for more time. This was Turkey's first formal answer to Menshikov's demand. Menshikov, informed of it on 14 May, flew into rage. He had expected total victory; he had steeled himself against defeat; but for vacillation and discord at so supreme a crisis he was unprepared. He saw

Russia threatened with a blow to her prestige more serious than loss of a battle. Twelve hours passed before the courier who had brought this ominous message was again dispatched to the palace with the Russian's reply. It expressed the amazement of Menshikov that there could be hesitation or doubt. It declared that a "solid agreement" was the only way that Russia and Turkey could get on in peace. It announced that the feelings of Nicholas could not be tampered with and that Menshikov would at once put to sea.

The tsar remained unmoved by these events. He told the French ambassador: "The four of you could dictate to me but that will never happen. I can count on Vienna and Berlin." [12] He instructed his troops to trespass into Moldavia and Wallachia late in May; after much wrangling, they did so on 7 July 1853. The crisis had now reached its term. What motivated Nicholas? Did he suppose that a fresh display of force would break Turkish resistance? Was he taken aback by Menshikov's failure? Did he shrink from withdrawing his demands on Turkey once they had been launched? It is impossible to tell which feather turned the scale. Economic objects were, it seems, lacking in this desire—at best, glosses on the fundamental conflict, not its cause. Otherwise he would not have run the risk of antagonizing the British, the major suppliers of Russia's machine tools and her biggest customer in the grain trade. So too with religious grievances. Perhaps Nicholas saw the Turks as the Jacobins had seen the old monarchies—"infidels" and "pagans" with whom there could only be a fight to the finish. But this is doubtful. The dispute over the Holy Places had already been settled to his satisfaction: on 4 May the sultan had proclaimed that his Orthodox and Latin subjects would henceforth be treated alike. Nicholas's real motive was not far to seek. The outcome of the revolutions of 1848 had convinced him that Russia was the greatest Power in the world. The new European order seemed to work exclusively to her advantage. It never crossed the tsar's mind—or anyone else's—that in three years this order would be crushed by a defeat in war— a defeat that would shake Russian society to its foundations.

Nicholas was not inhibited by Austrian anxieties over his intentions. A curious incident showed it. In July he proposed yet another scheme of partition to Francis Joseph. He believed that Turkey would collapse in the wake of Russia's occupation of the principalities: Austria and Russia must therefore seize the initiative. He shrank from re-establishing the Byzantine empire: the best solution would be to allow Asian Turkey to continue to exist and to chop up her European lands. He offered to split the Balkans: Austria could have the western half, Russia the eastern. He offered to divide the Straits: Russia would take the Bosphorus, Austria the Dardanelles.

He had, of course, no success. Francis Joseph dared not spur Nicholas on by making an agreement at so perilous a moment. The Menshikov mission had provoked a fundamental split in British policy. The cabinet felt that they had been taken in by the Seymour conversations. The Menshikov mission threatened, or seemed to threaten, the independence of Turkey. More, it threatened their political lives: on 29 May Russell wrote Aberdeen that the government would fall unless some decisive stroke were taken. Stratford warned Clarendon that Nicholas would strike again and urged resistance. Prominent financiers and businessmen banded together and drafted a *Banker's Circular* which was peppered with statistics to show that an independent Ottoman empire was vital to British economic interests. Yet the government continued to walk warily. Aberdeen voiced his objections against pushing the country to the brink of war and speculated that the collapse of Turkey "may or may not be inevitable." Besides, "I should as soon think of preferring the Koran to the Bible as of comparing the Christianity and civilization of Russia to the fanaticism and immorality of the Turks."[13] Aberdeen still believed that conciliation was the wisest course, if it could be brought about; only now the alternative of war must be put more clearly before the tsar. He hoped that there was a rational Nicholas whom force would deter. He feared that there was an irrational Nicholas whom force would provoke. He steered uneasily between hope and fear. What followed after May was a change of emphasis, not a change of course.

The immediate emphasis was on firmness, and no wonder. For at this uneasy moment Napoleon III offered the British an alliance to defend Turkey against Russia. This cheered the advocates of a strong line. Nicholas would, it seemed, be "hit on the head" at last, and with two clubs instead of one; the Russian threat against Turkey would be checked, broken. Napoleon's proposal for an entente was accepted by the cabinet at the end of May. On 1 June the British cabinet dispatched the fleet to Besika Bay, next door to the Dardanelles; a French squadron pulled along side a forthnight later, and the entente of October 1849 was recalled to life "literally by a side wind."[14] The entente was formalized on 10 April 1854 when Great Britain and France bound themselves to each other to protect Turkey against Russia.

This was a political event of the first importance, the first time in 200 years that Great Britain and France had fought on the same side in a war against a common enemy. Though the alliance broke down in Europe after the Crimean war, it continued to operate more or less efficiently throughout the rest of the world for the next thirty years. The alliance thus marked an end to the world rivalry that had blackened relations between the two Powers since the time of Louis XIV—a diplomatic overturn, and one unexpected by all observers.

Until the dawn of Louis Napoleon the "liberal alliance," as it later came to be called, was a phrase rather than an institution, and even as a phrase had not much reality. England and France had cooperated in the Near East in 1833 and even more in 1849; Palmerston had won France for alliance in 1834. Apart from these, the two Powers had been generally on cold terms. The great Eastern crisis of 1840 had brought Great Britain and France to the edge of war and relations between the two of them were not improved by a succession of crises which had unfolded during the next decade: the episode over the Spanish marriages; the coup d'état of 2 December 1851; repeated alarms over Belgium; the Don Pacifico affair; the *Charlemagne* incident. The legacy of suspicion persisted during the Eastern crisis of 1853. There is a very good illustration. On 29 November 1852 Aberdeen told Brunnow that he feared a French invasion of England. He spoke with increasing alarm about the state of British naval preparations. Besides, "even with equal numbers we should begin by being beaten on land: 50,000 Frenchmen would beat 50,000 Englishmen."[15] In his view the rulers of Europe, whatever their interests or personal concerns, were all pretty much of a piece; at any rate none of them desired the destruction of the settlement of Vienna. Louis Napoleon was the lone exception, a cuckoo in the nest, as restless against inaction and as fertile with plans as his uncle had been.

These views were not personal quirks. They had been held until recently by many politically minded Englishmen. They were the accepted doctrine at the time; and, by dint of repeated assertion, the doctrine won acceptance from many people who had formerly called themselves friends of France. For instance, it was generally supposed that Louis Napoleon was the predestined successor of Louis XIV and that it was only a matter of time before he stepped into his inheritance. Louis Napoleon liked to make out that his system was based on the British parliamentary tradition and preference for the rule of law. During the by-elections of 1853 this idea was attacked. Wood, president of the board of control, declared that the French system was sham and that Louis Napoleon was a dangerous demagogue who was debarred by his ancestry and political outlook from belonging to the European system of security; the most that could be expected was that he would postpone his plans for a revision of Europe while hurrying after British favor. These suspicions transformed the alliance into an uneasy partnership, punctuated by tension and mutual distrust. British sentiment swung back towards suspicion against France as it had often done before 1853. It doubted the sincerity of Napoleon III, became wary of his designs, and friendly towards his enemies. British statesmen were affected by this. They resented the preponderance of Russia which had, they supposed, threatened the independence of central Europe and caused the downfall of the revolutions of 1848. But they certainly shrank from underwriting every French grievance against the settlement of Vienna. Napoleon III's obsession with nationalism seemed not so much mistaken as exaggerated; and those British statesmen who sought to lull this obsession with a form of words supposed that an alliance against Russia would be a drag chain on his revolutionary ambitions.

Napoleon III of course thought otherwise. He fought Russia out of a desire to win Great Britain for a Europe that would be remade in his own mold. Though he realized the British interest was confined to the Near East, he supposed that an alliance, once cemented there, would open the door to cooperation elsewhere. Deeper convictions entered in. Napoleon III knew England and the United States better than most Frenchmen, and he believed passionately that the future of both France and of humanity lay with these Powers. It was only because he was of all statesmen most favorable to Great Britain that the alliance was made at all. Only a few ranters on the extreme Right kept up the old hatred of England; virtually none favored Russia. But many distrusted the constancy of the two Powers which had, they supposed, and not altogether wrongly, caused the collapse of French fortunes before— at Constantinople and in Egypt for example; some, intoxicated by "the legend," dreamt of restoring France to the position of European predominance which she had enjoyed before 1815. Napoleon III shared this feeling. Russian power was the strongest peg in the European system of legitimacy that he abhorred and wanted to overthrow; and he was confident that his personal charm and political skill would erase any lingering suspicions which his enemies might still harbor. Defeating Russia in a war would launch the era of liberalism that he had foretold and would raise his prestige. As well, it would eclipse the memory of 1812. More practical arguments than prestige could, of course, be found for going with England. Menshikov's demands were supposed to be a prelude to a new bout of Russian aggressiveness. Nicholas was expected to lay hands on Turkey; Great Britain and France must stand in his way. Whether valid or not, this conviction was passionately held in London and Paris. Both Napoleon III and the British, with the exception—admittedly a big exception—of Aberdeen and his supporters, believed that the independence of Turkey was vital to their security. This conclusion, once reached, pulled away all the happy calculations of Russian restraint and moderation on which the opponents of action had relied.

II

This was obviously true of the British. The Russian occupation of the principalities caused an uproar of public opinion. What is more, it further divided the government. Though Palmerston was home secretary, he could not keep his hands off the conduct of foreign policy. He harangued Clarendon and bombarded Aberdeen with long papers. He proposed resolute action by sending the fleet through the Straits; the cabinet, prompted by Stratford, overruled him. Napoleon III on his side was flickering towards Drouyn de Lhuys's idea of resolving the crisis through diplomacy and also favored caution. Diplomacy meant calling in "Europe"—that is, Austria and Prussia—to resolve the issue. Here was the guiding thread in the diplomacy of the Crimean war: "the attempt of the two conflicting sides to involve the Central Powers and so achieve a decision." [16]

A wholesale ideological war against Russia launched by Great Britain with the aid of "the revolution" in the person of Napoleon III immediately turned the screws on Austria and Prussia as the friends of Russia. Whether the war was about the Eastern question or about the swell of Russian power in Europe, it could only be fought to a conclusion if Austria and Prussia joined in. If the war were a fundamental clash of creeds between East and West, as some British radicals supposed, then Austria and Prussia ought to have gone with Russia against Great Britain and France—gone, that is, not only as members of the Holy Alliance but as Powers tied together by tradition and political outlook. But what if it were about Turkey? In such case, a war to choke off Russia from the Danube was even more Austria's war than it was a French or British war. The Crimean war was, in fact, two wars rolled into one; and Austria's policy reflected both of its sides. On the one side she was threatened by Russia. The occupation of the principalities was a dagger at her heart. Austria tried repeatedly to pluck up the courage to take the decisive step of fighting the battle for survival instead of leaving it to the French and British. All the same, Austria shrank from a war in which she would bear the full brunt. She had four times been mauled by the first Napoleon and her institutions had been shaken. She had already been pulled down by the revolutions of 1848; how much more devastating must the results be to her society of an out-and-out war against Russia. Such a war would bring "the revolution" in its train and, worse still, would pave the way for the triumph of Napleon III and his principle of nationality. These were not the only reasons which made the Austrians hesitate. Right down to the outbreak of war in 1866 Prussia was bent on equality with Austria in Germany if not superiority to her. Only a few Austrians appreciated the extent of the Prussian ambitions; this did not make them any less suspicious of her. The Eastern question was sheer gain for Prussia. It was bound to disturb the Holy Alliance and perhaps even to estrange Russia from Austria but there was no danger of estranging Russia from Prussia. The Prussian object was simple: to keep the war from German soil. The Prussians calculated too that they had everything to gain from Austrian anxiety and resentment. The more Austria was driven into hostility towards Russia, the more the Prussians would have a free hand between the Holy Alliance on the one side and commitment to the western Powers on the other—a free hand, that is, to refuse both. All the same the issue was never in doubt: the Prussians, to all intents and purposes, did nothing between 1853 and 1856, and did it very well.

Austria thus had the best reasons for not wanting the war to be fought at all and the best reasons for not wanting either side to win. Hence the Austrian policy of acting sometimes against Russia, sometimes against England and France. From start to finish Austria's policy was the desperate, feeble kick of the last monarchy of the "old school" and, when we consider some parts of the European record, not all that feeble. In the first months of the crisis, Austria's policy was not fully worked out or fully applied but its principles had been established, and as Austria's stake in the issue became clearer her eagerness to call off the conflict increased also, particularly to the detriment of the Russians. It is said that Metternich regretted this policy of Austria's. There is little record that he provided any alternative. The critics of Austrian diplomacy, from the exiles in London to the ministers and generals in the imperial circle, were merely afraid what would happen if war spread to their borders. Here too the Austrians were pushed by geography into paths along which they were not happy to go. Obviously the object of their immediate concern was the evacuation of the principalities; and they concentrated all their efforts in the summer of 1853 to secure this object. The tsar did not respond. Austria therefore shifted her weight against him. Yet this was part of the broader, the vital Austrian aim of restraining both sides and of bringing the war to an end as soon as possible. To pursue this sleight of hand required consummate skill if it were to be achieved without making Austria the enemy of both Russia and the western Powers—a formidable task if ever there were one.

Buol, who took over foreign affairs in 1852, was a symbol of this policy. His predecessors, Metternich and Schwarzenberg, had posed alternatives: Austria must follow one line or the other. Buol chose both. All his diplomacy aimed at bringing together the two opposing sides: to satisfy Russia without offending the western Powers, and to satisfy the western Powers without offending, or rather humiliating, Russia. This was in keeping with his

personality. He was, without doubt, of a higher private character than any
of his predecessors with none of Schwarzenberg's brutality or Metternich's
shiftiness. Cultured, sympathetic, honest, he ran over with good intentions:
desired good relations with Great Britain; a reconciliation with France; fair
play for the oppressed nationalities; and even cooperation with Prussia. The
lithograph of 1854 is instructive—long fine nose, neatly combed hair
brushing the ears, thin lips faintly curled, smooth delicate hands, manicured
fingernails, black cutaway coat, narrow bow tie—altogether a pleasant
picture. His erect shoulders, pink cheeks, large blue eyes, and firm, upright
chin suggested a man of cast-iron resolution and singleness of purpose;
contemporary observers found him otherwise. In appearance and manner he
remains an enigma. His name was, or rather became, a symbol of equivocation—abused by conservatives, praised, though more rarely, by liberals. An
acute critic of his policy writes: "He seems colorless, his personal attributes
and talents subject to widely differing interpretations, his previous career
unremarkable, though not unimportant, his relation to the Emperor and his
colleagues unclear." [17]

Buol played most diplomatic problems competently, though others did
better with less fuss. Hard-working and impatient, he was good at his job—
a job that was not as easy as is sometimes supposed. His job was diplomacy
and in particular to maintain the greatness of the house of Hapsburg. He
brought settled conviction to his office: he knew that friendship with Russia
was in immediate jeopardy once the Eastern question burst into flames. He
knew, as well, that the disputes between Russia and Turkey could never be
ended by merely contesting every issue as it arose. New disputes would arise
unless there were a general settlement. The great aristocrats at court wished
to return to a policy of conservative solidarity with Russia; Buol believed that
this was impossible. Russia's intervention in Hungary in 1849 did more than
anything else to encourage the architects of Hapsburg policy to take their own
line—even if, as Buol urged or was to urge, this meant alliance with Great
Britain and France.

Did Buol sow the seeds of destruction by breaking with the conservative
tradition of forty years and thereby ruin the Hapsburg monarchy as a Great
Power? The answers by historians have gone up and down with the years.
Immediately after the outbreak of war, when the Russians, prompted by
Austria's ultimatum, evacuated the principalities, Austrian historians asserted
that Buol had wielded the bow of Metternich and had done so more
efficiently and with greater resolution; after the war, Russian historians
roundly condemned him as a villain who had gratuitously blackened the eyes
of his country's best friend and got nothing in return. The Russian view won

widespread acceptance at home and elsewhere and became the standard
orthodoxy for more than a century. In recent years, Buol has crept back into
favor as a man who did the best he could with what he had—a traditionalist
who broke with tradition only after all other means had been exhausted.

The latest view is the most sensible. Buol was not, as is sometimes alleged,
an inexperienced amateur. On the contrary, few men were better qualified
to be foreign minister of the Hapsburg monarchy. Metternich and Schwarzenberg, though more successful than Buol, thought highly of him and sent
him all over the map of Europe as their ambassador. The names of his
embassies are worth recording: Stuttgart, Turin, St. Petersburg, Dresden,
London. Towards the end of the Crimean war opinions were reversed and
Metternich presented Buol in sackcloth and ashes—a bungling incompetent
who had thrown away the conservative inheritance bequeathed him. The
contrast between them, in this period as in others, was overdrawn. Both
desired a settlement of the Eastern question that would check Russia without
humiliating her; both desired it on diplomatic terms profitable to Austria. At
all times they saw the specter of "the revolution" on the horizon if the Eastern
question broke away from diplomatic control. Both men, as foreign ministers,
knew that their policy would not be tolerated by their opponents at home
unless it left Austria more secure and enhanced Austria's prestige; hence they
sometimes seemed to the ambassadors at Vienna to be devious and not above
cheating their allies. The ultimate object, a general settlement of the Eastern
question by the methods of diplomacy, did not alter.

Buol had, however, two great handicaps which threatened to hamstring his
policy. The first was the condition of Austria. The revolutions of 1848 had
brought the monarchy to the ground; its rulers still lived in their shadow.
Antagonism among the nationalities had not really disappeared with the
revolutions of 1848. All were discontented. All had tasted the promise, if not
the reality, of victory in 1848, the Germans more than the rest. They resented
the demands imposed by the army, and resented, as the wealthiest and best
educated class, the mess that the Hapsburgs had made of the financial affairs.
Unbalanced budgets were the rule, not the exception, in the Austria of the
1850s; loans from abroad even more. Railway building, which featured so
conspicuously in the economic development of the other Powers, lagged
behind in the Hapsburg lands—an ominous reflection on its strength. These
weaknesses were bound to affect Buol's diplomacy. Foreign policy is, after
all, the product of deep social and economic forces; it is not crudely
manufactured in chancelleries. Bismarck as usual was right when he likened
Austria to a worm-eaten galleon; equally right when he said: "The Emperor
of Austria has many ministers, but when he wants something done, he has
to do it himself."

Buol had a second and more profound dilemma. He was the foreign minister of Francis Joseph, Emperor of Austria, Apostolic King of Hungary, King, Archduke, Grand Duke, Count, and Lord of this, that, and the other, to say nothing of being titular King of Jerusalem. Francis Joseph was a gentle, puzzled young man of twenty-three, not very bright, with a romantic sense of devotion to his dynastic duty. He had, as archduke, been plain Francis; the additional name stuck on to his title evoked Joseph II, the People's Emperor. This was a deception. Francis Joseph had nothing in common with his illustrious predecessor. He had none of Joseph II's innovative spark or reforming zest. His ideas were dusty. He was rigid and narrow. "He called himself the 'last monarch of the old school' and imagined himself at one with Charles V or Louis XIV. Their pride had rested on unquestioning self-confidence; his was always conscious of the challenge of 'the revolution.' He represented traditional beliefs and institutions when these had been forced on the defensive; like them he lacked faith even in himself. He always expected failure and disappointment, and he always got them." [18]

Here, then, was another obstacle in Buol's path, adding to the clamor, threatening the direction of Austrian policy. Nevertheless, in the hard circumstances of June 1853, Buol could not afford to hesitate. A Danube under Russian control would mean the strangulation of the Hapsburg monarchy; this was the opinion even of Buol's opponents at court, the great aristocrats who sighed for a new Holy Alliance. Hence Buol's desire to resolve matters with a plan that would strengthen the independence of Turkey and yet meet with the approval of the tsar—a classic definition of Hapsburg policy in Metternich's time.

His first attempt came in the summer of 1853. A series of concessions had been made by the Turks in a document that came to be called the "Turkish ultimatum." It had been drafted by Reschid with the help of Stratford, and sent to a four Power ambassadorial conference which Buol had convened in Vienna. The "Turkish ultimatum" attempted to settle the Eastern question by reciting the concessions granted by the sultan to his Orthodox subjects over the last century. It referred to the peaceful attitude of Turkey despite the Russian occupation of Moldavia and Wallachia. Most important, it promised that "the ancient privileges professed by the Emperor of Russia and by the great part of his subjects have been fully confirmed in perpetuity." [19] The French jibbed at this wording; in their view, or at least in the view of Napoleon III, the affair was between France and Russia; and they insisted that any formula for peace reflect this. Buol acquiesced. The Vienna note—the fundamental document that would dominate the attention of the statesmen of Europe for the next two months—therefore laid down that the

Porte would not alter the conditions of the Christians "without previous understanding with the Governments of France and Russia." [20]

The Vienna note raised problems from the start. It had to be enforced by the Great Powers; it could not, as it were, enforce itself. This was obviously true in regard to the Turks. Few Turks accepted the note as a fair settlement among equals. Most Turks meant to shake off some part of the note as soon as it was convenient to do so. They differed as to timing—some wishing to repudiate it at once; others wishing to postpone it until the Russians had been put in the wrong. Enforcing the note ran against practical difficulties quite apart from these general objections. Its formal, though secret, submission to the Russians beforehand offended Turkish pride. The "Turkish ultimatum" had saved Turkey's face by making "Europe" witness to her promises to Russia. "Europe" fell out of the Vienna note. Turkey was made accountable to France and Russia—beautiful example of using the machinery of peace against the victim of aggression.

The Vienna note was sent off to Constantinople at the end of July. A week's lull now relaxed the rigors of diplomatic negotiation. The Eastern question, as it was now called, still monopolized general attention—a clear threat to the peace of Europe. The Austrians, including Buol, were again waiting, though they did not know for what. For a conciliatory gesture from the Turks? Or for a new bout of negotiations? Their minds told them that it ought to be the first; practice gradually led them towards the second. After all, they could, with enormous effort, extract such concessions from the Russians as would quieten the crisis, or so they supposed. They could do little to influence the Turks. For there was a problem of communications. There was a telegraph line from most capitals to Vienna; there was no line from Vienna to Constantinople. This was a considerable handicap. The five Great Powers had indeed designed a solution to the crisis. They could not secure the acceptance of the Turks over the wires; a week or ten days was needed to get a message through.

The Russians accepted the Vienna note on 5 August. This decision threw British policy into disarray. The hardliners in the government were now haunted by the fear that the negotiations might succeed and that Russia might scrape through the crisis with her prestige unsullied. They had a deeper worry still. Stratford was now exasperated with the negotiations and ready to bolt. He insisted on a straight confirmation of the "Turkish ultimatum" by the ambassadors at Vienna; he shrank from forcing a Franco-Russian protectorate down Turkish throats. He believed that the Turks had stretched conciliation a long way by the concessions which they had made in their "ultimatum" of the previous month; he balked at the prospect of asking them for more. The Turks, on their side, saw matters in exactly the same light. They argued over the Vienna note for a fortnight; and on 19 August turned it down, insisting instead on amendments. For instance, they made the position of their Christian subjects dependent solely on the benevolence of the sultan; in addition to this, they struck out all references to the treaty of Kutchuk Kainardji. The Russians rejected their amendments out of hand. The negotiations deadlocked once more.

Were the Turks justified in their decision? Should the Austrians have been as suspicious of Stratford's influence on the Turks as he was of their dealings with the Russians? For that matter, could Stratford have won the Turks for the Vienna note if he had tried? No questions are more overlaid by controversy or more confused by hindsight. Certainly Stratford enjoyed a position at Constantinople. The other Powers could boast of no champions to balance his influence. No doubt he foresaw the Turkish objections. No doubt the Vienna note ran against his better judgment. This is not to say that his intervention would have produced a different reaction. The Turks would have rejected the Vienna note with or without Stratford. Indeed they had always assumed that Russia would twist its words to her own advantage; they did not take seriously her acceptance of the Vienna note; and Buol's assurances to the contrary did not move them. What was surprising is that their rejection of the note was not more categorical or high-minded. Stratford was a heavy-handed operator on many occasions, particularly in his later dealings with the French, but the charges against him have, on this occasion, been exaggerated.

Stratford's own mind was clear: by confining himself to official encouragement he would incline the Turks more readily towards agreement. Musurus pasha, a good judge of British affairs, was convinced throughout August that the cabinet would back the Turks, no matter what they decided. There is even better evidence. On 18 August Reschid pasha visited Stratford. He was concerned to show that the sultan would make a better deal with Russia by amending the Vienna note than if he waited for a more militant ministry to break out on the tormentors of Turkey. On the following day he carried the grand council for his policy. The Turkish decision sprang from their independent resolve. No advice from Stratford would have changed it. If there is to be a criticism of Stratford, it must be that he did not keep the government informed of the mounting indignation in Turkey. This indignation was itself the logical by-product of British indecisiveness and hesitation. Moreover, the British lacked a directing hand to insist on priorities. It was easier to acquiesce to immediate impulses and to drift with events. This encouraged the Turks to suspect the worst in the Russians and to turn their backs on the negotiators at Vienna. Not that their fears were unjustified. The Turks had rejected the Vienna note because they believed that it was a cover for more aggressive designs. As a matter of fact they were proved right by events. For the Russians still had the religious protectorate up their sleeves. A small incident proved it. On 7 September Nesselrode, with curiously uncharacteristic bluster, asserted in the German press that the Vienna note gave Russia everything that Menshikov had sought—by which, of course, he meant the protectorate over the Orthodox Christians of Turkey. This may have been an exaggeration of events, squeezed up to satisfy public opinion; its consequences could not have been worse. When news of this "violent interpretation" reached London, the government, or most of them, at once became convinced that the Russians had tried to cheat and that the Turks had been right to break off. The British regarded Nesselrode's declaration as tantamount to a new Menshikov mission and to the demand which the tsar had tacitly repudiated when he had accepted the Vienna note. From this it was a short step to thinking that the Russians were aiming at the dismemberment of the Turkish empire and—a worse offense—that they had deliberately deceived the British by their offers of cooperation over the Eastern question in 1844 and in January of the present year.

The statement is not totally accurate. Some British statesmen—Palmerston for instance—had already determined that the western Powers could not force the Vienna note upon Turkey in the event that Turkey rejected it, as indeed they hoped she would. They were not alarmed by Nesselrode's announcement. Rather the reverse: they regarded it as ammunition for their own argument that Russia must be resisted at all costs. The tsar's acceptance of the Vienna note had strengthened the hands of their opponents at home. During the first part of September the cabinet went from one provocative muddle to another. Clarendon behaved like a referee in a boxing ring, supervising the combats of others, not as a reconciler of differences. Each minister ran his own department in isolation and constantly sniped at his colleagues. Proposals to pass the Straits were aired by all the activist forces— by the Whig newspapers, by Russell, by Palmerston most of all. Aberdeen stamped on these proposals and insisted on abstention. In his view the Ottoman empire was not worth preserving and he would have liked to settle the crisis on the basis of the proposal that Nicholas had made to Seymour— Russia would strengthen her principalities, consolidate her reactionary hold over Europe, and Great Britain would console herself by taking Egypt. But Aberdeen's powers were shorn. Palmerston and Russell were too strong for him. Abstention was merely the last negative of a coalition cabinet that had failed to coalesce. The proponents of action could not shake their colleagues.

They were stuck for evidence of Russian bad faith—stuck, that is, until Nesselrode unwittingly handed it to them by his "violent interpretation" of the Vienna note.

The western Powers now swung round. On 22 September Walewski proposed to Clarendon that the two fleets should advance to Constantinople. Clarendon and his colleagues had no plausible excuse for this move. They therefore trumped up some false stories of inclement weather in Besika Bay; and with this decked out the order to the fleet on 23 September. This was the decisive step, though not in the way that was subsequently imagined. In the two weeks that had preceded the allied decision there had been reports of imminent insurrection in Constantinople. The friends of England and France feared the consequences of popular hysteria on their ongoing deliberations and proposed to bridle it by asking the allies to send their fleet into the Dardanelles. At the end of September they received what they thought was good news. Stratford had been authorized to call up the fleet. It might be supposed that the Turks deliberately exaggerated the threat of insurrection in the hope that this would sting the British and French into action. This too is not the case. The Turkish ministers knew, of course, that Russian resentment over the Vienna note had been accumulating and was not likely to be relaxed by the presence of the two fleets in the Straits. But they were more apprehensive as to civil disturbance and wished to do all they could to stave it off. What appeared later as a step towards war was made as a security for peace.

For the moment nothing happened. Stratford believed that the order was poorly timed and decided to postpone its execution. For negotiations had resumed in Vienna. Outcome of these was the Buol project, developed at a meeting between the tsar and Francis Joseph at Olmütz in the last week of September. Nicholas was alarmed and in a conciliatory mood. Pressed by Buol, he disavowed any desire to secure new rights in Turkey or to intervene in her internal affairs. His promises were to be submitted to the Vienna conference, which Buol promised to reconvene. They would be guaranteed by the Powers and transmitted to Constantinople. Nicholas knew that the "violent interpretation" had pushed matters to the breaking point. More, "he now wanted the alliance of the three Northern Courts' which he had evaded in 1851."[21] The Austrians would not hear of this. A revival of the Holy Alliance at so crucial a juncture would offend the British and French; and Austria would be stripped of her neutrality. Francis Joseph replied that Austria had to stick to Prussia and could make no alliance to which she did not belong. This was safe enough. Frederick William IV refused to be tempted out of his neutrality for the sake of a forward policy in the Near

East. Nothing the tsar offered (and he offered little) could make it worthwhile for Prussia to fight a war against England and France over the Eastern question. This was the line which Frederick William took when he met Nicholas at Warsaw. He insisted that Russia must first withdraw from the principalities before an alliance was concluded—a condition that, if fulfilled, would have made an alliance unnecessary. Nicholas had been importuned; it was his turn to be importunate. At Potsdam he denounced Prussia's policy as cowardly. Once more he demanded her support out of dynastic loyalty, and threw in for good measure an offer to defend her against a French attack on the Rhine. Frederick William listened patiently to Nicholas, announced that he was very interested, and did nothing.

Both the British and French governments watched the meetings at Warsaw and Potsdam with mounting apprehension. Drouyn was once more having second thoughts about launching a European war, especially a war between France and a revived Holy Alliance. This was the great issue in the autumn of 1853: whether the Holy Alliance could be revived before the Eastern question exploded into war. The meetings at Warsaw and Potsdam gave Drouyn good reason to expect that it could. Napoleon III feared, on his side, that the hole in the Holy Alliance that had developed as a result of the Eastern question was now plugged. He thought to transfer this fear to the British and proposed that they accept the Buol project as evidence of the tsar's moderation and good faith. The British refused to be caught. They were convinced that Russia and Austria had plotted to dismember Turkey; besides, they knew that Napoleon III, if forced to choose between England and Russia, would choose, indeed had to choose, England. They could talk of resisting Russia and if the French refused to back them it was the French, or rather the liberal alliance, which would suffer. These calculations had a curious result. On 8 October the cabinet met for the first time in six weeks. They determined that the Buol project was not enough: it did not extract from the tsar such promises as they could be content with. Clarendon commented: "I daresay that it would be a fatal mistake for us to force upon the Turks a scheme that they are likely to refuse. . . ; we would then place ourselves in great difficulty about affording them aid afterwards."[22]

This was true. The Buol project had as its aim the independence of Turkey; in fact it was virtually the same plan as the "Turkish ultimatum" of July. The Russians had abandoned their claims on Turkey; the original causes for war had become excuses for it. The British government were not below the average of normal times. But the times were not normal. With the Turks roaring at their backs and with British opinion astir, a diplomatic solution to the crisis was a damp squib; what they wanted was a dramatic decision, not merely the withdrawal of the current Russian demands. There was a further consideration. The government balked at swallowing a solution that had been devised behind their backs by the Austrians. This would not suit their prestige. The British wished to keep the Austrians dangling at the end of a string which only the British could pull. Though they wished to cooperate with Austria, they did not view this as a cooperation of equals. They therefore slipped into believing that the Buol project was an Austro-Russian trick or—what amounts to the same thing—that Buol had been bamboozled by the Russians in the same way that they had imagined themselves to have been deceived over the Seymour conversations. Russell laid down: "If Nicholas or Buol or Nesselrode were honest all might be settled in half an hour." [23] The Austrians imagined that there was a solution to the Eastern crisis and that negotiations would produce it. The British believed that the problem was insoluble in terms of negotiations and, more importantly, that the Russians were incorrigibly dishonest and could not be trusted. On the other hand, the Russians pushed this logic on. At Olmütz the tsar had developed another, though more temporary, way of postponing Austrian cooperation with the Western Powers. "Faithful to his old illusion," he praised his dream project of a partition of Turkey: "once more he talked of Constantinople as a Free City, offered the western Balkans to Austria, and even suggested a protectorate of the Danubian principalities, anything, in fact, to break the solidarity of 'Europe.'" [24] Without success. The prospect of Russian control of the Balkans turned the Austrian rulers pale. Nicholas could not bring himself to realize what was obvious to everyone else: the Russian occupation of the principalities threatened the security not only of Turkey but "Europe"; Russia had fallen out of favor when the first Russian soldier had crossed the Pruth. Nothing could turn the Austrian flank until she withdrew.

This was obvious to the British government. On 8 October they instructed Stratford to summon the fleet at once. In part this was done to cement their alliance with France; in part to confront the tsar with an overwhelming display of force. As well, it sprang from anxiety over public opinion at home. In any case the decision was unanimous. On 2 October even Aberdeen confessed himself apprehensive that the fleet was not at Constantinople. He said to Colloredo, the Austrian ambassador: "England must prevent Turkey from being left to ruin. Public opinion will not allow us to abandon her." [25] Clarendon mumbled the same fear to Stratford: "The alarm here is universal among the educated and business and rational segments of the population." He claimed that the move was, at bottom, defensive: "Great care must be taken that the fleet doesn't give too much encouragement to Turkey. We have as yet no quarrel with Russia." [26]

Stratford was in a dilemma. He had deliberately refrained from calling the fleet at the end of September for fear it would make the Turks bellicose. Now he was given no choice. In any event the decision to move the fleet to the Straits brought Napoleon III back into the fold. He now limped after his ally: similar orders were issued to the French fleet two days after the meeting of 8 October. With this decision the western Powers passed the point of no return. In the words of Sidney Herbert, the youngest member of the cabinet: "We all agreed as to the objects in view. We must have a Power at the Bosphorous to hold the keys of the Mediterranean from the East. This Power cannot be Russia. We cannot allow Russia to encroach upon or undermine the power which is vital to us there. We are not bound by treaty to interfere, but we are bound by our own interest and by European interests, not to allow Turkey to be overborne. We are further bound in honour not to abandon Turkey in difficulties that have resulted from decisions made with our sanction or taken with our advice."[27]

III

Meanwhile, new alarms came tumbling in from Constantinople. Goaded to fury, the Turks had gone berserk. When they learnt that Russia had rejected their amendments to the Vienna note a surge of patriotic enthusiasm broke over the city. The passion for war reached a fever pitch; all lesser passions were laid aside. On the afternoon of 26 September the sultan held a council of war. Its members deliberated as Turkish soldiers paraded through the streets amid shouts from the multitudes. While the council met appeals for caution poured in from London and Paris. Stratford, on his side, warned Reschid that England and France could not back Turkey against Russia in a war which Turkey declared first. To no avail. The sultan and his ministers were determined to throw down the gauntlet. On 4 October 1853 they declared war on Russia; at Stratford's behest, they agreed not to take up arms. They soon broke their word. On 8 October Reschid sent a note to Stratford formally requesting the presence of the western fleets in the Straits. Stratford had not yet heard of the outcome of the Buol project, and put the matter off for a few days. Having learnt that the project had fallen to the ground, he determined that he could wait no longer. On 20 October he carried out his instructions; and two days later the British fleet followed by the French sailed into the Dardanelles. Now there was no restraining the Turks. On 23 October Turkish forces under Omer pasha passed the Danube "and killed some Russians."[28]

News of Turkey's declaration of war threw the British government into high alarm. On 24 October a dispatch was sent off to Constantinople warning that a "desire for war on the part of Turkey would be viewed with great displeasure in this country." [29] Palmerston objected: the dispatch must not be an instrument that the Turks must either take as is or reject, and demanded it be amended. He failed. Russell had better luck. The dispatch had demanded the suspension of hostilities by the Turks as a preliminary to negotiation. At the last minute Russell got Clarendon to add "for a reasonable period of time" after this phrase. This gave the Turks a loophole; and they took advantage of it. On 5 November they laid down their arms; and took them up again in less than a fortnight.

The British cabinet were now paralyzed by weak and divided leadership. Extreme answered extreme. Aberdeen believed that the ground had been cut from under him by Clarendon over the dispatch of 24 October. Palmerston attacked Aberdeen as a coward and called for immediate entry into the Black Sea. Clarendon said to Aberdeen: "You cannot be more averse to war than I am, but if our pacific determination is too clearly reckoned upon, we may render war inevitable." [30] In such circumstances, it was not surprising that the last attempt for peace—again the work of Buol—failed utterly. This was the protocol of 5 December, signed in Vienna by the representatives of the four Powers. The story of its negotiation is a complicated tangle, significant only to those who participated. Essentially it called upon the tsar to respect Turkey's integrity (a repeat of his pledge at Olmütz) and simultaneously instructed the sultan not to walk out on his promises to his Christian subjects. The protocol of 5 December was destroyed by the opposition of the British government. The cabinet claimed to approach the protocol of 5 December with detachment. In reality they came to it with their minds made up. First they were against the protocol; then they discovered the arguments to justify their opposition. They had displayed their unhappiness at every stage. They had jibbed at the wording of the protocol. They had swallowed almost every piece of Austrian phraseology with manifest reluctance. They now took steps which rendered it meaningless. For instance, they insisted on an amendment to make as a basis of negotiation any terms which the Turks dreamt up. This was a high fence to ride at. The Turks had skimped on concessions to the Russians; and the circumstances of the moment were not likely to make them more conciliatory. The machinery of peace had ground to a halt; and everyone knew it. At bottom the British balked at any scheme of which Austria was the author. The more the Austrians insisted on the protocol of 5 December, the more the British pressed against it. The British wanted a dramatic decision that would humiliate Russia and enshrine her defeat. The

Austrians wanted a decision that the Russians could live with without feeling disgraced.

The British fears were of little moment. On 30 November the Russians got the victory in war which they had failed to get in peace. On 13 November a Turkish flotilla had been sent to Sinope, supposedly on a pacific mission. Osman pasha, the admiral, had been ordered to keep on his good behavior and not to fire unless fired upon. Soon after he got there he sent back a dispatch complaining of six Russian sail of line which were just off port: "If reenforcements are not sent to us and our position continues the same for sometime, it may well happen that the Imperial fleet may incur disaster." [31] His appeal fell on deaf ears; no ships were sent to aid the flotilla at Sinope against Russian warships from Sebastopol, barely a hundred miles away. On the morning of 30 November the Russian squadron put in at Sinope, and demanded that Osman hoist the white flag. Osman refused and fired the first shot. Minutes later the Russian battleships answered his guns. Before morning was out every Turkish ship had been destroyed and 3,000 Turkish soldiers were killed.

Sinope was memorable as the most spectacular success in the history of the Russian Black Sea fleet. It was memorable for another, more important reason. For 300 years wooden sailing ships held their unchecked sway over the seas. Sinope was the last time they did so. During the Crimean war wooden ships fell out of fashion; armored men of war, driven by steam, took their place. Curiously enough, the Russians seemed to have recognized this new twist of fate. Sinope had no sequel. The Russian fleet made no appearance in the Black Sea; and before the Crimean war was over the Russian warships were finished off by their own crews. A historian of the technology of war has written: "Exact figures are lacking but it appears that in 1854 and 1855 the Russian fleet lost in this way 4 ships out of 120 guns, 12 84's and 4 60-gun frigates besides a large number of smaller vessels." [32]

The "massacre of Sinope" had a more immediate effect. It was decisive in its effect on British public opinion—"the symbol which removed all doubt." [33] Those who had railed against Russia from the beginning were at last proven right. They had said that Nicholas would never rest content: he would march from one conquest to another, and could be stopped only by force or the threat of force. The emotional outburst was soon translated into practical response. Early in December the cabinet had decided that the fleet should move into the Black Sea if Russian troops crossed the Danube. When the news of Sinope arrived the decision was changed; and the fleet was instructed to proceed into the Black Sea at once.

Of course it would be too simple an explanation for all that happened between 1853 and 1854 merely to say that Great Britain and France were pulled into war by the impact of Sinope. The Aberdeen coalition was already on the verge of disintegration. Palmerston had rebelled, had resigned over the question of parliamentary reform, and now Russell was threatening to resign too. Early in December he had told Aberdeen that he would resign unless the fleet were ordered to the Black Sea. The decision to make the Black Sea entry conditional on Russian passing of the Danube and then, after Sinope, to move in at once, was designed to satisfy Russell. It was also designed to satisfy Palmerston. It did both. Russell agreed to stay on and Palmerston withdrew his resignation on 25 December.

Nor was this all. On 19 December a strong communication was received from Napoleon III. It demanded that all Russian warships and transports in the Black Sea be intercepted and returned to port. Turkey would, to Napoleon's mind, never be safe until the western Powers "swept the Russian flag from the sea;"[34] and he announced that he would act alone if Great Britain refused. At the cabinet meeting Clarendon professed fear for the alliance if they rejected Napoleon's proposal. More pacific men—Gladstone (chancellor of the exchequer), for instance, most strongly—echoed him. Aberdeen resisted. At the last minute Cowley telegraphed from Paris with a compromise: "Offer the French Government to send the fleet into the Black Sea for defensive purposes and promise to adopt the full suggestion should peace negotiations fail."[35] Aberdeen would have liked to reject this proposal: "We must first know the outcome of the negotiations."[36] But in the end he came round and consented. He said to the queen: "It was stated categorically that the Emperor of the French would either act alone or that he would withdraw his fleet to Toulon. Public opinion in the country would not permit the dissolution of the Alliance at so critical a juncture."[37] The cabinet thought that they could yield to Napoleon on the fleet if they pledged him to urge the peace proposals in the protocol of 5 December. The decision to enter the Black Sea was typical of Anglo-French relations during the Crimean war: "from start to finish the maritime Powers were drawn along by the need to prove to each other their mutual good faith."[38] On 24 December simultaneous orders went out from London and Paris. On 3 January 1854 the allied fleets entered the Black Sea.

The allied fleets were in the Black Sea for pacific purposes—that is, to protect Turkish ships and to confine the Russian navy to its base at Sebastopol. All the same "the move was next door to a declaration of war."[39] Nicholas knew this; he supposed the time had come to call the Holy Alliance into action. Orlov was taken off the shelf and dispatched to Vienna with a fresh offer: Russia would cooperate with Austria in the Balkans and would not change things there without her approval. The Austrians responded as though someone had trodden on a sore corn. Buol argued that a revived Holy Alliance would incite French agitation in Italy. Francis Joseph went further and demanded the Russian troops withdraw behind the Danube. This was out of the question for reasons of military strategy: it implied that the Austrians desired to pin down Russia's land operations at the very moment the western fleets were entering the Black Sea and pinning down her naval maneuvers. The Vienna deliberations—if the word can be used for so empty a procedure—were therefore a broken reed. Budberg, at Berlin, struck the same note with Frederick William IV. Frederick William had an urgent reason for resisting Russia's promptings: he was in the midst of offering his neutrality to the British in the hope of receiving from them a promise of support in Germany. He received nothing. The British wanted Prussia as an ally against Russia; nothing short of this would do. All the same, Frederick William shrank from the prospect of incurring their wrath by making a bargain with the Russians; he sought to emulate Budberg in sincerity, if in little else, and to emphasize the breach between Prussia and the tsar. An anti-Russian coalition of Europe, against which both Orlov and Nesselrode had been struggling from the start, was inexorably growing to maturity.

The meetings at Vienna and Berlin were therefore futile formalities. Nonetheless they were not without effect on the western Powers. In France there was a strong current running towards reconciliation. The meetings between Orlov and the despots of central Europe convinced Napoleon III that the Holy Alliance had been recalled to life. This was the last thing he wanted. He was now resolute for peace where he had formerly been ripe for war. In January he appealed to the tsar for direct negotiations between France and Russia. This proposal, like those of Orlov to Francis Joseph and Frederick William, sounded daring; in reality, it did not amount to much. Napoleon III could not join hands with Russia without a swindle on the British government. An alliance with Russia, or even direct negotiations with her, must inevitably be anti-British. Either made sense only if the British were made to join; or, alternatively, if the Anglo-French alliance were destroyed. Napoleon wanted the first of these things. He therefore insisted that the British be told before the alliance was signed; the tsar, on his side, was equally insistent that it must be signed before the British were told. On 12 January he announced: "Russia will be in 1854 what she has been in 1812,"[40] and broke off. To some extent the French approach served Russia's turn. News of it reached the British almost at once. They immediately protested; and Napoleon III was once again faced with a choice between alliance with

Russia and entente with Great Britain. Of course, he would have liked not to choose. All the same the issue, once raised, was never in doubt: in his eyes the British connection was a vital necessity; good relations with Russia an agreeable extra. His appeal was symbolic—dying echo of the Franco-Russian bickering which began the Crimean war; presage too of their entente "with which it ended."[41] It was, as well, positively the last kick in the efforts of diplomacy to avert the war. Thus the two sides circled round each other like wrestlers seeking advantage before the clinch. On 4 February the Russian ambassadors in London and Paris asked for their passports; two days later they left. On 27 February an Anglo-French ultimatum, demanding the evacuation of the principalities, was sent off to St. Petersburg. When this was refused the French on 27 March 1854 declared war. The British followed the next day.

Chapter 6

THE FOUR POINTS

In 1848 the system of security against France devised in the treaty of Vienna was still complete; French hegemony was checked; Louis Philippe was impotent; the victors were ostensibly united; and the system, or the most conservative part of it, was reinforced by the Holy Alliance. Eight years later all this had changed. International stability was first shaken by the collapse of order in Europe that began in February 1848. But "Europe" weathered the storm. The French peril for example—never as acute as men thought—ended abruptly with the election of Louis Napoleon Bonaparte as president of the Second Republic in December 1848; the president was the "guardian of order," dependent on clerical support; and he showed this as much in his foreign policy as he did in home affairs. Hence the first military action of the Second Republic was against a republic led and defended by Mazzini and Garibaldi and in favor of Pope Pius IX. Again, Italian nationalism had made much noise in the early months of 1848—as much in fact as French nationalism from a territorial point of view. It did not raise more than a shadow even of local war, never a shadow of general upheaval. The Poles too had bickered with Prussia over the Posen question; and had later presented themselves to revolutionary France as an unsatisfied "have not" people. The most Poland could do was talk big, not raise an alarm. The German problem stood alone.

The Crimean war first bore witness to this. The history of Europe during the war revolved round the German question, or to put it another way, "the attempt of the two conflicting sides to involve the central Powers and so achieve a decision."[1] The watershed in the diplomatic history of Europe commenced in the summer of 1853 when Drouyn de Lhuys began to devise schemes that would tempt Austria and Prussia out of their neutrality. From that moment change and upheaval went on without interruption until the representatives of the five Great Powers (and a doubtful sixth) met at Paris in January 1856. Why all the fuss? The answer is not far to seek: the Eastern crisis had driven a wedge between Russia and the central Powers—or rather between Russia and Austria on whom western policy mainly turned. The "Austrian question" soon became the dominating topic of international affairs and in Great Britain and France the theme of passionate domestic controversy as well. The controversy was further inflamed by the events of March 1854. In Vienna, the "liberal party" led by Buol was preaching alliance with the western Powers; his persistence in this line stood European diplomacy on its head and brought on a series of events that determined the future fate both of the Hapsburg empire and of Europe.

II

Buol presented his policy in skeleton form at a ministerial conference of 16 January. He presented it again at conferences of 23 January and 31 January. On 21 March he sent a memorandum to Francis Joseph appealing for its adoption. The memorandum of 21 March became the foundation-stone of Hapsburg diplomacy for the next year and is therefore worth looking at closely.

That afternoon Buol saw Francis Joseph at the imperial palace. Buol did most of the talking. He began with a general disquisition on the Eastern question; and he left no doubt that the friendship between Austria and Russia that had existed almost without punctuation since 1815 and which the tsar had taken for granted in his dealings with "Europe" of the past year was at an end. There was no mystery about this. The Russian troops in the principalities were a threat to Austria's existence as nothing had been since the French Revolution—a turning point in Austro-Russian relations that had shaken every assumption of traditional diplomatic practice. Something had to be done to remove this threat. But what? Here Buol did not hesitate. The Russian occupation of the principalities had, he asserted, taken place in July 1853—six months before the western Powers had moved their fleets from the Straits into the Black Sea. Austria could not accept Russia's presence in the principalities without inviting disaster. Her escape from this danger was to be an alliance with Great Britain and France. Such an alliance with the western Powers seemed to him a safe course so long as it brought increased security for Austria and not merely an obligation to support "the revolution."[2]

Buol thereupon unfolded the stages by which the alliance would be made. The first step would be for Great Britain and France to renounce to Austria any thought of territorial acquisition. Austria, on her side, would make a similar renunciation to Great Britain and France. Each of the three would work with the others for the destruction of the Russian protectorates over Serbia and the principalities. The memorandum did not mention Buol's belief that the western Powers would permit Austria to occupy the principalities after the Russians had been driven out. But the idea was there though the phrase was not. No negotiations with Russia were to begin until the object of the alliance had been realized. This was in keeping with the principles that Buol had laid down in the negotiations that had produced the Vienna note. Here he was saying the same thing: he wished to avoid any solution to the Eastern question that was not comprehensive—that is, not satisfactory to all concerned. Without this, new crises would arise. They would grow more frequent, more disastrous, and more difficult to overcome. He ended with a clause that invited Prussia to join in, though he did not, for reasons which soon became clear, say when or on what conditions.

Buol's memorandum caused a considerable stir in Austrian politics. Hess, the chief of staff, had decided long before his colleagues in the army did, that war with Russia would mean the ruination of the house of Hapsburg. This was a reflection of his character and background. He had learnt the principles of absolutist rule from Schwarzenberg and, though these principles were shaped by the Vienna revolution of 1848, their immediate origin was the experiences of the Austrian army in Italy. Taking all this at its worst, most commanders would have diagnosed no more than stupidity or cowardice on the part of the Austrian rulers. Not so Hess. On 25 March in a meeting with Francis Joseph at which Buol was also present, he unfolded his case:

> Should Russia retaliate Turkey would cease to be independent and should fall under the protection of the three Powers who are purporting to promote her independence.
>
> What should come of this? Unquestionably a European war, a war no longer confined to the Near East. This will open a Pandora's box. Poland will rise. Italy will stir in Austria's rear. Austria will be pulled down from her high estate in Germany. . . . French influence will rise to new heights and will stretch across Europe to the frontiers of Russia and Turkey.[3]

Hess demanded further information from Buol and proceeded to cross-examine the foreign minister of Austria as though he were a hostile witness or a criminal. An anti-Russian policy would anchor Austria to Napoleon III with whom Hess, as a conservative stalwart, associated the belief that "the revolution" was waiting at the doorstep. This would fly in the face of her policy of the previous forty years—that is, friendship with Russia. How could Austria depart from this tradition? Buol answered the question: Russian inactivity in the Eastern question had been the essential condition of Austro-Russian friendship. A western alliance would confront the tsar with solid opposition in the principalities and would show him that Austria meant business when she told him to get out. Hess questioned the answer: hard geographical reality, Germany, stood between Russia and the maritime Powers hardly a comforting prospect. Hess had by now talked himself into a position of extreme anxiety and had increased it by his effort at precaution. But he had made his point all the same. Buol had to look round for arguments that would overcome Hess and break his opposition. The dispute dragged on for three hours. Each man waited cunningly until his opponent was forced to the wall. Time and again Hess expostulated; time and again Buol answered his arguments—or tried to.

III

A new difficulty now arose. Austrian hegemony in Germany was vital to all concerned—vital to Buol as a counterweight to Russia; vital to Hess as a barrier against France; vital to Francis Joseph as a symbol of tradition and dynastic prestige. Prussian cooperation with Austria in Germany, if not subservience to her, was the essential condition of all three; without it, the status quo there could not be maintained. The Eastern crisis had taken the Prussians unawares. Alone among the Powers, they had no ambitions in the Near East or even any interest there. They were concerned neither to endorse the Russian claims over the Christians of Turkey nor to thwart them. On the other hand, they were terrorized by the thought that, if the war with Russia got out of hand, it would become revolutionary and wash over into Germany. It was therefore vital to them that the fighting be localized lest it become a war of all against all. On 17 March they offered to guarantee against a Russian attack all of Austria's possessions as well as "certain Turkish territories" which, for reasons of military strategy, the Austrians might have to occupy. In return, Austria and Prussia should bind themselves to each other for their mutual protection. Hess jumped at this opportunity: alliance with Prussia offered the prospect of tying Buol down; Austria and Prussia could stand aside while Russia and the western Powers cut each other's throats. He therefore posed a stern choice: alliance with Prussia or total abstention from the Eastern question. Buol posed an equally stern choice on the other side: alliance with the western Powers whatever the price. His firmness over this made matters difficult; but he deserved far more respect from his critics than he received. For the emperor wavered. He wanted to have his cake and eat it; somehow to ally himself with Prussia and yet retain his freedom of action. He shrank from any clear-cut solution—much as he was to do during the endless negotiations with France which preceded the war of 1866. Francis Joseph was overawed by the Eastern question: he was inclined to bow to Buol's argument that the question should be settled in cooperation with the western Powers. Hess remained adamant. The emperor gave way. Eager for compromise, he decided to postpone alliance with the western Powers until agreement with Prussia had been reached. Remorsefully Buol went along. He asked only that the negotiations commence quietly behind the scene and commence without delay. Francis Joseph agreed. Hess was packed off to Berlin as negotiator.

The Prussians, as much despite their offer of 17 March as because of it, could not yet take a consistent line, though most of them still wanted agreement with Austria. Frederick William IV was too elusive and too unstable for any resolute action. Besides dissent within his own government was already blazing into the open. Manteuffel, the prime minister, wished to sit still and do nothing. Gerlach, the military expert, upheld legitimism and wanted a conservative solidarity with Russia. Bunsen, the king's closest friend, urged from London partnership with Great Britain. A few rejected all three lines, Bismarck, the delegate at Frankfurt, most of all. With characteristic ruthlessness, he wrote: "Let us frighten Austria by threatening to fight with Russia, and frighten Russia by letting her think that we might join the Western Powers." And in February 1854: "I should be alarmed if we sought protection from the approaching storm by tying our neat sea-worthy frigate to Austria's worm eaten old battleship."[4] In Bismarck's vision, Frederick William should mobilize 200,000 men in the hope of warding off a Russian attack; then he should demand from Austria the control of Germany, and neither Austria nor Russia nor the western Powers, absorbed by events in the Near East, could lift a finger to stop him. Frederick William replied: "A man like Napoleon could pull off this sort of stroke but not me."[5] Bismarck would not be so easily put off. Conflict with Austria was his overriding consideration during his years at Frankfurt, and he sacrificed to this all other questions of foreign and even of domestic policy.

In the spring of 1854 the outlook of the Prussian rulers, both military and civilian, very much concentrated on more immediate objects. They were faced by a considerable dilemma: how to break the impasse in their negotiations with Austria. These turned on the question whether Prussia would back Austria militarily as well as diplomatically in a war that sprang from Austria's intervention against Russia in the principalities. This the Prussians refused. The only war that they would enter was a war against "the revolution"—in other words, France. On 2 April Manteuffel discussed with Hess the possibility of extending the alliance to the Germanic Confederation—a suggestion ultimately brushed aside after opposition from Vienna. As to the principalities, he would assist the Austrians if they promised to take no further action without consulting Prussia. Hess would have liked to accept this. Buol overruled him. Deadlock followed.

Events soon pushed the Prussians towards Austria. The formal declaration of war against Russia by the western Powers at the end of March and the Anglo-French alliance of 10 April shook Frederick William's nerve. In his view the German states should band together for their mutual protection. In the middle of April agreement was, after much sordid wrangling, at last reached. This provided that the question of future consultation should be put on the shelf and that Prussia should join Austria in the latter's ultimatum to St. Petersburg. One difficulty remained. Frederick William still shrank from a breach with Russia. As always, the revolutionary excesses of 1848 weighed heavily upon him; and he was obsessed by the thought that if the provisions of the alliance were made known, the tsar would rise up in wrath against him. Hess had a fresh resource. He offered to exempt Prussia from the proposed ultimatum in return for her support, armed and unconditional, in the event of a Russian attack on Austria. Frederick William snatched at this proposal, asking only that the clause be suppressed. Hess agreed. The issue was resolved; the alliance was made.

Or was it? Hess's objective was alliance with Prussia, not her enmity. Frederick William's objections were tiresome preliminaries to be got out of the way. As before, Buol kept them in the way. So long as these objections stood between Austria and Prussia, he could evade the embarrassing offer of a Prussian alliance and so, he thought, preserve Austria's freedom of action. This calculation broke down. Hess and Frederick William, somewhat ashamed of the anti-Russian slant of the treaty, slapped in a clause that it would operate only if the Russian rejection of Austria's ultimatum were categorical and unconditional. This clause, though not a binding promise, had awkward consequences later on. It was another way of saying that Hess did not wish to act if the Russians attached conditions to their withdrawal from the principalities. After fierce bickering, Buol and his advisers accepted this clause as a necessary condition of the alliance. It was signed in Berlin on 20 April. The Austrians, it seemed, had got their way: a Prussian guarantee of Italy; Prussian support in the principalities. The antagonism between Prussia and Austria, long a-growing, appeared to have abated, much as Hess had hoped.

This was a misreading of the situation. The treaty of 20 April brought Prussia and Austria together—ostensibly a conservative alliance to replace the moribund Holy Alliance; in fact, no more than a military convention of disputed validity and no political significance. The treaty carried within itself the germ of a mortal sickness: Prussia did not promise to mobilize immediately in the event of war. The Austrians could congratulate themselves that they had secured Prussian mobilization in the event of a Russian attack; they could take comfort from Prussia's promise to support the mobilization of the forces of the Confederation under the same conditions. There their gains ended. These could only have been consolidated if there had been an Austro-Prussian agreement, possibly with the lesser states as a third party, to give Austria a free hand against Russia. Few Prussians wanted this, Manteuffel least of all. The Crimean coalition was as unwelcome to him as it was to be for Bismarck twenty years later. On the other hand the prospect of cooperating with Russia against it was equally unwelcome. Manteuffel's solution anticipated Bismarck's policy by twenty-five years: "the defence of Austria as a German, but not as a Balkan power."[6]

The treaty of 20 April was another bad knock for Russia. The directors of Russian strategy had assumed that, with Austria and Prussia safely in their debt, the entire might of the Russian army could be flung against the western Powers. Everything went wrong. The Austrians were hostile. The Prussians were evasive. It had been generally supposed that the tsar could put a million men on a war footing at a moment's notice. As a matter of fact, he had all he could do to muster half of that; the vaunted efficiency of his army collapsed almost before the first shot had been fired. There was now a new danger. The Russian generals were convinced that the Austrians were preparing to attack them. This was their nightmare. As a consequence, it brought a change in the way their campaign was conducted. In the first months of 1854 the Russian army had pushed across Moldavia and had besieged Silistria. Now the Russian generals, led by Paskevich, urged that the siege be lifted. Nicholas rejected this advice. The siege, he argued, had to be pursued if only to show persistence under fire. The generals shuffled. Russian strategy was falling to pieces. The high command was a muddle; the army short on supplies. Dramatic change was at hand. Russia's rulers had their hands full trying to keep her going. The Russian colossus, so universally feared, was already creaking at the joints.

IV

The Austro-Prussian alliance was greeted with studied indifference by the western Powers. The allies had already convinced themselves that any Austrian ultimatum to St. Petersburg would mean war between Austria and Russia. Besides, troubles breaking out in Greece and the southern Balkans threatened to turn Austria into an active belligerent at once. Greece had proved a problem for Europe since 1821. Her independence, established by two treaties of 1832, had been guaranteed by Great Britain, France, and Russia. The treaties merely papered over the difficulties. Greek nationalists envisaged a restored Byzantium. More, there was much antagonism among the three guarantors. In 1850 the crisis which exploded over Don Pacifico had pushed England and France to the brink of war. The British disliked and despised the king, Otto of Bavaria; they supposed that he was a French puppet. Fresh trouble broke out in 1853. A Russian admiral, Kornilov, was sent to Athens with an offer of Russian support in a Greek insurrection against Turkey. Kornilov won Otto for "Greater Greece." This would bring Epirus and Thessaly under Greek control; Greece would then be the dominant power in the southern Balkans. Otto strode into action. He encouraged dissident Greeks under Turkish rule to foment rebellion. By 1854 revolutionary turmoil had lapped to the borders of Macedonia and Chalcidice. Peremptory dispatches from Constantinople demanding that the Greek government suppress the revolt fell on deaf ears. Turkey broke off relations with Greece in protest.

The revolt made some sort of western intervention in Greece inevitable. But what sort? The French supposed that the trouble was the result of Russian influence and Russian gold. They wanted to retaliate immediately and snuff out the disturbance before it spread. The British on the other hand saw the revolt as a legitimate protest against Turkish misrule and decided to go easier. Aberdeen did not rule out some kind of action. All the same he shrank from using British troops against Christians in revolt against Turkey. The allies finally decided to call upon Austria. The Austrians refused to intervene. Their main concern was to get Russia out of the principalities—and get themselves in. They dreaded the thought of offending the tsar by direct action against Orthodoxy. Buol would only agree to send a few warships to the western coast of Greece; he refused to use the Austrian army unless the revolt reached Albania. The western Powers now decided to take matters into their own hands. In June British and French troops were sent to Athens. After some bickering Otto agreed to summon a new pro-western ministry. It was headed by Mavrocordatos, his old enemy. Greece went into the background. Still, the episode widened the gulf between Austria and the western Powers. The allies resented Buol's refusal to use force; Buol resented the allied attempts to draw Austria into war over an issue he believed to be trivial.

The failure of the British and French to find new belligerents was soon repeated. As early as March 1854 they had launched efforts to extend the theatre of conflict to the Baltic. This meant engaging Sweden as an ally. An unsettled quarrel between Sweden and Russia over Finmark, the northern tip of Norway, had embittered Russo-Swedish relations for several years. In 1852 Russia had shut her frontier to Sweden. Strong anti-Russian sentiments were voiced in the Swedish press. A large segment of the population, led by the crown prince, was in full cry for a war with Russia. But the king, Oscar I, was resolute for inaction. On 26 October 1853 both Sweden and Denmark proclaimed their neutrality; all the same they agreed to open some of the ports to British and French warships. Meanwhile the crown prince had fallen into talks with the maritime Powers over an alliance. The negotiations were conducted in a confused, muddled way: demands for territory by the Swedes; equivocation by the allies. There was much debate between the British and French about exploiting the advantages of Swedish sea power. The debate, too, was run up in the slapdash fashion which had characterized the negotiations. There were no maps, no intelligence reports, no systematic preparations. By June 1854 the negotiations had fallen apart. The allies assumed that the alliance had been made; instead the Swedes answered with a clause that Austria must enter the war first. The crown prince argued, sincerely enough, that Sweden could not bring down the united wrath of Germany by taking on Russia alone. The operation could work, if at all, only with the active cooperation of the Austrian government. The Austrians refused to be drawn. Buol telegraphed to Stockholm: "Should be very happy to join, if we respectively want each other, but till we do, *silence*."[7] Austria was the rock—somewhat flaky, but a rock all the same—on which the allied schemes broke.

V

Even so, war between Austria and Russia still seemed likely in the summer of 1854. The Austrians continued to prepare for it. They tried to line up the German states behind them. This meant getting approval of the Austro-Prussian treaty of 20 April 1854. However, like Prussia, the middle German states did not wish to offend the tsar. Nicholas had anticipated this. Foreseeing the Austrian ultimatum he tried to sweeten German opinion by appearing as the aggrieved party. He therefore made concessions to Austria: he promised to guarantee the freedom of the Danube and to evacuate the principalities if Austria promised to guard his southwestern frontier. The concessions were contemptuously turned down by the Austrians. Buol insisted that Russia's withdrawal must be unconditional. The western Powers would take offense otherwise and Austria would be stripped of her neutrality. Still, the Russian offers stirred up German opinion against Austria. Nicholas had shown himself to be moderate; Buol intransigent. This encouraged the middle German states to take an independent line. Some of them now demanded that the Austro-Prussian treaty be amended—Saxony, for instance, whose foreign minister, Beust, sought to organize the middle states into an independent association. At first the movement made little headway. The middle states could not agree on a common program; they were more likely to quarrel as allies than they were if unattached. But Austria's refusal of Russia's conciliatory offer got the ball rolling. On 22 May 1854 Beust called a conference of the middle states at Bamberg to consider the Austro-Prussian treaty. Opinion was however still divided. Neurath, the foreign minister of Württemberg, wanted unconditional adhesion to the treaty; he believed that the participation of the middle states in the coming Austro-Russian war was inevitable and urged the conference to open negotiations with Prussia and Austria to fix their obligation as low as possible. He got nowhere. Beust did a little better. At his urging the conference on 3 June issued a circular which laid down the conditions under which the Germanies would accede to the treaty of 20 April. The main condition was for reciprocity in the Austrian ultimatum: any summons demanding Russia's withdrawal from the principalities must also call upon the western Powers to simultaneously evacuate the Black Sea. Austria must also renounce the use of force in her dealings with Russia.

The Bamberg conference seemed a bad blow for Austria. This was more appearance than reality. The conference was crippled by divided leadership; this took the sting out of its circular. Indeed the way in which the circular was adopted pointed to the division. Only Beust considered it a categorical declaration of policy; and even he was uncertain whether its conditions were a *sine qua non* or simply a statement of recommendations. It made no difference. The Austrians had already drafted their ultimatum to Russia. On 29 May a ministerial conference considered three dispatches which would go to St. Petersburg. The first demanded that Russia halt her offensive beyond the Danube and set an early date for the evacuation of the principalities. The second warned the tsar that this was the only way out of his predicament. The third laid down that Austria would fight to remove Russia if she refused to leave the principalities voluntarily. These three demands would be in the Austrian ultimatum. The conference rattled through its work in a matter of hours. Only Hess objected. He wanted reciprocity and an armistice from the western Powers and overwhelmed Buol and Francis Joseph with warnings that they were throwing overboard "monarchical solidarity" and the conservative cause that had given Austria security for the previous forty years; worse, they were becoming the lackeys of Napoleon III and "the revolution" and thus inviting catastrophe for the future. Buol answered that they need not worry about the future; the future was with them now. Austria could not tolerate the Russians in the principalities; nothing could atone for this—not the conservative cause, not monarchical solidarity, not even the Russian offer of the western Balkans. Francis Joseph agreed: Russia must get out of the principalities unconditionally and at once; Austria must allow her no loophole. Besides, the ultimatum was flexible: Austria was committed to no dates. The exact time and method of her action could be decided later.

The Austrian ultimatum was presented at St. Petersburg on 3 June 1854.[8] This was the greatest event of the last six months—by far the greatest in magnitude and also greatest in consequences. Many consequences of the war were predictable, destroying what was already rotten or putting things back where they were before. European frontiers were little changed except where Russia was concerned, and the same was true of European institutions with the same exception. Prussia was already a disgruntled Power. The Austrian empire was already in decline. It had already become clear, as the Hapsburg rulers themselves appreciated, that the Holy Alliance of Metternich's day was a broken reed, and almost equally clear, as some French observers recognized, that the Savoyards of Piedmont-Sardinia would ultimately become the champions of Italian independence. But Russia was, in Kossuth's words, a despotism wrapped in an immeasurable evil. Would the Russian menace continue to overshadow Europe? Was there no limit to Russian power? The Crimean war gave the answer, and the ultimatum of 3 June gave the first hint.

The ultimatum of 3 June 1854 had an immediate effect on the Russians. No longer was Austria content with impassive neutrality: she was now confronting them with the prospect of war on the Danube. The Russians, on their side, were still suffering from the nightmare of coalitions that had dominated them since the end of 1853; and they were not happy to see Austria closing with their enemies; this is what was happening. Vienna had been transformed into a battleground of rival ideologies. Opinion in St. Petersburg was not all one way. The tsar determined to punish Austria immediately: "for the first time the Russians saw clearly that Austria might oppose them in the Balkans; and the phrase was first heard in St. Petersburg that the road to Constantinople lay through Vienna."[9] This threat was too daring for the Russian diplomats, many of whom were, like Nesselrode, also German; like all the tsar's threats against Austria of the last six months, it was a pistol with the safety catch firmly locked. After all, as the Russian generals themselves had realized, war with Austria outstripped Russia's strength. Strategical considerations too told against it. Russia was already facing Turkish and allied armies in the Crimea and a potential enemy in Austria on the Danube. If the storm of war blew westwards, there was no telling what might happen in Germany or, for that matter, in Poland. From whatever point of view they looked at it—strategical, political, economic— the generals and the diplomats came up with the same answer: there were too many enemies already.

The Austrians did not foresee this. They hoped that their ultimatum would frighten Nicholas with the terrible prospect of an anti-Russian coalition of Europe and thus force him to give way. All the same they believed, understandably enough, that Austria having delivered her summons must be prepared to back it up. Buol therefore instructed the Austrian generals to prepare for the coming war with Russia. But he held out that agreeement on war aims must first be reached with the western Powers and that this agreement be specific as well as unconditionally binding. The generals approved. As usual, they disliked being provoked into action and welcomed any excuse for delay.

The debate over Austrian policy made little difference to the British. Palmerston, in particular, saw in it only great betrayals—betrayals in which the Austrians were working hand in glove with the French to call off the conflict. He could never see any sense in Drouyn's infatuation with the Austrians. He said to Newcastle: "Austria has, as usual, been playing a shabby game. When she thought the Russians likely to get on, she bragged of her determination to be active against Russia. As soon as she found our troops at Varna, she changed her tune. Now she says she shall not enter the principalities and the Russians must be driven out by the English and the Turks and the French." [10] This reproach augured ill for Buol's attempts to end the war by negotiation.

Palmerston may have hoped that diplomacy was over. Drouyn de Lhuys did not. The impetus of the previous diplomacy carried Drouyn forward of itself. This was the first war that the French people had fought under a Bonaparte since 1815 and Drouyn doubted whether he could restrain Napoleon III's revolutionary zeal if he allowed it to get out of hand: far better to restrain him by the tried method of diplomatic negotiations.

Thus Buol's decision to inquire of France for a statement of war aims was music in Drouyn's ears. Together with Hübner, he gradually formulated, behind the backs of the British, a series of war aims, the Four Points, with Buol's assistance and under Buol's prompting. These were supposed to represent the objects with which the allies had started the war and the bases on which they would end it. Beyond this, the program sprang from Buol's desire to pin down Anglo-French ambitions or—in practice the same thing— to temper their force. It sprang too from Drouyn's conviction that a war fought on such a scale ought to have a great, enabling outcome—a new constellation of Europe to take the place of the Holy Alliance. On 7 July Drouyn revealed to Clarendon what was afoot, and tried to carry the day in favor of Austria by proposing that the Four Points be committed to a protocol and signed in Vienna. Clarendon refused: "We must not get entangled in negotiations." [11]

This attitude did not last long. On 3 July Alexander Gorchakov became the Russian minister in Vienna. He arrived with a fresh offer—a promise to evacuate the principalities on condition that Russia was given an armistice and assured by Austria that Austria would not ally herself with the western Powers. The Austrians rejected this. They had demanded unconditional evacuation; they had already entered into negotiations about a possible peace settlement. They could not allow Russia's withdrawal to depend on an armistice; the western Powers would never accept it, and nothing would be achieved at all. This did not trouble the tsar. He knew in advance that Austria would reject his conditions. His motive was simple: to cause a stir against Austria in the Germanies. He succeeded. The middle German states once again protested against Austria's intransigence. They demanded that her mobilization be suspended. Worse things followed. The Austrian generals concluded that, since Russia's reply had been refused, Austria could not enter the principalities without going to war against Russia. This made it vital for Austria to get what Buol knew she must have—that is, prompt military aid from the western Powers. Drouyn agreed at once: 100,000 French troops for a campaign on the Danube.

A shadow hung over this promise. From the moment Buol approached Drouyn, he expected that a considerable portion of the British army should be directed towards the principalities. The British willingly produced fanciful figures showing the armies available for the various theatres. They were less forthcoming in the practical consideration of coordinating their strategic plans along the lines envisaged by Drouyn de Lhuys and Buol. Though Clarendon believed that a large allied force would "set Austria going," British military experts pronounced the idea of a Danubian campaign worthless and unnecessary. Its only objective could be to defend Constantinople against an attack by the Russian army, and for that there was no need. Palmerston and the bulk of the British military wanted to hit Russia in Georgia, Circassia, and the Crimea; in particular, they wished to concentrate on smashing the fortress of Sebastopol and thus finish her off as a Black Sea power. The French wavered. Drouyn argued that the allies should first aid Austria and then pursue their own objectives. Napoleon III rejected this advice.

Napoleon III's attitude was cold comfort to Buol. Nor was this his only disappointment. Austria's relations with Prussia had run downhill. Frederick William was indignant at Buol's treatment of Russia; he insisted that any future answer to the Austrian ultimatum be submitted to an Austro-Prussian committee. Buol refused. Frederick William retaliated by threatening to destroy the alliance of 20 April; he warned Buol that should a breach occur between Prussia and Austria, Prussia might go with Russia and attack Austria in Galicia. Tension continued to mount; it rached its height when Frederick William and Manteuffel were both on Austrian soil at Teschen. Frederick William quickly lost his nerve. In his more rational moments he recognized that he could not abandon Austria unless he were willing to see her join hands with the western Powers. Should that occur the war would become general, would spread to Germany—Prussia's *bête noire*. As well, Frederick William's threat was too strong meat for his conservative generals who still clung with romantic attachment to Austria. All the same the Prussian threat to tear up the treaty produced panic in Vienna. It appeared as though Austria and Prussia had, after many false alarms, finally and decisively fallen out. Hatzfeldt, the Prussian ambassador at Paris, raised the cry that the Austrians were cheating on their promises and added that the treaty of 20 April 1854 was not worth the paper and the ink with which it was written.

The Austrians did not take these blows impassively. After some fumbling, Buol hit on the idea of offering the western Powers a treaty of alliance in return for a defintion of their war aims. On 9 July Hübner had written from Paris recommending "a treaty which will bind us together in pursuit of a common policy—a policy which, at the very least, will be defined by the four points."[12] Buol accepted this idea: alliance with the western Powers. On 24 July Hübner received orders to begin negotiations with Drouyn de Lhuys concerning a treaty. But his instructions were guarded with a vital reservation that the negotiations were in no way binding upon Austria. Buol still hoped that the Russians would retreat peacefully from the principalities. For the moment he was disappointed. Not so the French. Alliance with Austria was the object of all Drouyn diplomacy; how it was achieved was unimportant. Drouyn de Lhuys therefore snatched at Buol's initiative and began drafting a treaty. He also sought to satisfy Buol on war aims by resurrecting the Four Points.

All these negotiations between France and Austria strengthened the British conviction that Drouyn was ready to sell out. Drouyn was knocking harder than ever at the Austrian door. The British could not listen in. The prolonged negotiations were shrouded in secrecy. Buol had summarily ordered Colloredo not to breathe a word of them. On 26 July these orders were suddenly changed. Hübner said to Colloredo: "Communicate the scheme to Clarendon. Waste not a day." [13] In executing these instructions Colloredo was cold-shouldered by Clarendon and abruptly told that, since the French had made the treaty, they must carry it through by themselves.

If matters had depended on Drouyn alone, the treaty of alliance would have been signed and the statement of war aims turned into a full-blown diplomatic instrument. Hübner and Drouyn formally proposed this to Buol at the end of July. The difficulty came, as had other difficulties, from the British. Palmerston's first reaction was to attack the treaty as sham. On 28 July he saw Clarendon. He displayed his old doubts about Austria's intentions, described the difficulties awaiting a campaign on the Danube, and casually slipped in the accusation that French policy could not be pinned down by dealing with Drouyn. Still, though Palmerston and Clarendon both resented the work of Drouyn and Buol which cast doubt on French good faith and impeded their efforts to get on with the war, they shrank from revealing a breach with France. A way out now presented itself: the treaty of alliance would surely mean war between Austria and Russia. This is what Drouyn de Lhuys had been preaching all along. His expostulations had gone unregarded a fortnight earlier. Now they were taken seriously. The French drafts were also accepted in Vienna. Westmorland rubbed his hands: "Buol agrees to proposed Notes and treaty—in short, buckles to everything." [14] Hübner announced: "Great news is at hand." [15]

There followed a fantastic event that upset all the careful calculations of allied diplomacy: the Russians began to evacuate the principalities. The rulers of France received this news with common consternation. Cooperation over the principalities was the main concession that Drouyn de Lhuys had offered to the Austrians, and the Russians, by evacuating them, knocked this card out of his hand. Now there seemed to be no new device in the arsenal of diplomacy. The tripartite treaty which had seemed indispensable to Austria a fortnight earlier now became an immeasurable danger—a means by which she might be drawn from her neutrality. On 5 August Buol announced to Bourqueney and Westmorland that Austria would sign the treaty only on condition that the Russians were not going to evacuate the principalities.

Bourqueney protested that "unless the treaty is accepted we wash our hands of the Four Points."[16] Drouyn overruled him. He could not bring himself to break with Austria and, in the high confusion of the moment, thought to trap Buol by accepting the notes and the notes alone. Westmorland, a man of straw, who had, in any case, been instructed to stick to Bourqueney, readily gave way. The Four Points were thus under way.

According to these, peace between Russia and Turkey could not be restored unless (1) the Russian protectorate of the principalities were replaced by a European guarantee; (2) the navigation of the Danube were "freed"; (3) the Straits convention of 1841 were revised in the interest of "the Balance of Power in Europe"; (4) the Russians renounced their claim to a protectorate over the Orthodox subjects of Turkey and instead the five Great Powers obtained from the Turkish government security for the Christians. No negotiation was to take place with Russia save on these points. This promise was a fraud on the Austrians and maybe even on the British. It could only have meaning if the Four Points represented settled allied policy. They did not. The agreement of 8 August 1854 was for Buol a final settlement; for the allies, or rather for Drouyn de Lhuys, a payment on account.

Drouyn had not been precise in his dealings with Buol. Though parading his loyalty to the Four Points, he nonetheless insisted that the allies were entitled to coordinate new aims. Drouyn had a bright idea. The Austrians had objected to too strident a formulation of war aims for fear of being tied to "the revolution"; then let the allies reserve unto themselves the right to demand further concessions from Russia should circumstances warrant it. Buol gave way. But he posed an essential condition: the new concessions must arise from an interpretation of the Four Points—that is, they "could not be entirely new."[17]

In retrospect it is tempting to say that the Four Points merely confirmed what had already been decided. To adapt Taylor once again: "Points 1 and 2 had been tacitly conceded by the tsar when Russia withdrew from the principalities in August 1854. Point 4, the original source of conflict, had been conceded when he accepted the Vienna note in July 1853, and again in September when he repudiated Nesselrode's 'violent interpretation.' The Crimean war was therefore fought over point 3; since a mere revision of the Straits convention was not enough, the decisive conflict centered on the question of Russian naval power in the Black Sea. Though this affected Turkey and the Near East, its basis was 'the interest of the Balance of Power in Europe.'"[18] Why did the allies press this point so ruthlessly and so persistently? Was it merely an excuse for escaping negotiations with Russia? Perhaps. But the point had to be raised and settled. The Russian fleet in the

Black Sea had brought Turkey within an ace of destruction the year before—a menace that had, the allies believed, to be overcome if Turkey were to be secure as an independent Power.

The Four Points were the most celebrated diplomatic achievement of the Crimean war—an instrument supposedly binding and a concrete basis on which to build up the foundations of peace. But their strength depended on the continuing unity of the three Powers who had made them, each of whom was set on a different interpretation. There was a rift between Austria and Great Britain with the French more or less completely on the British side.

Most Englishmen had not noticed the Four Points until the middle of July. Now they snatched at the idea that they had been cheated by Drouyn just as in earlier times they had snatched at the idea that they were the victims of an Austro-Russian conspiracy to overrun the Near East. Clarendon emerged from the ordeal more dissatisfied than ever; and Palmerston dreamt of some fantastic military success that would destroy the Four Points altogether. The Whig backbenchers were for resistance. Russell was always sensitive to the conscience of the nation and took a hard line. Landsdowne and Graham both held that the Four Points would not do. Uneasiness therefore overcame the British, or rather it was the unmistakable by-product of the events of 8 August. Still there was no way out.

VI

Diplomacy was now eclipsed by military action. It was never eclipsed totally, so much so that it is almost possible to write about the diplomacy of the Crimean war without mentioning the military history and, for that matter, to write about the military history without bringing in the diplomacy. Almost possible but not quite. The diplomats in all the belligerent states took an extremely active part in military affairs and by no means treated diplomacy as an isolated department of national policy. It was generally supposed—in Great Britain at any rate—that the war would be over quickly; the decisive battle would last a few weeks; afterwards it would be a matter of mopping up the scattered remnants of the Russian armies. The deadlock in the Crimea exploded their high expectations. Hence the disenchantment of the civilian ministers with the generals. The same sort of pattern developed in Russia, only more rapidly—due no doubt to the incompetence of the military machine to cope with millions of potential recruits. As a final disappointment, the two western Powers were plagued by a problem that had already raised its head in their first military conversations: whether their armies should be put under a single commander. The two countries never argued this difference out to a conclusion and their diplomacy was bound to suffer because of it.

In the middle of September 1854, an allied expeditionary force landed in the Crimea. The force totalled 50,800 men as against the total Russian force in the Crimea of 35,000. The first armed combat took place in the southwestern corner of the peninsula. Early on the morning of 19 September long lines of British, French, and Turkish troops began to move across the hills while their fleets moved correspondingly across the Black Sea. The troops continued to advance the next day until they were just outside the village of Alma. Here they ran into a sharp blast of enemy fire. This did not deter them. Soon they were splashing their way across the tiny Alma river. Beyond this point the major strength of the Russian army lay. The offensive was a complete success. The allies confronted the enemy on the ground above the river; and by sundown the Russians were retreating in complete disarray. They had a death roll of nearly 2,000; over 5,000 of their soldiers had been hit. Against this, allied losses were slight: only 365 British killed; about 1,600 wounded. French casualties came to something over 500; of these, about 60 were fatal.

Allied rejoicing was however short-lived. On 25 October the Russians attacked the British, French, and Turkish soldiers at Balaclava—a narrow valley which was bordered by a low ridge. Soon Russian guns were established on both sides of the ridge and at the end of the valley. The Light Brigade was ordered into action to clear the ground of enemy artillery. The order was mad: the Light Brigade was no match for heavy guns; besides, it was outnumbered hopelessly. No logic went into the command—it was given in desperation and utter confusion. When the charge was over, 113 British soldiers lay dead in the valley; 134 were wounded. The news of the Charge of the Light Brigade was telegraphed to London by W. H. Russell, the correspondent of *The Times*. It was soon recounted endlessly in verse and prose. Indeed, the Charge of the Light Brigade provided the concentrated meat extract of all the emotions that the generation of the 1850s had experienced during their lifetime. It has been rightly said that no military engagement until Dunkirk so moved the British people or so excited them. The battle as a whole proved a standoff; new fighting broke out a few days later at Inkerman. This was the decisive encounter. Once again the Russians took the initiative and unexpectedly attacked the allies. The battle was largely a series of isolated fights in the brushwood. At first the Russians had things their own way; but the arrival of French reinforcements tipped the scales in favor of the allies. Soon the Russians were defeated in every part of the field:

3,280 dead; 11,664 out of action. British losses were 638 killed; 1,938 wounded. French casualties were 2,675.

In the meantime the allies had attacked Sebastopol—their main objective. They supposed that taking it would be easy. The fortress of Sebastopol was a museum piece. Its defenses had not been improved in twenty years. A large part of the city was undefended by any substantial works. The only serious obstacle was the White Tower or Malakoff bastion. This was a semi-circular work of stone which covered the approach to the marine suburb of Karabelnaya. Sebastopol might have collapsed at once had it not been for allied incompetence and the wisdom and energy of a great engineer. The engineer's name was Edward Ivanovich Todleben—the only man who was, by his feats of genius in the Crimean war, able to lay a claim to the veneration of posterity. Under Todleben's direction the defenses of Sebastopol were quickly modernized. This task, to the realization of which the other military commanders never ceased to place obstacles, involved the whole population. Children pushed wheelbarrows; women carried earth in their aprons. Work continued during darkness under the glare of torches. When the allies finally struck on 17 October it was evident that the determination of the people had paid off. The fortress stood up well under repeated and heavy attack; and in the end the Russians gunners were able to beat it off. The British and French fleets sailed away and the armies now settled down to a siege, their main object having eluded them.

The allied offensive was petering out. Rain was falling. General Disease took command. British transports stuck in the mud. Allied artillery could not move forward. The ground was too cold to find effective cover in. British soldiers, without winter clothing, froze to death at their posts. Allied ships found themselves on stormy seas and sank. These events in the Crimea threw the British government into disarray. The deadlock there corresponded to the deadlock in the Baltic sphere. No one had prepared for this; no one knew how to handle it. Military action had been tried to get round political difficulties. It produced new difficulties of its own. The allies could not take Sebastopol; the Russians could not drive the allies out of the Crimea. So the two sides drifted on, operating on a narrow margin, but no longer counting on quick victories achieved at little cost.

Chapter 7

THE AUSTRIAN AND SARDINIAN ALLIANCES

Diplomacy had by no means been interrupted by military preoccupations. No sooner had the Austrians agreed with the allies over the Four Points than Buol began to press them upon the tsar. Drouyn de Lhuys, on his side, now determined to take up where he had left off in July—to take up, that is, the question of the Austrian alliance. He was concerned more generally to build the barrier that a well-armed Austria, allied to France and Great Britain, would raise against Russian hegemony in the Near East. Drouyn supposed that Russian intransigence would deliver Austria into his hands. He was very nearly right. On 16 August the Four Points were formally presented to Russia by Esterházy, the Austrian ambassador. The Russians denounced the transaction as "a piece of impertinence." Nesselrode pulled Esterházy into the corner and asked: "Is this how Austria responds to our latest sacrifice? Is this our reward for evacuating the principalities? Is this fair?"[1] The tsar ostentatiously drew up a project for war with Austria. Then Nesselrode intervened. He saw clearly that, if Russia went against Austria, "instead of three enemies we shall by spring have to take on 'Europe.'" The tsar backed away. Still, this did not shake the Russian resolve to reject the Four Points. Esterházy lamented: "It is scarcely possible to find here a man who will even talk about them."[2]

News of the Russian decision reached London and Paris on 1 September 1854. The expedition to the Crimea, long pent up, was at last on the verge of sailing. Drouyn de Lhuys now resolved to launch a new effort to win Austria for the triple alliance. He produced a scheme at the end of August and at once sent it off to London. The British government accepted it immediately, and for good reason. An open repudiation of Drouyn's scheme would, they thought, provoke a row with France. Their initial solution, as they had revealed in a conference in the middle of June, was to hope for a conflict in the principalities between Austria and Russia. Then, as Cowley put it sometime in August 1854, Austria, threatened by Russia on the one side and by Prussia on the other, would become the dutiful servant of the allies, loyally accommodating herself to their aims and to their wishes.

This plan too rested on a misconception: it overrated Russia's capacity for a second front. But whether the war over the principalities came off or not, it was worthwhile to prepare the situation in Austria by putting out feelers. On 15 August 1854 clear-cut orders were sent to Vienna. Westmorland was instructed to keep in step with Bourqueney over the notes of 8 August; not only that, "the Governments of England and France are agreed that the conditions attained in the Note shall be regarded as the Bases of Negotiation with Russia."[3] The negotiations were to commence swiftly; the French must be given no excuse to complain.

On 5 September 1854 Drouyn's draft treaty was sent off to Westmorland and Bourqueney with instructions to press it on Buol. Westmorland and Bourqueney failed miserably. This was not surprising. The western Powers had supposed that Russia's rejection of the Four Points would bring a decisive split with Austria. They were wrong. The Austrians were not surprised by the Russian rejection; on the contrary, they had expected it. Nor did they take Nicholas's tirade seriously: the Austrian high command knew, as did Nesselrode, that war with Austria outstripped Russia's strength; no fighting had yet taken place; the Russians had evacuated the principalities; thus there was no reason for Austria to do anything.

II

This situation soon changed. The convention with Turkey of 14 June 1854 had empowered Austria to enter Moldavia and Wallachia. Austrian troops occupied them immediately; their presence was supposed to be temporary— ostensibly to prevent anarchy and restore order. But once in, the Austrians showed no signs that they intended to get out. Coronini, the Austrian commander, behaved like a dictator. He interfered with Turkish military maneuvers, and launched schemes for tying the principalities to Austria by railway and telegraph lines. Bruck (now minister of finance) developed plans for incorporating Moldavia and Wallachia into his central European customs union. Austrian military leaders—Hess, for instance—wanted the principalities for Austria's defenses, and urged the construction of fortresses on the lower Danube and the Prut.

Buol liked none of these schemes. It was indeed no part of his policy to annex the principalities. He had long believed that the principalities were a

European problem, and this implied a diplomatic solution. He shrank from coercing the inhabitants of Moldavia; he had no wish to stuff the Empire with millions of new subjects; he would have liked to silence the military men.

This object was not realized. On 13 August, Austrian troops crossed the border into Wallachia. Once in, the Austrians encountered difficulties. For the allied plenipotentiaries at Bucharest soon expostulated that the Austrian commanders were bent on remodelling the principalities according to their wishes. Buol denied this with every display of offended honor; and an examination of the secret records made during the occupation shows that this denial was more or less correct. Still, this did not change Buol's dilemma. The British and French divided over the future organization of the principalities. (Point 1 of the Four Points had stipulated the removal of the protectorate held by Russia since 1829, but otherwise had left their postwar status uncertain.) Napoleon III, faithful to "nationalities" and "self-determination," wished to make the principalities independent—the type of government to be decided by plebiscite. The British, at the other end of the scale, were not clear what they wanted. Unlike the French they lacked a directing hand that settled policy requires. There was a series of disagreements. Stratford proposed that the principalities be returned to Turkey on condition that a constitutional regime was set up; Cowley proposed to hand the protectorate back to Russia on condition that Russia hand Great Britain territory in Asia; Palmerston proposed to use the principalities as a bargain counter to buy the Austrians out of Italy; Russell proposed to tail along with Napoleon III. The ministers wore themselves down. No one could carry the cabinet.

None of this mattered. All their schemes cut across Austrian ambitions in the principalities—or so the allied statesmen believed. The British and French could make up their differences when the war was over; they could not allow Austria to take advantage of their preoccupation in the Near East. Austria was supposed to be "on the make" in the principalities; against this the allies fought with pride and determination, usually also with despair.

The wrangling bred suspicion and suspicion bred more wrangling. Buol took alarm. In his view (and not in his alone) the existing political order could not lurch on much longer. The Austrian position seemed desperate. Danger was everywhere. The Russians were estranged over the Four Points; the Prussians determined to exploit the situation in Germany; and the British and French anxious to press on with the war before it deadlocked. At bottom, there was an impassable cleavage between Russia and Austria, a cleavage of ideas as well as of policy. For half a century Metternich had insisted that the Ottoman empire was fundamental to the security of the Hapsburg monarchy, as Gentz, his right-hand man, bore witness when he laid down in 1815: "The end of the Turkish monarchy could be survived by the Austrians for but a short time."[4] Buol held the same view; and in his case Austrian fear of Russia in Turkey was reinforced by the events in Hungary in 1849—at once a new incentive and a new danger. In 1849 the Hapsburgs had succeeded in breaking the dream of a great independent Hungary. Yet this was an illusory success. It had been accomplished only with Russian military aid and depended on continued Russian support. The tsar's self-confidence was increased and with it his belief that Austria and Prussia were his political satellites. Buol resolved to show him that Austria could not be taken so lightly—resolved, that is, to compel the Russians to evacuate the Danubian principalities by the threat of intervention. He passed a true verdict in September 1854: "That peace which is necessary for us we can only gain in alliance with the Maritime Powers. Russia will never give it to us."[5] Buol certainly believed that Great Britain and France were less of a danger to Austria than Russia, and therefore put his weight more with them. Nevertheless balance between the two sides rather than the victory of either was his object.

Buol was bound to feel that alliance between Austria and the western Powers was within his reach. He was genuinely exuberant over the professions of friendship that Drouyn de Lhuys was making to Hübner; this effect was multiplied by the allied victory at Alma on 20 September. Buol had already convinced himself that there was enough cement to bind Austria and the allies; this cement was a common hostility to Russia. He therefore determined to display this hostility in London and Paris. He wired congratulations to the allies over their victory at Alma. On 1 October he took a further step. He told Westmorland and Bourqueney that he was prepared to sign an alliance. The next day copies of the draft treaty reached London and Paris. The treaty was wholly the work of Buol. But Buol feared that, if this were known, a rejection of the treaty by the allies would widen the rift between Austria and the western Powers. He therefore paraded the scheme as the project of Bourqueney and Westmorland, hoping that the label stuck on it would bluff the allies into acceptance. Of course he bluffed no one: the British and French governments knew that the treaty was entirely Austria's and never referred to it as anything else.

The language of the treaty shook off Buol's disguise: nowhere was there the slightest hint that Austria would lift a finger—a finger, that is, against Russia. The treaty emphasized diplomacy. It was Buol all over; if he could not do something effective, he would do something ineffective. The only area in which he had any experience was diplomacy; and it was, no doubt, the area in which he felt most at home. From start to finish his object was to settle the war by negotiations; and negotiations were impossible until the allies had achieved some striking military success. British patience was now exhausted. When news of the treaty came through, Clarendon wrote: "I venture to think that we might borrow a favorite phrase of Austria, and reserve to ourselves 'an entire freedom of action.'"[6]

The French, too, were disappointed. Drouyn told Hübner that the Four Points could now scarcely be considered binding: "The Notes were exchanged under the supposition that there would be a further convention binding Austria to give us real aid." Hübner, on his side, warned Buol that it was a mistake for the Hapsburg monarchy to attach itself to such dying causes as the Germanic confederation and the Holy Alliance. Buol brushed this warning aside, and replied on 23 September 1854: "What more can the allies expect . . . Our task was to obtain—by force, if need be—the evacuation of the principalities. Russia decided to yield this region. The allies could not, I daresay, have realized this object without our assistance. Granted, the result has been achieved without the shedding of blood, but does this make it any less important?"[7]

Buol achieved nothing. The stumbling block in his project had been his failure to offer the western Powers any promise of aid against Russia. Disillusionment followed. The diplomatic muddle drove a further wedge between Austria and the western Powers—or rather between Austria and Great Britain. Palmerston was convinced that the allies had been bamboozled by Buol and called for fiercer war, no doubt in the hope of posing as the champion of popular indignation and impatience that was swelling inexorably to a crescendo. Yet even Palmerston recognized that the allies could not inflict upon Russia the wholesale defeat that he wanted without Austrian assistance. Essentially he wished to draw a line between Russia and the rest of mankind. He pictured rational civilization advancing by ordered stages once Russia fell out of Europe; and he regarded Austria's abstention from war as willful treachery to civilized virtues—organization, liberty, self-sacrifice. Yet Palmerston and his colleagues were stuck. They drifted helplessly, waiting on events.

The Austrian alliance now seemed to count for little. Drouyn de Lhuys could not however bring himself to pronounce the death sentence on it. He determined that the Austrian initiative should not go unanswered, and set out to devise some sort of reply. He produced a scheme at the end of October; and on 1 November a copy of Drouyn's project reached London. Its chief provision laid down that if peace had not been made on the basis of the Four Points by the following April "the high contracting parties will deliberate as to the best means of securing the object of their alliance."[8] In the British eyes this clause was a godsend. At the time the clause was drafted Russian acceptance of the Four Points seemed as far away as ever; hence the only clear implication was that the allies should develop war aims, and diplomacy could be casually flung aside. Clarendon purred contentedly: "We ought to be only too happy if Austria will agree to it."[9]

British enthusiasm for the treaty did not rest solely on its language. The deteriorating situation in the Crimea weighed heavily upon them. The British had gone to war to defend the independence of Turkey; they also supposed that they were defending European civilization against a barbarian. By November the glory and romance had gone out of the war—a profound change of outlook. The mutual slaughter of Balaclava and the frustration of Sebastopol shook the happy equation between victory and civilization. There was, too, the desire to maintain the Anglo-French alliance. Drouyn made the most of this desire and warned Cowley that France could not keep up the war without Austria as her ally. The British were trapped. If they broke with France over the Austrian alliance they risked defeat in the Crimea and humiliation at home. If, on the other hand, they decided to negotiate, they might be made by Buol to spell out their war aims. The British fell back on the second alternative as the lesser evil. Draft treaties were sent off to Westmorland and Bourqueney in Vienna on 6-7 November 1854.

By this time the diplomatic picture in central Europe had changed decisively, and that because of the mobilization of the Austrian army on 22 October. This was a diplomatic maneuver, not a military one, "since the campaigning season had passed."[10] Still, the Austrian mobilization was too strong meat for Frederick Willian IV. Throughout the autumn he had beat about for some device that would end the war without calling in "the revolution." Yet, he could not bring himself to act for fear of antagonizing Russia. Now, as the direct result of the Austrian mobilization, he plucked up courage. He said to the tsar: "The green table of the conference room is the sheet-anchor of the world."[11] In other words, by agreeing to negotiate, Nicholas I would secure for himself freedom from war with "Europe"—a spectre that had bedeviled his advisers since the end of 1853.

Nicholas duly obliged. He accepted the Four Points. Frederick William, for his part, determined to reward the Russian decision. Disputes over the Austro-Prussian treaty of 20 April 1854 had proved a grumbling undercurrent of discord in the relations of the two for the last six months; now, thanks to the mediation of Pfortden, the foreign minister of Bavaria, they were successfully resolved. On 26 November 1854 Frederick William IV agreed to defend Austrian troops in the principalities against a Russian attack. There were these conditions: Austria must (1) rule out an offensive against Russia; (2) promise not to sign a triple alliance with Great Britain and France.

The agreement of 26 November was certainly a score for Prussia though, as it turned out, a rather hollow one. The treaty seemed to tie Austria inextricably to neutrality. Austria was barred from alliance with the western Powers and so prevented from transferring the war from the Crimea to Galicia. Prussia could pose at Frankfurt as the defender of German interests—the Power that wanted to do nothing and had got its way. More than this, Austria now seemed hopelessly compromised: she has estranged the tsar by refusing to promise a resolute neutrality; she had estranged the western Powers by refusing to go against Russia. Frederick William IV counted on the agreement of 26 November 1854 to tame Austrian policy. This hope was to be disappointed.

For Buol was once again driven into action by events. The Russians were on the point of accepting the Four Points; now Buol determined to make an alliance with the western Powers in order to carry them out. This was not his only consideration. As always, Buol aspired to be a mediator, a reconciler of differences. For that he had to straddle between the two sides: he could not satisfy Russia over the Four Points without satisfying the allies over the proposed treaty. The situation was moving ominously towards deadlock. Buol meant to control the situation before it got out of hand. It was not of much moment to him that the German princes were furious over his behavior. Their revolt did not, as it turned out, go very far. The German Diet voiced its abhorrence of Buol's bargain, then acquiesced in ratification of the Austro-Prussian agreement of 26 November. In any case Buol now played his strongest card. He revoked the order of general mobilization. Practical considerations entered in. The mobilization had been intended as a stroke of diplomacy, not of military strategy; and diplomacy had done its work. Cancellation of the order would neutralize opinion in Germany. As an added bonus it would show the tsar that Austria was not bent on a show of force.

Buol's mind was still dominated by the calculation that had dominated it since the summer of 1853: Austria must, were she to arrest the advance of Russian power in the Near East and secure the independence of Turkey, act in concert with the two western Powers. Alliance with them was not only the best policy; it was in the eyes of some Austrians—Hübner, the ambassador to France, for instance most strongly—the only policy. A desertion now by Austria of Great Britain and France would, or so Hübner made out, launch "the revolution" in the person of Napoleon III. The Polish question would burst into flames: "This will permit Italy to stir. The ambitions of Sardinia will be encouraged and will soar. . . . England will fight

Russia in Asia while France resumes her military traditions on the Rhine and on the Po. The secondary states will transfer their sympathies from Russia to France while Austria, pinned down in the east and west, will come face to face with England, France and 'the revolution' and will find herself alone in the midst of chaos." [12] In all this Hübner saw only one thing: alliance between Austria and the western Powers. He was now knocking harder than ever at the French door. The tripartite treaty, on which he pinned all his hopes, seemed at hand. His dispatches rang with the cry of unbridled urgency. He said to Buol: "Let us sign, then let us sign! We have, unless I am mistaken, arrived at the decisive moment." [13]

Buol saw things in much the same light; and as usual, events were shaped by what men believed, not by what happened. He had been told by Bach, by his other ambassadors, by Bourqueney and Westmorland, that the time for action had come. Buol took the plunge. The order to cancel the general mobilization of the Austrian army had gone out on 21 November. Buol at once determined to win the western Powers for the draft treaty that he had turned down in August. Negotiations proceeded furiously between Vienna and the two western capitals: the Austrians hinting at what they would offer; the allies, and especially the British, at what they would demand. The foundation-stone of Buol's proposals was the French scheme that had arrived on his desk a fortnight earlier. Buol accepted this scheme. But he made an important change in its timing: "the end of the present year" was substituted for "the following April" as the deadline "for a satisfactory peace on the basis of the Four Points." The British agreed to Drouyn's project because it did not imply the opening of conferences; the Austrians because it did. The French exhorted the British to immediately accept Buol's offer. The British were in no position to refuse. Their strategic operations had faltered and broken. News of Inkerman was dynamite. On 22 November 1854 clear-cut orders were sent to Vienna. Westmorland was instructed to assent to the treaty. The same orders were sent to Bourqueney from Paris. The allied decision was communicated to Buol. He welcomed it enthusiastically. On 2 December 1854 Buol saw Westmorland and Bourqueney. The three men signed.

The treaty confirmed the Four Points and declared that the allies reserved the right to make further demands; it also repeated the timetable which Drouyn had devised and Buol had modified: it said that if, by the end of the year, peace were not assured on the basis of the Four Points the three allies "will collaborate to decide how best to secure the object of their alliance." This hope was shattered before the ink on the alliance was dry. "For the treaty of alliance was signed, on Buol's prompting, on 2 December; and the

Russians had accepted the Four Points unconditionally on 29 November." [14] The object of the alliance was, according to its preamble, "to bring the war to an end as soon as possible by the establishment of a just and secure peace" and this object could now obviously be best achieved by negotiations if the western Powers were sincere in their adhesion to the Four Points.

They were not. The French had used the Four Points to enhance the prospect of Austria's entrance into the war; they had used the prospect of Austria's entrance into the war in order to tie Great Britain to the Four Points. Despite the treaty the British nursed the hope that negotiations might be avoided; and they nursed this hope to the last. Palmerston and Clarendon somehow imagined that Buol had deceived them. In reality, they had deceived themselves: for they had all along been trying to pull Austria into the war by promoting schemes that they thought would never be implemented. The Russian decision turned the tables on them.

III

News of the treaty of 2 December 1854 was not long in reaching St. Petersburg. It shocked and disgusted Nicholas I. He believed, and for a long time continued to believe, that he had been given a black eye by his best friend. At the time when his physical powers were waning, the Austrian decision seemed all the more incomprehensible, all the crueler. Nicholas I became, in the end, physically an absolutely broken man. Yet he was always able to impress people, not only to inspire them again and again, but also to make them fear him. Buol appreciated this. He had fathomed with little difficulty the depth of resentment at St. Petersburg over the treaty of 2 December 1854. He now groped for some device that would assuage Russian outrage and so allow the tsar to recover his temper.

Buol had a bright idea. He had, as always, been at the center of events, yet would now somehow leave the impression that he was not connected with them. He therefore made out to Gorchakov that the treaty had been designed by the western Powers and imposed upon him only after an ultimatum from them.

The stroke miscarried. Esterházy reported: "The tsar today asked me, 'What are the names of the two most foolish kings of Poland? I will tell you: John Sobieski and myself: we both committed the supreme folly of saving Vienna from destruction.'" [15] Nicholas I was on his last legs, would live only four more months; it became the commonplace of his subjects that he had died of a broken heart. Nor did this belief wear thin with the passing of years.

Quite the contrary. An English traveller reported twenty years later: "During my journey through Russia I was struck by the marked hostility shown by all classes to the Austrians and Germans, the conduct of the former Power during the Crimean War having left bitter feeling behind it." [16]

The treaty of 2 December 1854 had the opposite effect in Paris. The treaty seemed a staggering example of French ingenuity and of French diplomatic skill. Napoleon III, in particular, was enthusiastic. When word of the alliance came through, he "embraced the Empress and for a long while held her closely to his bosom." [17] The Austrians did not sign the treaty for nothing. They had long wished to extract from the French a promise not to explode Italy; Buol had expressed this wish to Drouyn de Lhuys during the negotiations over the treaty of 2 December 1854; and now it had to be fulfilled. On 22 December France and Austria signed a convention guaranteeing the existing state of affairs in Italy and providing that, if Austria went against Russia in the Near East, France would assist Austria in Italy. Drouyn de Lhuys was satisfied. He was as eager as the most extreme radical to be rid of the Holy Alliance lock, stock, and barrel. The treaty of 2 December 1854 was thus music in Drouyn's ears. So was the treaty of 22 December 1854. The first estranged Austria from Russia; the estranged, or seemed to estrange, Napoleon III from "the revolution."

Buol was satisfied also. He had outdone even Metternich; he had secured alliance with a Napoleonic France that would bar the door against Russia in the Near East. Liberal opinion in Germany praised the Hapsburg monarchy to the skies. Buol had, it was said, squeezed concessions from Napoleon III. More than this, he had secured for Austria freedom from conflict in Italy. Now Austria was free to solve the Eastern question in a sense favorable to her. Buol could pursue, cautiously, a series of new victories.

The victory of Drouyn de Lhuys and Buol proved a false dawn. For there were two gaping holes in their system, each the result of the other. One was geographical. Austria lay smack in the center of Europe—a buffer interposed between Russia and the West: "with so much at stake both on the Danube and Italy, she dared not go decisively against either." [18] Or was rather unable to do so. The Hapsburg monarchy was in decline. The Napoleonic wars had had a devastating effect on the monarchy, the revolutions of 1848 even more. The Austrian rulers, and maybe even Buol, too—were unshakably convinced that Austria should not suffer a similar catastrophe.

The system of Drouyn de Lhuys and Buol had another, deeper, flaw. Though European in origin and policy, Napoleon III was estranged from Austria by "the legend," and even more by the settlement of 1815: "however great his need for the Austrian alliance, he would never permanently renounce his plans for remaking the map of Europe."[19] His mind teemed with ideas for a revision of Europe on national lines. Drouyn de Lhuys might acquiesce in the settlement of Vienna in the hope of securing an Austrian alliance. Not so a Bonaparte, and especially not Napoleon III. Though bound to Austria by the treaty of 2 December, France remained liberal, nationalist, revisionist—a fish too big for Buol's net.

Still, 2 December 1854 was an historic date. It marked the decisive crumbling of the Austro-Russian cooperation in European affairs that had begun during the Napoleonic wars (or perhaps earlier in 1772), operated by Metternich more or less successfully in the thirty years that followed, and on which Metternich's successors had staked much in 1848 and the tsar everything in 1853. Buol took the decisive step of his career when he signed the treaty. He did so without hesitation and it brought him only temporary advantage. He acted only when events had shattered the settlement of 1815. But conservative opinion outside Austria and especially the champions of that settlement within believed that Buol had destroyed it himself. He had, they said, pushed over the established settlement which had benefitted Austria most and from the fall of which she alone could not gain. No wonder then Buol's ears were tuned for new alarms. He said to Westmorland: "The revolution (for it is nothing less than that) has met with many and powerful opponents among certain segments of the army to say nothing of the bureaucracy and the civil service. The Emperor, who has much to overcome in his own mind, feels indignant towards those who did not accept the conversion to this new policy as quickly as he did himself."[20] By Buol's policy, that is, the policy of 2 December, Austria lost the two allies she had kept almost without interruption since 1815; she gained no permanent allies in return.

IV

Events in Italy during the next month bore witness to this. The treaty of 22 December 1854 certainly ended any prospect of French action against Austria there, but it did not automatically secure Austria against Sardinia. The French had signed the treaty; they had admitted an obligation; they alone could discharge it. In practical terms, this meant extracting from Sardinia a promise not to explode Italy in Austria's rear. Here was an opportunity for Cavour, since 1852 minister president of the Sardinian council. For over a year he had cast about for some device that would secure Sardinia in allied favor. Wiser than the revolutionaries of 1848, he recognized that only a Continental ally could redress Austria's superiority in manpower and liberate Italy under Sardinian auspices.

That Continental ally could only be France. The ostensible reason for this was Napoleon III's devotion to the principle of nationalities. Yet the Italian problem was for Cavour a problem in European diplomacy, not a matter of national sentiment. Still, this did not shake his faith in alliance with France. His father had fought in the *Grand Armée;* his grandmother had sat at Turin in the court of Napoleon I; and Cavour himself felt more sympathy with France than with any other Great Power.

There were other, deeper reasons why Cavour should try to turn to advantage events in the Crimea. Two defeats at the hands of Austria in 1848–49 as well as the abdication of Charles Albert had tarnished the prestige of the Sardinian monarchy; victory on the heels of these defeats would, Cavour supposed and not altogether wrongly, restore Sardinia's honor; Sardinia's claim to leadership of the Italian national cause would then be carried further to success. Cavour believed, and believed quite rightly, that Sardinia's influence in Europe rose or fell in inverse ratio to Austria's. He knew that the allies had been unable to win at a single blow and perhaps looked forward to a long war, one that could not be brought to a resolute conclusion without Sardinian aid.

Cavour also had a domestic calculation. As minister-president he had to straddle between Left and Right. Though himself a moderate he had intrigued himself into power with the help of the anti-clerical Left and so had estranged himself from conservative Sardinian opinion, that of the king, Victor Emmanuel II, most of all. Cavour, on his side, was alive to the resentment of the king and looked forward to the day when he could shake himself free of royalist intrusions into politics. This development was to occur only late in the day. Indeed at this very moment, when Cavour was sending feelers to London and Paris, Victor Emmanuel was intriguing with Pope Pius IX and with the parliamentary opposition against Cavour's religious policy, and—even more alarming from Cavour's point of view—was developing plans to call in the conservatives and thus wreck Cavour's government. The clericals were already Cavour's principal opponents and laws against them had just been passed. Nor did Cavour much care for Mazzini and the radicals who were constantly parading their grievances against the Sardinian mon-archy and whose republicanism had proved singularly unsuccessful in 1848–49. It would be a great stroke against conservative clericalism as well as against revolutionary republicanism if Sardinia acquired prestige and territory under Cavour's direction and one highly pleasing from a constitu-tional point of view. For just as the royalists intended to blame Cavour for any failure, Cavour was resolved not to allow the royalists credit for any success. He regarded Victor Emmanuel as an amateur dabbling in political questions and meant to strengthen his influence and his independence against the crown.

A great stroke of policy was therefore attractive, even essential, to Cavour. For over a year he had followed, with sharp eyes, the war between Russia and the western Powers. During the first stage he kept Sardinia neutral. He gambled on a renewed Holy Alliance: should Austria go with Russia, Sardinia might ally herself with Great Britain and France. The gamble backfired. The western Powers wished to pull Austria into the war on their side; they dared not risk alienating her by flirting with Italian nationalism. As early as March 1854 Drouyn warned Cavour that Sardinia must not use the Eastern question to explode Italy against Austria: "If Austria comes to fight along with us in the East, we shall regard as a diversion hostile to ourselves every movement which the revolutionary party might provoke in Italy." [21] The message convinced Cavour that he must get ahead of Austria in the competition for allied favor. He told Hudson, the British ambassador, that Sardinia might be persuaded to send 14,000 or 15,000 troops to the Crimea. Hudson posed the decisive question when he asked Clarendon: "Can Piedmont take part in this war, and on what conditions?" The need for military aid was obvious to every competent British observer immediately after the first battles were fought; there were obvious difficulties in getting it. Hudson noted: "So far as Piedmont is concerned, I am convinced that she will act with good faith in any case. But she would be placed in a dilemma. She would feel that she could not draw the sword for Austria and against the Italians. She would do nothing. She would be neutral and neutralized and of no use to herself let alone to the western Powers, and a source of constant anxiety to Austria. An Italian revolution would tend to the advantage of Russia and in great measure palsy the action of Austria."

Hudson did not yet despair. He went on: "Piedmontese statesmen hold that the proper position of Austria is that of a barrier to Russia on the Danube and on the Black Sea. They say: Give Austria Bessarabia, the provinces of the Danube and the Crimea; make her an Eastern bulwark of Europe. In exchange for the Danube give Sardinia Lombardy and Venice." [22]

And then? Nothing. Cavour's power did not extend beyond the hall where the council of ministers met. The council objected that the allies must satisfy Sardinian grievances over "the condition of Italy" in return for an alliance. Cavour thought otherwise. It was inconceivable to him that this objection could ever be met as long as alliance between France and Austria lay on the horizon; and he would have liked to strengthen Sardinia's hand with the western Powers even at the cost of being associated with Austria. Not so his colleagues. They were insistent that, since the allies had refused to take up "the Italian problem" an alliance of the kind envisaged by Cavour was out of the question. It was bad enough that Cavour and Hudson had negotiated behind their backs; the results of these negotiations were worse still.

These objections were repeatedly voiced at Turin during the summer of 1854. Their immediate effect was to launch Cavour on the path towards closer relations with France. Some of the more radical of the Sardinian ministers hoped to win Napoleon III for a ringing declaration of support for the Italian cause and for full-scale opposition to the Austrian occupation of north Italy; others, more modest, hoped that Napoleon III would provide enough encouragement as to future rewards for Sardinia in order to break the deadlock in the council. Since Napoleon III had already written about "doing something for Italy" and since hostility to Austria, the country of Metternich and of legitimacy, was, or was to be, the overriding theme of his foreign policy, this seemed a plausible or even a reasonable expectation. But the Sardinian ministers, including Cavour, expected from Napoleon III more than he was in a position to offer. For though his professions of sympathy for Italy were genuine, he had at the moment certain fundamental reservations: there was, for instance, his fear of the French clericals and their indignation that a forward policy in Italy was bound to excite. There was Drouyn de Lhuys and the Austrian alliance. Most of all, there were serious economic and social problems. The French people had at best been half-hearted about the war against Russia. Now they were genuinely anxious over the incompetence and disease that were ravaging the allied troops. Napoleon III did not in any case wish to upset the status quo on his frontiers before he had finished with Russia; therefore he must break off. "Italy" went into the background: no serious fighting for six months; no contacts between the allies and Sardinia; mounting losses in the Near East.

At the end of the year things changed. On 13 December 1854 two letters reached Turin from London. Both requested Sardinian troops. There was no mystery about these requests. The grim situation in the Crimea and the disasters of the Baltic campaign made the last two months of 1854 the gloomiest time of the war for the British people. Popular feeling wanted some dramatic action. The agitation crystalized around the inefficiency and the incompetence of the British army. Hence the government had a powerful incentive to tread the path hewed by the French: faced by dwindling resources in the Crimea, they looked covetously at the Sardinian army: "small but undeniably efficient." [23]

There was a secondary consideration that gradually moved up to first place. The British high command was painfully aware of its military inferiority compared with that of the French: they shrank from allowing the war to continue merely to shower prestige on Napoleon III's army. Cavour called a cabinet council and won it for adherence to the Anglo-French alliance of 10 April 1854. There were these conditions: the western Powers must (1) press Austria to lift the law of sequestration in Lombardy; (2) affirm that the Franco-Austrian treaty of 22 December 1854 had in it no clauses detrimental to Sardinia; (3) agree to discuss "the condition of Italy" before making peace. These proposals represented the program of collaboration between Sardinia and the western Powers that the bulk of Sardinian ministers had hoped for. But the western Powers made it clear that there was one condition which they could not fulfill: the question at issue between Austria and Sardinia over the sequestrations in Lombardy. The negotiations reached deadlock.

The French were much disturbed. They believed that the Sardinian ministers would surrender at discretion when they contemplated the choices confronting Sardinia and the consequences of intransigence. They therefore stepped up their provocations to Sardinia: "they even threatened to go over to the conservative side by seconding Austrian complaints against the Sardinian press." [24] King Victor Emmanuel blinked at this threat; he had grown weary over the innumerable obstacles against Sardinian action that his ministers were presenting to the allies; more, as a military monarch, he relished the prospect of going to the Crimea with the Sardinian army, himself as its supreme commander. He said to Guiche, the French representative: "I believe we ought to ally ourselves in full trust without restrictions or reservations or not at all. If we are beaten in the Crimea we shall manage to get along somehow; and if we win? Well, that will be worth to the Lombards more than all the articles they want to put in the treaty. . . . If my ministers won't go ahead, I shall get rid of them and call in ones that will." [25]

A confused interlude followed. Neither Cavour nor the cabinet as yet had any inkling as to what was afoot. As ever the Sardinian ministers wished to bind the allies and, as ever, the allies meant to disappoint them. The foreign minister, Dabormida, was insistent that it would be crazy for Sardinia to join hands with Austria without receiving in return some concrete reward. For the time being he got his way. More than this, the other ministers were persuaded by him that the allies were about to give way. There was some ground for this belief. On 28 December 1854 Hudson had received a letter from Clarendon. Its hard core read: "Though we rule out a treaty with secret articles we nevertheless recognize the deep-seated concern of the Sardinian government in ameliorating the deplorable conditions on the Italian penin-sula. . . . We promise the Sardinian government our support for the efforts that they have made to improve these conditions in a manner consistent with our existing obligations by treaty."[26]

Dabormida had an ingenious idea. The council, including himself, had been resolute for a treaty between Sardinia and the western Powers—on condition, of course, that Sardinian demands were satisfied. Dabormida now hit on the idea of dropping the treaty in return for a "reverse note"—a device that would, or so he made out to his colleagues in the cabinet, incorporate the concessions to Sardinia implied in Clarendon's letter of 24 December 1854 but would do so in less rigid form.

There was one awkward flaw in this happy plan. Though it had been worked out by Dabormida it ignored the opposition that the "reverse note" was bound to incite among the French. Drouyn de Lhuys could not have accepted it without repudiating French policy of the last six months; Dabormida's plan made sense in Paris only on the assumption that France was prepared to risk a breach with Austria. This prospect did not trouble the British. Left to themselves they would gladly have jettisoned Austria if they could have won Sardinian assistance in exchange. They were too late: the treaty of 22 December 1854 had been signed; and the French could not conclude any agreement with Sardinia in an anti-Austrian sense. The negotiations deadlocked once more.

France and Sardinia held rigid positions. The directors of French policy, Napoleon III and Drouyn de Lhuys, were agreed that Sardinian adherence to the Anglo-French alliance should be immediate and unconditional. France was committed to Austria by the treaty of 2 December 1854 and even more by the treaty of 22 December 1854. Neither Napoleon III nor Drouyn nor Guiche wanted a row with Austria; the Sardinian cabinet refused to budge. The confusion was heightened by personal differences of outlook. Dabormida never wanted association with Austria except on impossible terms. Guiche was inclined to say, "Now or never." Impatient in temper, choleric in disposition, he reined in his nature and strove for compromise. Cavour, on his side, wished to spin out the negotiations; he proposed to send his minister of war, La Marmora, to Paris ostensibly to sort out the confusion over the "reverse note," really in the hope of provoking a better offer from Napoleon III at the decisive moment. This temporizing gesture was rejected by the western ambassadors. Guiche was indignant. He said to Cavour: "It's not for me to tell the Minister of War to keep out of Paris. But I assure you that he isn't going to change the mind of my government—it is already made up. . . . What are you up to? We have reached a dead end: further discussions are impossible. . . . Do you suppose that your Minister of War can persuade

Drouyn de Lhuys and Lord Clarendon to change their minds? You must be out of your mind if you . . . think that."[27]

Cavour backed down. His policy had failed to avert the crisis. Time was running out. Decision rested with the council of ministers. Sardinian policy was considered at a ministerial conference of 9 January 1855. Hudson and Guiche attended. Though still anxious to avoid a breach, the Sardinian ministers, and especially Dabormida, walked a little nearer the edge. Reports of French dissatisfaction with the Sardinians were growing, and these reports were well-founded. The council, it was expected, would soon act. But how? and still more important, when? Guiche complained that the allies were being deluded and led astray by the intemperate bickering of the council; he added, more indignantly, that the Sardinian ministers were bent on neutrality. Cavour replied: "Oh, that just isn't so! Here we are, discussing our policy in the very same room as you—that itself should tell you where our sympathies lie."[28]

Cavour still hoped that a moment would arrive when the western Powers and Austria would fall out. At the very last he came to realize that this hope would not materialize, was illusion. There was an extraordinary epilogue. Cavour had been very much a man "on the make." He had come to power by intrigue with the Left; he now saw danger from the Right. Victor Emmanuel had told Guiche, but not Hudson, of his intention to wreck the ministry by throwing out his ministers. Probably Victor Emmanuel had been hoping all along that the council would prove intransigent and thus provoke a monarchical intervention. In any case a French diplomat now unwittingly spoilt Victor Emmanuel's scheme by blurting out the story to Cavour. For this reason Cavour now agreed to accept the treaty unconditionally. Cabinet opinion was all against him. But personal opinion took over. It would never do for the council to be turned out of office by monarchical decree. The council must coordinate its diplomatic and military policies with those of the allies. Dabormida raised hot objections: the government could not bind itself without concessions from the western Powers. He asked Cavour: "What possible good can come of this treaty?" And Cavour answered: "Maybe not much. But what else can we do?" Dabormida persisted: "What is the object of the treaty? What does it give us?—nothing. No promises, no prestige, no satisfaction of our honor."[29] With this he shrugged his shoulders and passed out of events.

Cavour attempted to consolidate the cabinet. He made himself foreign minister. The other ministers, with little wrangling, agreed the next day. On 10 January 1855 Sardinia adhered unconditionally to the Anglo-French alliance; this was followed by a military convention two weeks later. The

decision of 10 January charted the history of Italy for the next five years.
Cavour wrote: "Events have driven Sardinia to take an unequivocal position
in Italy. . . . This position is hazardous . . . yet it was imposed upon us by
honor and by duty. Since Providence has determined that Sardinia alone in
Italy should be free and independent, Sardinia ought to use her liberty and
her independence to plead before Europe the cause of the unhappy peninsula.
We shall not draw back from this task. King and country are determined to
carry it through to the end." [30].

The allied demands were met; Sardinia had been won for war. Later on
the alliance looked like a first step towards the unification of Italy, and its
significance was therefore not grasped. At the time it seemed a step the other
way. By Cavour's stroke public opposition in Sardinia was brought to white
heat. It was hardly cooler in Lombardy. Everywhere men were stirred by
righteous indignation and thrust forward eagerly to condemn the government.
La Farina spoke for contemporary liberal opinion: "So we shall be allies of
the allies of *the* ally." He was echoed by the liberal press and by the
revolutionary pamphleteers. Mazzini said: "By this act the King's government
have once and for all announced 'We are with Austria.'" [31] Ignorance
inflamed passion further. The Red party bombarded the troops with petitions
urging defiance of military service. Army officers charged that the foreign
office was crammed with guilty secrets. The merchants of Genoa railed over
the loss of their grain trade with Odessa.

These were understandable objections. It was not easy to see the
advantages of the treaty, as contemporary critics insisted. The treaty of 10
January 1855 certainly did not improve Sardinia's position in Italy. Quite
the contrary. Sardinia was made to turn her attention away from Italy to the
Eastern question. And for what? No promise of an indemnity, let alone of
territory; no mention of sequestrations; nothing about the "condition of
Italy." Sardinia had been won, though not easily; this seemed another score
for Buol and Drouyn de Lhuys.

This was a misreading of the situation. As a matter of fact, the treaty of
10 January 1855 was as much a victory for Sardinia as the treaties of
December 1854 had been for Austria—maybe more: "though Great Britain
and France had promised not to back the cause of Italy, Cavour had not
promised to give it up." [32] Indeed the treaty of 10 January 1855 gave the
decisive blow to the treaty of 2 December 1854 and all the paper structure
that followed from it. The Austrian threat could no longer keep France and
Sardinia apart; Sardinia had to be won over by the French if Italy were to
be checked. Nor could Austria count on Great Britain any longer to restrain
France in Italy, as Great Britain had done with comparative success in

1848–49. The British welcomed the aggrandizement of Sardinia in northern Italy as a matter of general principle, and this involved hostility towards Austria in any case. Besides, Great Britain and Austria were at loggerheads over the treaty of 2 December; each insisted on her own interpretation of the treaty and these were fundamentally incompatible. To the Austrians the treaty of 2 December meant negotiations; to the British it meant war. The British had insisted on an agreement for military cooperation before negotiations began; the Austrians would agree to military cooperation only after negotiations had failed. Hence the moment had arrived that still seemed like war to the British but like peace to the Austrians. The treaty of 10 January 1855 at last enabled Cavour to compete against Austria on grounds of Sardinia's choosing: "in realist fashion this was a competition that he could win." [33]

V

The treaty of 2 December 1854 infuriated Frederick William IV, and no wonder. In his view, the treaty gave decisive proof that Buol was not contemplating cooperation with Prussia in Germany and probably was not contemplating cooperation with Prussia anywhere. Frederick William IV therefore hoped that the treaty would be revoked. Buol hoped, still more strongly, that it would be enforced. Frederick William was the more anxious of the two; after all, the treaty flew in the face of the Austro-Prussian alliance—to say nothing of Buol's express promise not to make it.

Frederick William, therefore, once again charged forward as a diplomatic negotiator. He first proposed to follow Bismarck's advice and mobilize 200,000 men in Silesia—ostensibly a gesture against Russia; really a stroke against Austria. Such a move would in his own words " . . . inspire Austria with the courage to deal vigorously with Russian peace initiatives." [34] This was too much for the Prussian liberals; it could not be accomplished without risking the hostility of the western Powers.

In January Frederick William IV turned the other way. He sent a special envoy, Usedom, to England to negotiate an Anglo-Prussian alliance no doubt in the hope of stealing a march on Austria whose intimidation he had vowed never to accept. He had a more immediate motive. Usedom had bewitched him with the idea that the Catholic Powers of Europe, with Austria at their head, were plotting the destruction of Prussia. This was an absurd exaggeration. All the same, it was enough to goad Frederick William IV into action.

Usedom proposed to bustle Queen Victoria and Prince Albert into an anti-Austrian combine.

He had, of course, no success. What could Prussia have offered in exchange for British favor? There was some desultory talk of stationing several divisions on the Russo-Polish frontier. These were important only in revealing the illusions in the mind of Usedom, illusions to which the Austrian ambassador drew attention when he remarked, a little condescendingly, "Prussia will mobilize an army that will do nothing." [35]

This was the crux of the matter—the point of fundamental difference between Prussia and Austria; and it was the point that gave the death blow to Usedom's offer and, for that matter, to all Prussian attempts to outbid Austria in their competition for Anglo-French favor during the Crimean war: "an Austrian mobilization inevitably threatened Russia and diverted her military resources from the Crimea." [36] The Austrian rulers already knew this; the allied ministers knew it; and the tsar of Russia knew it most of all. After all, it had taken the Austrian mobilization of 22 October to bring Nicholas to accept the Four Points. War against Russia was never contemplated seriously by Prussia, and therefore a Prussian mobilization would not serve any purpose except to put a neutral zone between Russia and the western side. Besides, the British government knew very well that Frederick William IV was too bewitched by the tsar to be taken seriously. As Prince Albert said: "It is known to the most gullible-minded simpleton in St. Petersburg that Prussian troops will never go against Russia." [37] The negotiations died away.

Similar failure awaited Prussian policy towards France. Frederick William IV disliked and distrusted Napoleon III as "the revolution incarnate"; at the time the impending conference at Vienna gave a new twist to his policy. General Wedell, intimate friend of Manteuffel, prime minister of Prussia, came to Paris. Not much happened—at any rate from a practical standpoint. The French would have liked to push Prussia into the allied camp in order to create a great coalition against Russia. The terms that Frederick William IV put up made this impossible. Wedell demanded an invitation to the Vienna conference before an alliance was signed; the French answered that the alliance must be signed before an invitation was given. Drouyn de Lhuys became impatient and said of Wedell: "He brings us nothing but the King's tears." [38] These negotiations too broke down.

Was there ever any sense in them? In a curious way, yes. Throughout the winter of 1854–55, Frederick William IV appeared to be vacillating between a pro-Russian position and a pro-western one. To pro-Russian Prussian conservatives like Leopold and Ludwig von Gerlach, and to pro-western Prussians such as Prince William and the liberals of the Prussian Landtag, the king's course must have seemed confused, inconsistent, erratic. At bottom, however, Frederick William was resolved on neutrality; despite occasional swings this way and that, he calculated and calculated rightly that Prussia had nothing to gain from either side: not from promoting the aims of the western Powers nor from threatening the interests of Russia. Prussia made no promises to either side, estranged neither.

Whenever two Powers or groups of Powers have fallen out, it always seems immoral to them for another Power to try to dance with both. Prussian policy came in for accusations of shiftiness and duplicity during the Crimean war; and no doubt these accusations were true. All the same they ignored the fundamental calculation on which Prussia's policy rested: a genuine indifference to the affairs of the Balkans and a belief that the right course was to hold aloof, to do nothing—a belief vindicated by events.

The fundamental task of the Prussian government was now to persuade the states of the German confederation that Austria should not be allowed to involve them in her troubles. This was pretty small beer in the eyes of the western Powers. Their running sore was and always had been Austria; and Austria meant diplomacy once more. The way was thus paved for a new bout of negotiations—that is for a conference at Vienna.

Chapter 8

THE VIENNA CONFERENCE

A peace conference at Vienna raised the question of the Four Points. The Four Points raised deeper questions, point 3 most of all. The allies never dreamt that they would be faced by this question. They believed that by the treaty of 2 December they had committed Austria to war. Now Russia had accepted the Four Points, thereby committing the allies to negotiation. The acceptance meant that the third point would have to be defined more clearly: "revision of the Straits Convention" was an empty phrase, an unsatisfactory basis for negotiation. The British wanted a "full and frank" definition of point 3—that is to say: "the demolition of Sebastopol and of the other Russian fortresses on the Black Sea and the limitation of Russia's Black Sea fleet to four ships." [1]

The French jibbed at this suggestion. Drouyn de Lhuys, in particular, was disturbed. The British scheme would, he asserted, create panic in Vienna, would vindicate the opponents of Buol. Even worse, it would destroy the alliance of 2 December 1854—Drouyn de Lhuys's peculiar achievement, *chef d'oeuvre* of his diplomacy. Thouvenel seconded him. As early as 6 October 1854 he wrote: "If we refuse Austria everything she will escape us . . . we must commit her against Russia." [2] It may have seemed a little awkward for Thouvenel to take this line; he, more than any other minister in France, was the enthusiastic executant of Napoleon III's policy of nationality; and this involved opposition to Austria no matter what Drouyn de Lhuys might do. As a matter of fact Drouyn believed that it was only out of expediency that Thouvenel supported him. It was not only out of expediency. It was also due to the encouragement and inspiration that Thouvenel, while sometimes disagreeing with Drouyn policies, sought to give him as foreign minister.

The bickering between the allied governments put Napoleon III in an awkward position. He wished, of course, to promote "the liberal alliance"

in order to fulfill his dreams for revising the map of Europe; at the same time
he wished to conciliate Austria. Left to themselves the British would gladly
have abandoned the Austrian alliance which they regarded as a nuisance and
a distraction. Paris forbade such a break. Drouyn de Lhuys thought he saw
a way out. The French ministers—or at any rate Drouyn de Lhuys and
Thouvenel—were insistent on a moderate interpretation of point 3 so as not
to estrange Austria. The British were equally insistent on a strong interpretation so as to have done with her. Then mix the two together. Great Britain
and France should secretly commit themselves to each other, that is, they
would agree on the "full and frank" definition the British had wanted. With
Austria, on the other hand, they should pose as champions of moderation.

This policy was duly implemented. On 17-19 December the British and
French governments secretly exchanged notes; on 28 December they signed
a protocol in Vienna. The first defined point 3 as the British had envisaged
in their statement to Paris; the second vaguely asserted that "the preponderance of Russia in the Black Sea must be brought to an end." Drouyn de
Lhuys was deliberately dabbling in the politics of duplicity; he knew very well
that he was running the risk of being discovered, but he clearly expected to
get away with it. The Russians would, he imagined, accept the interpretation
of point 3 in the protocol of 28 December; Austria would then be ensnared
in his trap, would go to war with Russia over the strict one.

This calculation misfired. On 7 January 1855 Gorchakov accepted the
version of point 3 laid down in the protocol of 28 December. Many factors
entered into the Russian decision. A personal factor: the tsar's poor health
brought back into events men of a more conciliatory disposition—Nesselrode, for example, most strongly. A practical factor: the military stalemate
in the Crimea was sapping Russia's economic resources and her manpower.
There was the fear that the war, if not soon ended, would take a revolutionary
turn. There was the calculation that Russia would gain sympathy in the eyes
of the German states by yielding on point 3. Most important, there was the
assurance from Francis Joseph that the western Powers would not pitch their
demands too high in a peace conference. The Russian answer arrived in
Vienna six days before it was due. This was perfect timing: it made nonsense
out of western claims that Russia was using the time to delay the opening
of a conference. Once more the allies had counted on Russian intransigence.
Once more the Russians had disappointed them.

The Russian answer delighted Buol. He believed that a "glorious peace"
was at hand. In the middle of January he launched a scheme for German
mobilization at Frankfurt. In this way he hoped to force Prussia and the other
German states into line behind Austria during the peace negotiations and to

confront Russia with the prospect of a European coalition against her in the event that they collapsed. He failed. He then sent a protocol to the middle German states exhorting them to accede to the Austrian request and place their forces under her command in case of war. Here too he failed. Russia's evacuation of the principalities had convinced the German states that she had ceased to be a threat to anyone. Indeed in their eyes the real threat was Austria. Buol's schemes seemed to bear out the suspicion, rampant in the Germanies, that Austria was bent on destroying the confederation. Pfortden went further and asserted that she was trying to regain the imperial crown. An anti-Austrian circular denouncing Buol was hawked round Germany. At Frankfurt Bismarck expostulated that Germany's only interest, the freedom of the Danube, had already been secured; on 8 February he drove the Diet into action and won it for a declaration of total neutrality in the war.

This was a dramatic event, heavy with consequences for Bismarck's later policy—the policy he followed during the Eastern crises of 1875–78 and 1885–88: the maintenance of the Hapsburg monarchy as a Germanic Power, but no support for her ambitions in the Balkans. This was the note that he first struck in his speech at Frankfurt on 8 February 1855. By the beginning of March Frederick William IV's zest for adventure had dwindled, dissipated; and he at last settled down to play the role for which Bismarck had cast him. Infuriated over allied inflexibility, bewildered by the divisions among his advisers which had confused Prussian policy all along, dreading "the revolution," suspicious and contemptuous of Austria, eager to maintain favor at Frankfurt, anxious to maintain conservative solidarity with the tsar, he determined to wash his hands of diplomatic negotiations—"this filthy mess,"[3] as he called them—and to break off once and for all. Henceforth he regarded the Federal resolution of 8 February 1855 as the key to Prussian policy.

II

The two western Powers had always regarded Frederick William IV as little more than a nuisance who had to be tolerated but not respected. For Drouyn de Lhuys, in particular, the temptation was now irresistible to round on those Prussians, such as the Gerlachs, who had wished to harass France and to declare that, thanks to the Russian decision of 7 January 1855, France was now bound to negotiate in Vienna. Or rather: Drouyn de Lhuys thought that the more he convinced Buol of his willingness to negotiate, the more likely the prospect that he would not have to; hence the greater acceptance in Vienna for his argument that there was no clash of political principle dividing Austria from the West serious enough to prevent her from joining in the war against Russia.

Here was the curious feature of French diplomatic activity at this time. All their interest centered on Austria. It was felt, quite understandably, that there was something peculiarly perverse in attending a peace conference and at the same time vowing to continue the war until military victory had been achieved. The French ministers therefore tumbled over themselves to get out of their mess. Drouyn de Lhuys thought to evade the negotiations by reviving an idea of Russell's and demanding that Russia first evacuate the Crimea. The British cabinet rejected this as too risky: Clarendon feared that the Russians might accept it and thus commit the allies even more. Drouyn's next impulse was to demand that the Russian acceptance of the protocol of 28 December be put in writing. Once more British opinion was too strong for him.

And not only British. French opinion too was moving against the war in a way which shocked Napoleon III's nerve as supreme master of France. By 1855 the Crimean war was generally believed to have been a mistake. The course of the war and its failure to "come off" pointed the same way. One observer noted: "If difficulties continue, if the war drags out for too long a time, perseverance will . . . weary and this . . . weariness will become a source of discontent, a veritable complaint against the government."[4]

Napoleon III was nothing if not a man of the masses. The radicals of 1848 had made out that they and they alone had brought the masses into politics. The claim had little validity. Napoleon III, not the radical republicans, had let the genie out of the bottle; and he determined from the start to shape his policy according to public desire. As Hübner once noted: "Louis Napoleon will always permit himself to be guided by what he believes to be the opinion, the interests and the will of his country."[5] Historians who have studied the diplomacy of the Second Empire, with L. M. Case at their head, have demonstrated this beyond peradventure. Napoleon III fully appreciated the power of opinion in wartime and knew now, if he did not know earlier, that popular enthusiasm for the war was waning, in need of a shot in the arm. He was also acutely aware that as head of the army he could not allow things in the Crimea to stand still, and he therefore had urgent motives for seconding British objections. The divergence between Drouyn de Lhuys and the British government became particularly marked. Indeed for Cowley the real question was: "Who is the greater rogue in the political game, Drouyn or Buol?"[6] The French foreign office was held firmly by Drouyn de Lhuys to the line of preserving good relations with Austria at all costs. Persigny, the minister of the interior who was responsible for ascertaining public opinion, was an old-fashioned radical who disliked Drouyn de Lhuys and who would not stomach a soft line. The bulk of the ministers supported Persigny. French policy fell into confusion.

The British position was more complicated. Diplomatic negotiations were inextricably connected with French policy—or at any rate with the policy of Drouyn and Thouvenel. With the British, on the other hand, diplomacy counted for little, diplomacy with Austria even less. Aberdeen's policy had rested on the dogma that the Russians were acting in good faith. He could not now reject this line without accepting Palmerston's argument that Russia's policy of dominance and expansion had brought the war on in the first place; nor—a more important point—could he admit the failure of his government to wage war effectively. This had a decisive result. Failure to wage the war effectively had been the decisive weakness of Aberdeen's government in the public eye. In consequence the storm of opinion now blew with unrelenting fury against Aberdeen himself. This storm had been long pent up; and its origins are worth looking at closely.

The Crimean war had been jubilantly welcomed by various segments of British opinion. *The Times* gave out on 9 November 1854: "The nation is in essence what it was forty years before—sound to the core and true of itself." The statement was a significant pointer to a trend that the war had ushered in. While political leaders fumbled towards new outlooks, the newspapers were busy shaping public opinion and official policy, or so their editors imagined. *The Times* was indeed a power behind the throne. The position of its editor, Delane, on the great questions of the day excited as much interest as the positions of the most prominent political leaders. In fact, the two positions often ran together. In the words of its official *History:* "Nothing is more notable in the history of *The Times* than the part it played in the Crimean war. It was not only the chief recorder of events, it can be counted among the chief protagonists."[7]

The popular enthusiasm for war and the rigmarole of affairs in the Crimea did not mix well. Dreams for resolute action against the Russians were shattered by the end of 1854. The war was being fought in the Crimea, "the eye tooth of the bear"; worse, it was muddled by persistent diplomacy. The chaos provoked radical segments of British opinion to rail more loudly against the incompetence of the government in London than the wickedness of the Russians. Indeed some radicals pronounced the war a hoax, and believed that Russian wickedness was a myth, a story launched by the government in order to delay social reform. This was the view of Cobden, the apostle of free trade, who had led the fight against the Corn Laws ten years before. Cobden had visited Russia and had taken the line that Russia, not Turkey, could become the civilized community of British ideals. A

Russian takeover of Turkey would help everyone: "Not merely Great Britain but the entire civilized world will have reason to congratulate itself the moment that the territory falls under the sceptre of any European power whatever." He described the advantages which Constantinople would gain from Russian rule—noble public buildings, learned societies, the end of slavery, polygamy, and plague—and concluded: "To assert that *we*, a commercial and manufacturing people have an interest in retaining the fairest region of Europe in barbarism and ignorance—that we are benefitted because poverty, slavery, polygamy, and the plague abound in Turkey is a fallacy too gross even for refutation."[8] His argument appealed to some of the high-minded of British society, the Peelites most of all. This was as far as he got. Public opinion was not moved by his arguments. It was thoroughly distraught by the muddle and disappointment over the war; and Cobden was ineffective while the war went on.

Most societies have an underworld of crackpots and layabouts. Opposition to the government was transformed into a mighty force by another radical, David Urquhart. He did not begin as a radical. In the 1820s he had supported the Greeks in their war of independence. Afterwards he became a transplanted Turk. He believed that western society was sliding into irremediable decay and that only Turkey and Turkish institutions offered a way out. He was the first to promote Turkish baths in England and to advocate them as a cure against all the maladies of mankind. In his eyes Turkey was a Heaven on earth, and he was convinced that she could survive forever if she were not shackled with western projects of reform. In his view, it was the western Powers who should emulate Turkey, not the other way round.

Urquhart was bewitched by his obsessions. The strongest of these was his hatred of Russia. Some radicals regarded Russia as a mere nuisance. To Urquhart she was the Devil incarnate. He saw the tsar stirring up wars between the civilized peoples of Europe while at the same time holding aloof, keeping out of them. When all the civilized countries had cut each other's throats, Russia would step in and run the world. The swell of indignation against Russia that arose in Great Britain on the outbreak of the Crimean war put wind into Urquhart's sails. The military stalemate convinced him that the war was a fraud—run for Russia's benefit; and he determined that he alone could pull the chaos into order. He stumped the country on a wave of popularity, harangued lower-class audiences, launched the story that the members of the government, especially Palmerston, were in Russian pay. From this his deduction: Russia was on the march to world conquest: she would be in Constantinople one day, Persia the next, India a fortnight later.

Urquhart's doctrines were strong meat, aimed at working-class radicals, as restless and as opinionated as himself. He sought to convince them that their plans for reform at home and especially their demand for universal suffrage were a gigantic red herring; what was needed was the right foreign policy. Once this had been achieved, Russia would be destroyed, the nations of Europe would treat each other in a civilized manner; and the radicals would get universal suffrage without difficulty.

This argument and many others like it were music in the ears of working-class radicals. They believed that the war was a fraud on the British people; and believed even more strongly that the foreign office was crammed to the hilt with guilty secrets. To Urquhart's enthusiastic audiences the study of the blue books became a modern scholasticism, each sentence combed over and analyzed as solemnly as Holy Writ—a whirlwind of activity designed to prove Palmerston's guilt. For Urquhart taught not only that all diplomacy was immeasurably evil; this evil could be found in the contemporary records that the diplomats themselves had made.

In 1848 Urquhart convinced Antsey, a fellow radical, to open an impeachment of Palmerston on twelve fantastic charges. All memory of the affair was washed away by the revolutions of 1848, and in retrospect it seems a trivial episode hardly worthy of record. But it left its mark all same. Urquhart had no standing in established circles. He had never been a member of a government. Yet Urquhart came nearer than any other single man has ever done to unhorsing the accepted spokesman for the foreign policy of a Great Power. Urquhart's one-man crusade stirred up a hornet's nest. It drove Palmerston to the wall and was not settled until Palmerston announced to a startled House the famous phrase that England has no eternal friends, no eternal enemies, only eternal interests.

By 1854 the tables had been turned. The campaign against Palmerston got off on the wrong footing. Palmerston determined not to let Urquhart steal a march on him—determined, that is, to win over radical opinion. In any case Urquhart sealed his own fate. He believed that the only way to end the war was through open diplomacy and demanded that the queen convoke the privy council in order to do so. This proposal was defeated in January 1855 by the foreign affairs committee of workingmen at Newcastle, one of 145 such committees that Urquhart had set up in the autumn of 1854. This defeat gave the death blow to Urquhart's hopes of toppling Palmerston. By the end of the war Urquhart had given up the British radicals and, though never converting to Catholicism, turned to the pope as the only dependable shield against Russia.

Dissent continued nonetheless. Though the radicals were divided, the Crimean war gave great impetus to radical attitudes. Cobden and his followers had hoped that the mounting unemployment and high food prices of the hard Crimean winter of 1855 would swing opinion for peace. Not at all. If anything, economic discontent paved the way for a new bout of bellicosity—a bellicosity that went deep down into the population. Early in 1855 an Administrative Reform Association was set up in London, "brought into existence by the exigency of the time." It demanded full information about the real conduct of "public affairs" particularly in the foreign office, "a region of unknown powers and undefined responsibilities. There must be an end put to every mystery of office; how the administration of the country is carried on must be made plain to the most ordinary capacity."[9]

Agitation in Parliament bubbled up from agitation in the streets. These were the halcyon days of the individual members. They were free to make their own way, follow their own instincts, lay down the law on high policy. The MPs jostled each other in debates, scrutinized the conduct of the government, demanded information. On 23 January 1855, Roebuck, a radical MP from Bath, introduced a resolution to set up a committee "to enquire into the condition of our army before Sebastopol." The motion sealed the fate of the government. Russell told Aberdeen that the motion could not be resisted, and on 24 January resigned his post as leader in the House of Commons. The next day Aberdeen announced that the government would stand firm. The writing was on the wall. On 29 January Roebuck's motion sailed through the House of Commons by a vote of 305 to 148; and the government fell.

Aberdeen resigned on 30 January, thus bringing the government to an end. A week's delay followed. Derby (leader of the opposition) tried to form a government. Without success. The next candidate, Lansdowne, lost his nerve, and "Russell, after a vain attempt, found that his former colleagues would not serve under him."[10] On 3 February Aberdeen told the queen to send for Palmerston. Within twenty-four hours Palmerston was prime minister. All the same, his government was shaky. For he was at first the captive of the Peelites: Graham, Herbert, and Gladstone agreed to serve under him only on condition that he perpetuate Aberdeen's policy. For instance, they insisted on early negotiations at Vienna and on the dropping of the demand for Sebastopol. They were also led to believe that Palmerston would resist the Roebuck motion, though they failed to get a formal guarantee. Palmerston, for his part, supposed that the Roebuck motion would be no problem. He had now achieved the pinnacle of his ambition, was not troubled by parliamentary opposition. He believed that he alone could govern England—

indeed that he alone was England. He supposed that, in the face of his personal popularity, all hostility in the Commons would melt away.

Things did not work out like this. On 16 February Palmerston appeared in the House of Commons. He declared that a parliamentary commission was now absurd; the new government would itself be the commission. But the MPs would not budge, and Palmerston beat a retreat. The next day he told the cabinet that the inquiry could not be resisted. This was too much for the Peelites. They saw the Roebuck motion as a breach of constitutional practice, an intolerable encroachment of the legislature on the executive. On 22 February they resigned. Three posts fell vacant. Palmerston filled two of the posts with "new" men: Lewis succeeded Gladstone at the exchequer. Wood moved to the admiralty in place of Graham. The colonial office went to Russell. Russell had already been named British plenipotentiary at Vienna: Palmerston had agreed to send him there in order to satisfy the Peelites. Russell had, from the beginning, been an anti-Russian fire-eater; at the present time he was however locked in a ferocious competition with Palmerston for control of the Whig-Liberal coalition. This had a curious result. Russell resented playing second-fiddle to Palmerston, and he now hoped to elbow Palmerston aside by returning from Vienna as a conciliator-in-chief with a triumphant peace pact in his bag, or as Palmerston put it, "an olive branch round his temples." [11]

This is not the only reason why prospects for peace had improved. In February 1855 the political situation in Russia changed. Nicholas fell ill. His ministers, and all those in positions of authority in St. Petersburg for that matter, expected him to die, and on 2 March 1855 he did so. The significance of this event is not always appreciated. According to Hugh Seton-Watson: "It has been suggested that Nicholas I committed suicide. Perhaps it would be more correct to say that he had lost the will to live, so that his powerful frame could be destroyed by a minor illness—" [12] a verdict that could have been passed on the death of Stalin one hundred years later.

The successor of Nicholas I was Alexander II. Himself a weaker man, he was thought to be in no position to stand out against pacific sentiment. He was, in his own words, a Russian "pure and simple"; his deepest wish was to improve the condition of the Russian people, "and not to shoulder crusades against 'the revolution.' " [13]

This development was welcomed in Paris. Hitherto the bulk of the French ministers had wished to skip the conference at Vienna until decisive military success had been achieved or, in the case of Drouyn de Lhuys, until some device for curing it of practical meaning had been hit on. All this was changed by a dramatic event of 16 February 1855. Napoleon III, frustrated by the rigmarole of events in the Crimea, announced his intention of going there himself. Uproar followed. The French ministers became, in the words of the official history, "one vast rumble of disapprobation and alarm; these servants of the Emperor, usually so quick to disagree, were united this time in unanimous agreement." [14]

Nor were they alone. The British ministers too had urgent reasons for seconding French fears. For one thing they knew that Napoleon III was the built-in force behind "the liberal alliance"; it had little reality in the minds of the French people. What was to become of the alliance while he was in the Crimea? And, for that matter, what would he do once he got there? Steal their thunder and make a separate peace with the enemy—"an alarm later justified by the similar way in which he ended the war against Austria in 1859?" [5] Napoleon III waved these doubts aside; hence the eagerness of the French ministers for the conference that they had once hoped to avoid. Drouyn de Lhuys said to Cowley: "Let us solve point 3 by limiting Russia's Black Sea fleet to its present number." [16]

III

The peace conference got underway on 15 March at Vienna. As expected, it got off to a good start. The first two sessions coasted along, seemingly free of the antagonisms and discontent that were to later rear their heads. Russia agreed to give up the protectorate over the principalities that she had held since 1829. The Danube was to be put under a European commission. Having cleared away the underbrush, the plenipotentiaries were now face to face with the decisive issue on which the conference was henceforth to focus—that is to say, on point 3. The two western Powers had, as already described, agreed with Austria that point 3 should have as its object "the elimination of the preponderance Russia in the Black Sea." This was a vague definition. It was now for the allies of 2 December to push through the cloud of words to the realities beneath—to agree, that is, on a settled meaning.

This was not easy. Russell and Bourqueney were insistent that Russia's fleet in the Black Sea be limited to a set figure. Gorchakov would hear nothing of the kind. Buol sought to break the deadlock. He proposed to Russell and Bourqueney that point 3 be defined by a counterpoise—the Russians could keep their present fleet: if they increased it the two western Powers could send warships through the Straits to match the increase. The allied plenipotentiaries rejected this proposal.

Buol was not yet dismayed. He realized that the Russians would never accept any limitation of their Black Sea fleet. He therefore sought to dodge the problem by inviting the Russians themselves to define point 3—a most ingenious device for stopping the clock. For the moment Buol's efforts were sidelined by events elsewhere. Napoleon III's projected trip to the Crimea had alarmed everyone. The alarm died away. On 13 March Queen Victoria invited him to visit Great Britain. Drouyn de Lhuys resolved to take advantage of the delay in order to produce his own solution to point 3. The Russians had complained that direct limitation infringed their sovereignty; the allies had answered that Russia's sovereignty had to be infringed if Turkey were to be protected from future attack. Drouyn de Lhuys now hit on the idea of neutralizing the Black Sea—that is, barring it to the warships of all Powers. The Russians would be placed on an equal footing with the Turks and with everyone else; more than this, Austria would be won by the allies. There was not much ground for the latter speculation. Neutralization was anathema to Buol. Russell too was inclined to rule it out. He said to Clarendon: "It puts us out quite sadly. I hope it will not be renewed." [17]

Drouyn de Lhuys brushed these objections aside. He knew in advance that neutralization would find rough going in Vienna. He therefore determined to go there himself and carry the day for it. The French foreign office shared Drouyn's sublime confidence in neutralization. Yet they too anticipated difficulties. Thouvenel's anxiety was directed towards the Turks. As Benedetti explained to Thouvenel: "It will not be easy to secure from the sultan either the destruction of his navy or the destruction of his fortresses in the Bosphorus and the Dardanelles. What to his mind are symbols of personal greatness cannot easily be turned into impersonal abstractions." [18]

Thouvenel considered various remedies. He thought to emphasize the practical advantages that would accrue to the Turks under the French scheme and to emphasize even more that, since the Turks could maintain warships in the Sea of Marmora, they could always dominate the Black Sea in time of war. The hard-headed leaders at Constantinople did not take kindly to this argument. They brandished their opposition to neutralization. Their objections anticipated those that the Russians were to make when neutralization was presented at Vienna a month later.

Turkish opposition was not the only difficulty confronting the French at this time. Drouyn's decision to go to Vienna put the British in a panic, Cowley most of all. He said to Clarendon: "I have no opinion of Drouyn's political integrity. . . . I am sure that although he was the greatest advocate in France for war he is for 'la paix à tout prix.' The consequence will be that when he, Bourqueney, Lord John, Westmorland, and Buol get together, they will concoct a peace of which I am sure both countries will hereafter repent." [19] Cowley therefore proposed to Drouyn de Lhuys that the trip to

Vienna be put off and that Drouyn first go to London to take soundings of the British ministers.

Drouyn de Lhuys agreed. On 30 March he promised Palmerston and Clarendon that "neutralization or limitation and nothing else would be proposed." [20] If Austria refused to make Russia's rejection of either scheme a cause for war, neutralization would be presented to Russia in the conference by France alone, and all negotiations would be stopped.

Drouyn appeared in Vienna on 6 April. On 7 April Buol examined his scheme and threw it out: neutralization would expose Russia's Black Sea coast to enemy attack in time of war; worse, it would infringe Russia's sovereignty by depriving her of the right to defend her borders. On 9 April he took a further step. The Russians had, he said, behaved well over points 1 and 2, and because of this, "Austria was not," in Russell's words, "prepared to go to war on account of the refusal of Russia to limit her naval force in the Black Sea." [21]

Drouyn de Lhuys had by now run out of steam. All along this most paradoxical diplomat of the Second Empire had never intended to break with Austria. From start to finish he had assured himself that if only he stuck to his guns, Austria would at some point give way, would go to war—perhaps when the Austrian ultimatum to Russia had been presented; perhaps when the treaty of 2 December 1854 had been signed; or perhaps when his own plan of neutralization was brought in. Drouyn had little desire to go further. The bluff, to which he had encouraged himself, was not succeeding, and in the usual way of those who get into this position, he proposed to play for time, in other words, to do nothing.

This was not a bad idea. The other plenipotentiaries shared Drouyn's desire; they had no wish to see the negotiations break down. Russell had already unfolded his plans for dealing with point 3. As early as 8 March he had written what he called a "Memorandum on Modes of Carrying into Effect the Third Point." Its key passage warned against the dangers that the destruction of the coalition of 2 December must involve: "If Russia shall find when peace is established that the present alliance is dissolved, she will watch her time and, acting with more rapidity and boldness than in 1852, she will trust to her influence and to her diplomacy to postpone, or avert altogether the interference of other Powers to prevent the accomplishment of her designs. If, on the other hand, she is convinced that three such Powers as Austria, France, and Great Britain will act with promptitude and vigor for the protection of Turkey she will hardly play so hazardous a game." [22] Whether this proposal was a realistic plan for the general pacification of Europe will be considered later. Realistic or not, Russell was now landed in an awkward predicament, and Drouyn de Lhuys with him. They were caught between insistence on their own schemes and a breakdown of the conference.

They were not alone. Hitherto Buol had hoped that the terms expressed in the protocol of 28 December would be the foundation-stone of a general settlement of the Eastern question. He now learnt that he had been bamboozled. He was no doubt disgusted to learn the truth of allied intentions; yet, like Russell and Drouyn, he shrank from letting things stand where they were. Fear of rupturing the negotiations weighed him down; and as well, Buol wished to show Drouyn and Russell that he was not the weak, irresolute character that he was so often alleged to be—deservedly or no. Buol knew that Drouyn's entire foreign policy rested on an alliance with Austria. This was the trump card on which Buol had relied all along. He now played it. He told Drouyn that he would prepare a compromise on point 3 that would end Russia's preponderance in the Black Sea, but would spare her the humiliation of neutralization and limitation. In return, Austria would ally herself to France and Great Britain. Drouyn de Lhuys agreed at once; he told Russell that if a rupture with Austria occurred, all his efforts of the last twelve months would be shattered, and the object of his foreign policy destroyed. In this way Drouyn de Lhuys, having been bewitched by the idea of neutralization, was swept into uncharted waters and drifted into acceptance of a scheme which was both unsatisfactory and incompatible with the promises he had made to Palmerston and Clarendon.

The running was now taken up by the men in St. Petersburg. Russian policy was considered in a special committee at the beginning of April. On 17 April the conference reconvened. Gorchakov was ready. He announced: "Russia will not consent to the strength of her navy being restricted to a fixed number either by treaty or in any other manner." [23] More wrangling followed. The plenipotentiaries divided deeply and bitterly over point 3, as much as at any time in the war, and perhaps more so. Gorchakov created a sensation on 22 April 1855 when he proposed that the sultan open the Straits to the warships of all nations. This scheme suited Gorchakov's book, but his alone. No one else would consider it. Russell raised the alarm that his instructions were exhausted and his energy equally so. Drouyn de Lhuys refused to give up. Once more he fell back on neutralization. Once more Gorchakov rejected neutralization out of hand. Gorchakov's ingenuity produced yet another scheme on 23 April. Let the sultan, he said, close the Straits in time of peace and thus keep intact the convention of 1841; there would be this exception: in time of emergency the convention would cease to operate and foreign warships could pass the Straits at the sultan's request. This proposal too was as good as dead. The western Powers, and the Austrians as well, for that matter, could never admit it if they believed that the preservation of Turkey was worth their while. Gorchakov sought to get round this objection by parading his conviction—flattering but untrue—that Turkey could not stand on her own legs unless left alone. He was fumbling in the dark. As a matter of fact, his two schemes were really irrelevancies and the others evaded their own predicament by denouncing them as fraud.

Real events now moved into the back rooms. The Russian announcement of 17 April should have been the death knell of the conference. Nothing of the kind. Buol exasperated himself by devising schemes to keep the conference alive. On 10 April he revealed the workings of his mind to Russell and Drouyn de Lhuys. He had, he said, produced a compromise providing for (1) the closing of the Dardanelles in time of peace; (2) a European guarantee of the integrity of the Ottoman empire; (3) the resolution of point 3 on the basis of counterpoise. Under counterpoise or, as it has more recently—and euphemistically—been called, "graduated deterrence," [24] Great Britain and France could each send into the Black Sea half as many warships as Russia had, if Russia increased her fleet beyond the status quo afloat. This condition would be in an ultimatum that Austria would send to Russia. There was also the alliance between Austria and the western Powers for the purpose of holding Russia back in future years. Its provisions were simple. Great Britain, France, and Austria should promise each other to go to war if Russia's Black Sea fleet became "excessive"—that is, if it exceeded its prewar (1853) strength.

The behavior of the allied plenipotentiaries did not go unnoticed at home. Quite the contrary. Paris and London hummed with criticism of their respective representatives for duplicity and bad faith. Cowley foresaw, and was indeed already experiencing, the controversy that was to come: the advocates of peace, with Drouyn de Lhuys at their head, on the one side; the advocates of war, led by himself, on the other. Cowley exploited to the full his old weapon of the personal approach. At his urging, Napoleon III on 23 April wired Drouyn with preemptory orders to break off the negotiations. The telegraphs in London tapped out similar orders to Russell. To no avail. Despite the orders from London and Paris, Drouyn and Russell determined to return home to fight for the compromise that Buol had worked out.

IV

Russell returned to London on 29 April. The first signs were all in his favor. The cabinet, or most of them, would have liked to reject Buol's scheme.

The reality was different. In the circumstances they dared not risk conflict with France. Napoleon III had just returned to Paris from England: "he had been welcomed most enthusiastically, and this convinced him that the British alliance was worth a serious war."[25] What is more, he readily accepted a British suggestion to drop his plan to go to the Crimea. Now more than ever the liberal alliance had to be preserved.

The decision not to go to the Crimea was made on 26 April. Drouyn de Lhuys got back to Paris four days later. He saw at once that the tide had turned against him and that his position had been gravely weakened during his absence by the influence of Cowley. This convinced him that he could not get the Austrian project through unaltered; and he resolved to bring Napoleon III and Buol together by cheating them both. He therefore laid a false trail. He suppressed the clause of the treaty that dealt with Russia's Black Sea fleet: the allies would, he asserted, go to war if the Russian fleet in the Black Sea exceeded the number of warships currently afloat, not the number afloat in 1853. He also changed the ultimatum. He told Napoleon that it would require Russia to limit her Black Sea fleet to its present number. The changes turned the trick: Napoleon's bellicosity was gradually broken, and on 1 May Drouyn finally won him over. Immediately Drouyn telegraphed to Walewski and Russell in the hope of swinging the British government behind the French decision.

In the meantime Russell, too, had been busy. On 30 April he told Clarendon that "if the Government refused to make peace such as was now within their grasp they would commit the greatest blunder that any Government ever committed."[26] On 2 May Drouyn's plan reached London. It created a sensation. Cornwall Lewis, chancellor of the exchequer, expressed the opinion of some of the ministers when he said he "thought that our acceptance of these terms offered a reasonable ground for peace."[27] Clarendon did not know which way to turn. He sent a copy of Drouyn's plan to Aberdeen. Aberdeen replied: "Rejection of peace upon such conditions would be subject to very sharp criticism."[28] There was even stronger pressure. On 3 May Prince Albert, on the prompting of his German tutor, Baron Stockmar, wrote the cabinet a memorandum urging the abandonment of limitation and the serious consideration of Drouyn's plan. By 3 May, too, even Palmerston was inclined to give up, and gloomily anticipated Napoleon's final approval.

This was given and then snatched away again. In both cases Drouyn de Lhuys proved his own worst enemy. On 1 May he had won Napoleon III for counterpoise. This was the utmost he was capable of. Napoleon III had consented grudgingly and he refused to do more.

On 4 May 1855 the crisis reached its term. Drouyn de Lhuys was summoned to the Tuileries by Napoleon III. Cowley and Vaillant, the minister of war, were also present. Drouyn's reasoning was full of flaws; and he suffered a disastrous argumentative overthrow. Cowley, "though without instructions from his own government,"[29] demonstrated that Buol's proposal would leave Russia where she had been in 1853—that is strong enough to bring Turkey within an ace of destruction. Drouyn de Lhuys flagged—in Cowley's words, "got out of temper and was regularly crestfallen."[30] Vaillant gave the decisive answer to Drouyn's scheme when he announced: "Anything more dishonorable to the army could not well be imagined."[31] This was enough for Napoleon III. He rejected the Austrian plan. Drouyn de Lhuys duly resigned. The issue once decided in Paris the outcome in London became a foregone conclusion. Clarendon wired Cowley: "All is right. We agree with the Emperor."[32]

The tug of war over the Austrian plan left a deep mark on Drouyn de Lhuys—the first time, though not the last, that the Franco-Austrian alliance on which he based all his policy proved a will-o'-the-wisp. The same fixation was to underline his diplomacy during the war between Austria and Prussia over the fate of Germany eleven years later; once more the result was the same. Drouyn's bitterness was considerable. He wrote on 7 May 1855: "My position had for three days been eroded by the silence of the Emperor, only to be undermined and finally destroyed by the malicious advice of a foreigner."[33]

Drouyn's interpretation should not be carried too far. As so often with Drouyn de Lhuys, his policy was wrecked by his own worst instincts—in this instance by his refusal to trust even those who were on his side. Blindly confident of his own strength and contemptuous of others, he conducted his policy in autocratic isolation. He played a game of bluff with everyone—with the British government, with Napoleon III, even with himself. There is a very good illustration in his relations with Thouvenel. As political director of the foreign office, Thouvenel was second in command to Drouyn de Lhuys and, during Drouyn's absence at Vienna, the number one man in French diplomacy, aside, of course, from Napoleon III. Cooperation between Drouyn's and Thouvenel was essential if French policy were to operate clearly and consistently. Nothing of the kind took place. It did not become Drouyn de Lhuys to feed back to Thouvenel information as to workings of the conference. This had a curious result. As the record shows, Thouvenel was one of the few men in France who persistently favored the Austrian plan and who would have liked to get it through. It was easy for Cowley to chip away Drouyn's support when Drouyn's most energetic supporter was left in the dark, always days behind events.

No doubt more lay behind. The decision of 4 May was not surprising; any other decision would have run counter to the inmost nature of Napoleon III. France and Austria were estranged over the national principle of Napoleon III and by his intention to redraw the map of Europe. Drouyn's defeat was in large part due to the cleavage in political outlook and to the long-standing tradition on both sides of suspicion and hostility. Though bouts of Franco-Austrian cooperation were still possible after 1848, alliance between them was never practical politics except on terms of such dependence and humiliation as could only follow catastrophic defeat—of Austria in 1866, of France in 1870 and even then the alliance was sham.

At any rate, affairs in Vienna were now much in the nature of an epilogue. The negotiations ran on until early June; they were pointless. Buol's energies were consumed in trying to give the conference a decent burial. In practice this meant placing the onus for its breakdown upon the Russians. He proposed to do so by convening the conference once more; he would present Drouyn's scheme of limitation and urge it upon Gorchakov—in other words, he would support the plan diplomatically, though not as Austria's ultimatum. This did not suit the British. They wanted to wind up affairs in Vienna immediately, and would not swallow any proposal which might trap them into further negotiations. If the conference were to be reconvened it must only be to record that the participants had nothing to say. After some bickering the French agreed. Buol was at a loss to do more. The final session of the conference was a futile formality. Buol resurrected his original plan of counterpoise; Gorchakov, knowing what had happened, assented to it; Westmorland and Bourqueney repeated their previous objections; it was the end of the road.

V

The rigmarole over point 3 really amounted to little, though it did not seem so at the time. Limitation was intolerable to Russia because of strategic necessity and national sovereignty. Or—what is not quite the same thing—because of national prestige and national honor. Neither of these things could be appreciated by the generation of western statesmen who fought the Crimean war. Their overriding concern in waging the war was to win. Whatever their relations with the other Powers, their policy always revolved round Russia with a mixture of fear and hatred. Russia, they imagined, had grown too strong. Russian power was a threat to their vital interests; it had to be destroyed if these interests were to be secured. And shadowed behind this was the vague hope that the destruction of Russian power would somehow inaugurate a better world.

This reaction sprang from Russia's success in snuffing out the revolutions of 1848. For the allies as for everyone else the overriding impression of the years of revolution had been Russian power. From 1849 to 1851 Russia had had things her own way—in central Europe as well as in the Balkans. She had called the tune in the internal affairs of Austria; and she had decided the fate of the Germanies. She had twice occupied the principalities; and she had destroyed the Turkish navy. In the eyes of the British and the French, Russia had to be stopped—now or never. For them the war was a slugging match that had to go on until Russia fell down from exhaustion. If the allies had captured Sebastopol when they landed in April 1854, this object would not have been realized and the Russians would have evaded the challenge posed by the allied armies and the allied navies. For the allied operations aimed, as do most operations of war, not at the capture of a specific point, but at the reduction, if not the elimination, of the military strength of the enemy. This was accomplished after Russian resistance had been worn down by year's fighting round Sebastopol.

It could not have been accomplished by counterpoise in the Black Sea. Counterpoise would not have weakened Russia. It would have permitted her to rearm in the Black Sea up to the level of 1853. This would not do. The British and French had gone to war to reverse the situation of 1853, not to perpetuate it. The victors would have had no advantage, the defeated no handicap. Russian strength in the Black Sea could always be matched and even arrested if the two western Powers answered an appeal for assistance from the Turks and passed the Bosphorus—that was not the issue. The British and French aimed not to check Russian naval strength in the Black Sea but to destroy it. This would arrest Russian aggressiveness and so help to shatter the verdict of the years of revolution.

One writer has commented on the fact, bewildering to him, that the allies should have insisted on restricting the Russian navy without demanding the natural corollary and insisting on restricting the Russian army.[34] This is not really bewildering. The allies needed to secure Turkey against the Russian sea prong; and secure her against it as she had never been secured before. This would avoid a repetition of 1853 and, or so it was supposed, guard against future Russian aggressiveness. Turkey was secured against the Russian land prong, the Russian army, by geography—that is, by the Austrian army. Palmerston recognized this on 16 June 1854 when he said to Newcastle:

"There is not the slightest danger of Russia getting to Constantinople by land. The Turks are able to prevent that; but even if they could not, the Austrians would be compelled, by force of circumstances, to do so."[35] Besides, the Russian army, once called the gendarme of Europe, proved, almost as soon as the war got underway, a giant with feet of clay. The war of movement ended when the Russians dug themselves in at Sebastopol. A breakthrough could only be achieved by the accumulation of gunpowder and munitions, and this was hamstrung by the Russian system of supply, blind and unenterprising, over land and water.

This is very far from saying that limitation and neutralization were without punitive intent. In many ways they were more punitive than any terms presented to a Great Power in the whole of the nineteenth century. This was obviously true from the Russian point of view. The Russians could, if they had liked, have pointed to the wars against France forty years before. Then there was war in plenty—more persistent, more coherent, more profound. Yet even when the French were victorious and even when French satellites were set up by Napoleon I, as they often were, the defeated Powers were generously treated, with Prussia the flagrant exception. Much the same spirit prevailed in 1815. The victorious Powers were inclined to think that France should be generously treated; none for example—not even the Prussians— wished to impose upon France terms that infringed French sovereignty, as limitation and neutralization infringed the sovereignty of Russia—a dress rehearsal for 1919 and for the disarmament clauses that the Treaty of Versailles imposed upon Germany.

There is a deeper point still. Limitation and neutralization reflected the western view of Russia. In the eyes of the French, and especially the British, Russia did not belong in Europe—a semi-barbarous state that had to be pulled down from the ranks of the Great Powers and driven back into the inferiority from which it ought never to have escaped. They saw the war as a contest between two civilizations, and rightly so. The Crimean war was more than a struggle between belligerent states. It was a conflict between two ways of life. Like the Cold War a century later, the clash between the western Powers and Russia was dramatic, a clash of two worlds. The drama invaded real life. Events took hold of contemporaries and drove them to pronounce on the confrontation in almost apocalyptic terms. If yet another voice be needed for this view, it can be that of A. F. Tiutcheva, a young maid of honor at the Russian court and, as such, a woman close to the seat of power: "A terrible struggle has burst upon us. Monumental and contradictory forces are on a collision course: the East and the West; the Slavonic world and the Latin world. . . . Filled with dread and anguish, one asks, What will be the outcome of this struggle between two worlds?"[36] The Crimean war was fought to remake the European order—to sweep Russia from central Europe as well as to prevent her from encroaching on Turkey. The Powers of Europe fell out over what new system to create. In the end they failed to establish one.

In January 1853 Europe was in a state of peace that seemed relatively secure. By the end of 1853 Russia and Turkey were at war; within three months Great Britain and France had joined in against Russia. Austria teetered on the edge of war with Russia throughout 1854 and 1855, though she was never pushed over it. Prussia hardly stirred. Old Europe, the Europe of the Holy Alliance, perished; and no new Europe arose to take its place. New differences arose; and Europe was not to know unity again for twenty years.

Chapter 9

NEGOTIATIONS FOR PEACE

The breakup of the Vienna conference appeared to free the allied governments from negotiations: the British and French had tried diplomacy to escape war; now they could try war to escape diplomacy. This was by no means the case. Napoleon III did not break off with Austria on 4 June 1855. He had no intentions of doing so. As Cowley reported: "He still wants to maneuver in order to have Austria with us."[1] His advisers shared this feeling, Walewski, Drouyn's successor, most of all. Contemporary opinion dismissed him as a desiccated old maid, "at bottom for *paix à tout prix.*"[2]

There were other, deeper reasons why the French could not shake themselves free of negotiations. Opposition to the war which had been held by a sizable segment of opinion ever since 1853 was becoming more widespread. To judge from the press, the attitude of the ministers and the reports of the agents in the country—and we have little other guide—the French people were virtually unanimous in wanting to end the war, though they did not know how or on what terms. The allied failure at the Malakoff on 7 June 1855 reinforced this belief. The procureur of Bensaçon divined the outlook of the country when he wrote three weeks later: "The ups and downs of the war make the biggest impression at the moment. . . . The people are anxious over the outcome of the campaign; and our latest reversal there has given us a chance to see how easily public opinion can slide from confidence to gloom."[3]

The opposite was true in Great Britain. The collapse of the Vienna conference stiffened the will to fight on. Anything short of complete victory was regarded as an intolerable affront. The government did not benefit from this. The British had not won any striking success. The war in the Crimea was being fought at a snail's pace; victory was nowhere in sight. This was in part a legacy of the way in which Aberdeen's government had bungled the management of the war and an extension of the disputes over diplomatic

161

matters. The rancor was generalized. Once the Peelites saw Palmerston as a culprit in his immediate acts he became a culprit in everything. Conversely the more fervent supporters of Palmerston's government believed that a coalition that had run away from its responsibilities in 1853 was in no position to criticize now.

Personalities counted also. Russell had virtually ignored his instructions in Vienna in order to overthrow Palmerston and had played the role of Drouyn's chief supporter in the deliberations over point 3 when he returned. Drouyn's resignation bedeviled him. He considered it a matter of personal honor to share Drouyn's fate in defense of a policy which they had both supported. This posed a fresh crisis for the ministry. Clarendon took a hand. He made out to Russell that Drouyn had resigned for personal reasons, in particular, his failure to win Napoleon for a Continental League against Great Britain. He was successful. Russell swung round and formed the opinion that since Drouyn's resignation had nothing to do with counterpoise he was released from his earlier pledge to support it; and stayed in the cabinet, as enthusiastic for war as he had previously been eager for peace.

But not for long. In the spring of 1855 there took place in England a great debate over the conduct of the war. The debate was set off by the collapse of the Vienna conference as well as by the military stalemate in the Crimea. On 24 May Disraeli, the Tory whip, moved against the government in the Commons. He accused Palmerston and Clarendon of weakness, demanded that they carry out some great stroke of policy, and condemned the government's conduct of the Vienna negotiations as "useless and hardly honorable."[4]

Russell answered him. He defended the case for a "narrow limitation" of Russia's power in the Black Sea, and insisted that Austria's treaty obligations would compel her to come into the war. Disraeli's motion lost; and a concurrent peace resolution by Grey in the House of Lords was heavily defeated. Even so, the emotions and personal quarrels raised in the debate hung on. Clearly the government needed a vote of confidence. At Clarendon's behest, Charles Lowe, an M. P. from Birmingham, moved to blame the failure of the Vienna conference on Russia's refusal to limit her fleet in the Black Sea (4 June). The debate on Lowe's motion lasted for four days. Critics and defenders of the government both came into their own. Disraeli attacked the motion as a new piece of Whig claptrap; from the other side, Gladstone fired a broadside against it in what his latest biographer describes as "golden words of wisdom."[5]

Palmerston spoke on 8 June. He reviewed the history of the Eastern question, appealed for national unity, professed confidence that the tide was turning in favor of the allies. For the moment he got his way. Lowe's motion was carried; and the ministry pulled out of the scrape intact. Though no doubt intent to out-maneuver the Tories on the one hand and the Peelites on the other, Palmerston gave the impression that he was the instrument of national honor. He had courted Parliament with romantic respect; he had, it seemed, voiced the conscience of the nation. The critics of the government now seemed condemned to sterile resentment. Both Palmerston and Clarendon hoped that the country would weary of their carping and cheerfully contemplated grappling at last with the business of running the war.

Things went wrong. Buol, having learnt of the debate, dug out the protocol of the final Vienna conference and disclosed that both of the allied plenipotentiaries had supported counterpoise. The disclosure was Aberdeen's revenge for the Roebuck motion. His opponents were routed, Russell most of all. Russell had denounced counterpoise in Parliament; now he was forced to eat his words. He overrated his popularity; he counted wrongly on support from the ministers in the cabinet; he was shouted down in the House of Commons. Gladstone said: "A more ignominious conduct of a public official could not well be imagined."[6] Russell had relished the overthrow of Aberdeen and his government of feeble men; he dreamt of a revolt of the backbenches that would throw out Palmerston and put him in charge of affairs. Instead the gates of power seemed to close against Russell forever. On 13 July he resigned. It was now his turn to be a broken man.

II

All this time public opinion in Great Britain concentrated its attention on events in the Crimea. Cries for an energetic prosecution of the war had brought down the Aberdeen government; and they continued unabated even with Palmerston at the helm. This was not all. The civilian population felt that the war was drawing nearer to them. The casualty lists were no longer those of remote heroes. Now men could understand what was happening to the troops. The newspapers were larger; their circulation had increased; and the practices of modern journalism had been perfected. The postal service far outstripped that of the Revolutionary and Napoleonic wars. For the first time Englishmen could see photographs of the camps and the trenches. Moreover, opinion was less likely to tolerate mistakes. During the years of peace the standard of administrative efficiency had soared. The public expected more of its civil servants and departments of state; this slipped easily into expecting the same of the high command.

These hopes were disappointed. The army chiefs were supposed to provide a coordinated direction of the war, and this they never managed to do. In the military field they proved ineffective and in the medical field more so. Adequate care for the troops was difficult, if not impossible, under the circumstances, and few medical officers had any experience of a relevant kind. The British surgeon general, faced with complaints about the breakdown of the medical services, replied: "The medical services would have been perfectly adequate if it had not been for the casualties."[7] Such remarks strengthened the belief, already widespread, that the government was running the war in a singularly ineffective way. Anything to maintain the popularity of the war, anything to strengthen public confidence in the army became of great importance.

Florence Nightingale appeared on the scene. Support given to her by the home authorities at once strengthened her hand. Under her direction the hospitals at Scutari were cleaned. Drugs were introduced. Food improved. Her presence and that of the small contingent of nurses which she organized and placed under her control were of immense value. By the spring of 1855 the death rate among hospitalized British soldiers had gone down almost 80 percent. Disease was contained. Sanitation got better. By the spring of 1855 the worst defects had been remedied; and the main problem for the British army became cooperating with the French, not the problem of survival.

The two western Powers were still far from an agreed program of strategy that was compatible with a policy which would both win their diplomatic and military objects. Relations between the two armies, never on an immovable basis, had run downhill. Many in England believed that the Crimean war was becoming an exclusively French campaign in which British strategy would be politely determined by the directors of French policy. The French on their side had long groaned alongside "les malheureux anglais." A French colonel wrote: "The English army is a cannon ball chained to our feet."[8] The war had been tolerable to the French people only so long as it was fought on the cheap; once the fighting deadlocked they had little thought except that it should be ended.

Besides, there was a far wider divergence of outlook. Many in Great Britain, and not merely the Cobdenite Radicals, could not think why they had ever become involved in a war as the ally of Napoleon III; they remembered the long years when Great Britain had fought alone against his uncle. Napoleon III might parade his loyalty to the "liberal alliance," might insist that friendship with England was the key to his policy. Deep down the British—or at any rate many of them—did not trust him.

Thus Anglo-French affairs during 1855 moved on two planes. On the practical plane of war the allies tried to batter the Russians into defeat. The Russian army dug in and refused to accommodate them. Civilian life was becoming increasingly restless and discontented. Meanwhile the two governments tried to counter this feeling. An attempt was made to formulate more clearly the great details of the allied cause. The attempt happened at a peculiarly appropriate time. Queen Victoria was in Paris. The British and French governments thought to use the occasion to demonstrate to each other their mutual understanding and good faith. The alliance of the two Powers was confirmed "in the most satisfactory and solid manner."[9] At bottom this was a translation into diplomatic terms of the belief on both sides that something had to be done to assuage public opinion. Since the press was at this time the only means, apart from speeches, of influencing opinion at home, it was supposed that newspapermen should be employed to satisfy popular feeling. As well, Napoleon III wanted some striking public success to stem the rising tide of discontent against the rigmarole in the Crimea. French opinion, though impressed, hesitated. The procureur of Bordeaux minuted: "The business and commercial classes are still troubled . . . , hope devoutly for a return to peace."[10] The meeting between Queen Victoria and Napoleon III lasted from 18 August to 27 August; it no doubt helped put Anglo-French relations on a firmer footing. But it did little to satisfy the urge for peace that was threatening the stability of the Second Empire.

III

War-weariness was not the only political challenge to French statesmanship nor even, immediately after the queen's visit, the gravest. Problems at Constantinople reached their most acute stage. For some time in the summer of 1855 it seemed as though Anglo-French rivalry there would dissolve "the liberal alliance" into personal invective. The underlying issue, apparent from the outset and not resolved until 1857, was whether Stratford de Redcliff would continue his unchecked sway, so happily compounded of high purpose and high prestige. Stratford had always regarded the relations of Great Britain and Turkey as his private preserve and wished to grasp supreme direction of Turkish affairs for himself. This was at any rate the overriding impression of those in a position to know—the impression of the members of the British cabinet, the impression of other diplomatic representatives at Constantinople, the impression of the ministers of the Turkish government most of all.

In the summer of 1855 Stratford de Redcliff was clearly on top of the wave. He stood alone, outside party or class, a solitary figure following a line of his own devising. To others, especially to foreign ambassadors, Stratford attributed unworthy motives, jeering at their ambition for office, their political difficulties, or their personal appearance. Yet, paradoxically, the more Stratford got his way, the more he undermined his own position—a contradiction peculiarly felt in Paris. Napoleon III had long resented Stratford's refusal to treat France as an equal, the more so because the French were contributing the bulk of the armed forces in the Crimea. Previously he had confined his criticism to futile gestures of irritation to his ministers. At the end of May 1855 he became more resolute. Cowley reported: "His Majesty expects that Stratford will be recalled, for it is useless to hope for a good understanding between the two countries as long as he remains." [11]

This was too blatant a bid. The British ministers sympathized with Napoleon's demand. Clarendon said: "With all his faults Stratford can wring from the Turks more than any other single man ever could." But he added: "I have said in private twenty times that the French alliance is riskier at Constantinople than anywhere else . . . . At the first muttering of a storm, the Emperor will officially demand Stratford's recall, and this will prove most embarrassing." [12] With uncanny foreboding, Clarendon thus anticipated the course that events would follow for the next three months when the relations of the two liberal Powers skidded to their lowest point of the war. Still, the British refusal to accommodate Napoleon III bolstered Stratford's position: his grip on his office remained, or rather seemed, secure.

All this changed in July 1855 when Edouard Thouvenel, the most profound and original of Napoleon III's diplomats, became the French minister at Constantinople. Thouvenel inherited from his predecessors the conflict with Stratford over plans for reforming the Ottoman empire, and this conflict was threatening to become acute since the sultan intended to oppose all such projects which he regarded as an offense against Turkish pride and Turkish independence. His persistence in this line both antagonized Stratford and led to a crisis of relations between Stratford and Thouvenel. At the end of August the crisis exploded. The sultan recalled from exile Mehemet Ali pasha. This development put Stratford in a panic. Stratford bracketed Mehemet Ali with Thouvenel and the Abbé Borré, head of the Lazarist Jesuits at Constantinople and a name of ill omen in his book. Nor was this the only problem. Mehemet Ali was the arch-enemy of Reschid pasha, Stratford's protégé and the one man in Turkey whom Stratford could truly consider a loyal satellite. Stratford had leapt to his defense on more than one occasion and applauded his conduct. Stratford's indignation swelled over the recall of Mehemet Ali; and this was not the only occasion when, like the Greek subjects of the Porte in 1852, he claimed to have been the victim of a French conspiracy. He foresaw in the sultan's decision the eventual domination by France of the Turkish government and with it the severance of relations between the sultan and himself.

Stratford took the plunge. He sent Pisani, the linguistic-contact man at the British embassy, to rebuke the sultan for recalling Mehemet Ali and gave Pisani a letter of complaint with which he hoped to triumph. In an accompanying letter to Clarendon he aired his lucubrations about Thouvenel: "My colleague is laying himself out for an extensive acquaintanceship with men of all parties. He claims to make an exception of no one. Those who bear the most notorious stigma of culpability are sought after as diligently as those who command the greatest respect. I can not follow this line of conduct. My experience prevents it. What is pardonable for him would for me be wanton inconsistency." [13]

Other complaints followed. Stratford believed that Thouvenel was deliberately cheating. His letter to Clarendon on 23 August made no mention of his own provocative behavior and turned instead against Borré and the "secret, active, intriguing" party of clericals that he led: "Some ten or fifteen days ago this man . . . was received privately by the sultan after having been closeted once more with Mehemet Ali." Stratford also gave examples of Thouvenel's attempt to intrigue and conspire. His example of the latest attempt was peculiarly instructive and peculiarly dishonest: "I learnt of a secret meeting between Thouvenel and the Sultan which lasted over an hour, and of which His Excellency has not condescended to inform me. The absence from the meeting of any Turkish minister or even of the lowest official has made it difficult for me to learn what transpired." [14] No one would ever suspect from this that Stratford had had a number of secret meetings with the sultan before August or that he had repeatedly harangued the sultan about Thouvenel's shortcomings—never, it may be added, fairly or accurately. Stratford regarded Thouvenel as a devious man—or, as he explained to Clarendon, "rational, positive in his ideas, fond of ascendancy, and more alive to the attainment of specific objects than equal to carrying out a great policy." [15]

Clarendon was not moved by these expostulations. On the contrary, he believed that Stratford was deliberately rocking the boat and warned him on 9 September: "I cannot hide from you the fact that there exists towards you not inconsiderable jealousy and a belief that you cannot content yourself with equality but on the contrary are bent on superiority of British influence that will be established and recognized as such." [16]

Stratford waved this warning aside. In his view Mehemet Ali personified the superstitions, prejudices, and other pernicious accretions which had, over the years, sapped Ottoman society of its confidence, vitality, momentum. Therefore Stratford must impede his advance. This was by no means the first time that the sultan had been called upon to sacrifice an all-powerful minister for the sake of the irrepressible Stratford. Previously he had always complied. This time he refused. This unexpected rebellion suggests that Stratford had overplayed his hand and—a more alarming prospect from Stratford's point of view—that the sultan was at this time more Thouvenel's man than his own.

According to the evidence that Lynn Case has collected, it seems that Stratford's fears were largely imaginary. Thouvenel wished to strengthen his diplomatic position; this was his sole motive of policy. Equality with Stratford not domination of the Turkish ministry was his object. Indeed he emphasized to the Turks the virtues of conciliation and emphasized even more strongly the resentment towards himself that Stratford was bound to feel if the sultan behaved provocatively. He received cold comfort. Pisani's conduct infuriated the sultan. Turkish morality was outraged. The storm blew against Stratford. At the end of August Mehemet Ali was put in charge of the Turkish navy. The way was being paved for his political rehabilitation.

Stratford mobilized. On 1 September, returning from a trip to the Crimea, he called on Thouvenel, ostensibly for consultation, really in protest. He declaimed about the pernicious influence of the French Jesuits and added: "M. Boré is my enemy. He must be made to leave Constantinople." As to Mehemet Ali: "I shall have nothing whatsoever to do with him. I regard his nomination as dangerous to the point of inadmissibility." There was a final attempt to drum up support for Reschid pasha: "If one hair on his head is harmed, I shall at once break off relations and leave Constantinople."[17]

Stratford's attempts at intimidation were attended with little success. Thouvenel laid his finger at once on the exaggeration in Stratford's argument when he said to him: "I detest and despise all the sniping and intrigue . . . . You and I are too old for that [sort of thing] . . . . If you can prove that any member of my staff has intrigued against you I shall sack him and you shall be the first to know."[18]

Such assurances did Thouvenel no good. Stratford remained unmoved. Most Turks opposed him. They were virtually united on the political doctrine that the sultan alone should decide what ministers to put in his ministry. Some Turks in high places were "ready to support Lord Stratford de Redcliff."[19] This was an exaggeration. The Turkish ministers, visiting with their friends at court, soon learnt the strong feeling against Stratford, particularly, it is said, among the members of the sultan's family. No doubt the feeling was all the stronger from the brusqueness with which Stratford's demands were sprung on the sultan, as happened with Menshikov in 1853. Here was a constant element in the character of this redoubtable man: forever imposing himself on others and then girding himself against their opposition. Stratford was very historical in the sense that he loved the past. But from loving the past he took the step—in his case not a very great distance—to regretting that it had ever changed. Bluster was his stock-in-trade. He had to be boss, issuing orders without respect for protocol or the rights of others. When this position was denied him, he relapsed into cold rage and threats of retaliation.

The prolonged wrangling between Stratford and Thouvenel showed that Stratford was ill-suited to be an ambassador in such circumstances, a fact Thouvenel now fully appreciated when he wrote to Walewski on 2 September 1855: "What the sultan wants and what all of his ministers want with him is a balance, an equilibrium between the ambassador of France and the ambassador of England. Such an arrangement is, I must say with great sadness but also with great conviction, impossible so long as Stratford remains at Constantinople." [20]

At home he encountered resistance. Walewski and Napoleon III warmly approved of the pleas for caution which Thouvenel had urged upon the Turks. At the same time they were inclined to blame the trouble on "the excess of condescention" displayed by Thouvenel in his relations with Stratford. On 15 September in a private letter to Thouvenel, Walewski set down the code of conduct that Thouvenel would be expected to follow. A conflict over foreign policy must not, he warned, break out now, especially a conflict with Great Britain: there would be no conflict if Thouvenel endowed others with his own good sense; regarding Stratford de Redcliff, treat him "with the greatest respect and moderation, stretch to the limit your patience and conciliation." [21]

This injunction was unnecessary. On 10 September 1855 peremptory instructions were sent to Constantinople from London. Stratford was ordered to make up his difference with Thouvenel. Clarendon wrote: "It is not too much to say that the relations of the two embassies have constituted the only danger against which we have had to guard in the alliance. I have only occasionally told you of the battles I have had to fight for you. The Emperor has always yielded, though not always with good grace . . . . He anticipates having to recall Thouvenel . . . and is prepared to do so if he cannot maintain harmonious action with the English embassy. But I am certain that if he does he will expect a concession on our part and that if we decline to make it we shall be told that we prefer you to him and that we must each go our own way for the future." [22]

This was no more than the truth. Clarendon knew that Stratford was running into danger and even jeopardizing his position as ambassador. Walewski on his side had by now learnt of Stratford's behavior from Thouvenel—an account that was, in Clarendon's words, "highly graphic and no doubt strictly true." [23] Walewski said firmly to Cowley that he disliked and indeed detested the line that Stratford had taken. He would have liked to give the sultan a declaration of unconditional support for his ministry. Clarendon ruled this out as too risky. Though he would not approve Stratford's actions, he would not actually lead an opposition against them. He may have been calculating that opposition would blow up at home if Stratford were repudiated.

Still, the dispute between Stratford and Thouvenel had been transformed into a great international question, a question sharply posed to the British and French governments. Both governments wanted to settle the dispute, and wished that their ambassadors would do the same. Their principal motive was no doubt the desire to avoid a public row—a danger obviously threatening when rumors of Reschid pasha's impending return to the government were now spreading over Constantinople. The situation was deteriorating precariously. Walewski had at first thought to bring Thouvenel to heel; he now formed the opinion that Stratford was to blame for all the trouble. He hoped that Stratford might be impressed by warnings that France might demand his withdrawal from Contantinople if he overplayed his hand.

This expectation was not altogether without substance. While negotiations were proceeding between the two western governments, Thouvenel arranged several meetings with the Turkish ministers, as Stratford had done on earlier occasions. His own mind was clear. Stratford could not be allowed to infringe Turkish independence as he surely would if the sultan got cold feet and recalled Reschid pasha. On the other hand, Stratford must not be humiliated if "the liberal alliance" were to be preserved. Therefore there must be no more changes in the makeup of the Turkish ministry. This was the line that Thouvenel took on 30 September when he saw Fethi Achmed pasha, the sultan's brother-in-law and minister of war. France was, he said, opposed to Mehemet Ali as the Turkish naval minister; she would not protest out of deference to the sultan's authority. Further changes could not be similarly treated. For these were bound to excite speculation on who was running the Turkish government and so become a cause of probable conflict between Great Britain and France. It is hardly too much to say that Thouvenel had taken Stratford's place as the most influential figure in Turkish diplomatic circles, as Fethi, with unaccustomed deference, bore witness when he said to

Thouvenel at the end of their meeting: "Your presence here has given us a new outlook on life." [24]

Thouvenel went further in conciliation. On 1 October he saw Ali pasha, the prime minister. He repeated his concern for continuity in the Turkish government. He added a new element without appreciating how new this was. Because of his difficulties with Drouyn de Lhuys over the Vienna conference, he grasped that cooperation at this stage with Stratford would be easier if the Turks were made to understand that he was willing to raise up Stratford even if this meant pulling himself down. He therefore told Ali: "If I should, at some point in the future, press upon you demands that run counter to the interests of England, bound as these are to the interests of France . . . I should like you to remember that our conversation of today centers upon you the right to resist me to the hilt." [25]

Thus ended the great battle: no interference in Turkish affairs by the allied governments, no dismissal of Mehemet Ali by the sultan, and no recall of Reschid pasha for the sake of Stratford. Sniping continued, with the French government now on the offensive. Walewski persisted in his demands that Stratford be withdrawn, and put out feelers. His promptings brought no success. Stratford was not maneuvered out of office. Simply from a political standpoint, it was folly for Walewski to suppose that he could be. The British government appreciated that the prevailing cry of ministerial incompetence, reinforced as it was at this moment by the death agony of the army at Sebastopol, would be reinforced even more should Stratford be recalled.

Still, no one could deny the damage which the affair had done to Stratford's position. No longer could he use ministers merely to suit his purpose and then casually fling them aside. No longer could he deliver Olympian pronouncements in autocratic isolation. He had, at all events, been tamed, as he himself recognized when he wrote to Clarendon on 18 October 1855: "Our influence has fallen to nothing. I still see about me signs of respect for my position . . . these will soon be and indeed already are, wearing rather thin and that because of the crushing effect of my rival . . . . The decision of His Majesty to recall Mehemet Ali will, I need scarcely add, concentrate my attention for the foreseeable future." [26]

Stratford continued to seek vindication—an obsession that further undermined his position and strained his relations with Thouvenel. He deliberately antagonized Thouvenel and continued to harangue his critics in the Turkish ministry. His complaints, when this blustering failed, were those of an aging heavyweight who has been jostled by a younger, more agile opponent.

IV

Meanwhile, military events had taken a decisive turn. In the middle of May the allied forces in the Crimea had at last acquired a fighting spirit and in Pelissier, the new French commander, a general of experience and courage. Recognizing that nothing would be gained by further delay, Pelissier decided to risk the fortunes of war and his hopes were not disappointed. On 8 September 1855 he launched an assault on the Malakoff, the semicircular work of stone that controlled the central approach to Sebastopol. The assault was a complete success. MacMahon, the general in charge, reported: "Everything is great . . . . Here I am and here I stay."[27]

He spoke truly. The assault had obtained, as Pelissier had hoped, the supreme advantage of speed. It caught the Russians unawares. The general charged with the defense of the Malakoff was away from his post, lunching with his officers. The soldiers stationed there had already withdrawn, and their reinforcements had not yet arrived. Heavy mist completed the surprise. The Russian line was blown wide open and within hours the tricolor was flying above the Malakoff.

The British were less fortunate. They had set their sights on the Great Redan in the center. Their assault on it began almost immediately after the French advance on the Malakoff. It was a disaster. The chain of command broke down, as it had at Balaclava. To make matters worse, the troops were green. They were unprepared for a war of movement and fell back in disarray. Simpson, the British commander, faced defeat in the field. MacMahon rose undismayed to the height of the crisis. He held the Malakoff. That was enough. The Russians knew that the end had come. At nine o'clock in the morning of 9 September they evacuated Sebastopol. No doubt the morale of their army snapped under the strain of defeat. It is unlikely that the morale of the British army improved.

V

French prestige soared. Napoleon III seized this opportunity to reassert his authority. At the end of September he proposed to the British government a program that would knock Russia out of Europe—and would indeed destroy her as a Great Power—a program, that is, for the national reconstruction of Poland and of Italy as well. The British sheared off at once. Yet they took care to formulate their negative in the politest of terms. They had a very good reason. They wished to keep the war going. The fiasco at

Sebastopol weighed heavily upon them; and they sought to atone for this by demanding a more energetic prosecution of the war: "more amphibious attacks in the Black Sea and in the Baltic, until Russia was cut off from salt water altogether." [28]

The latter object was not beyond the realm of possibility. In October 1855 Napoleon III, egged on by Persigny in London, once again launched negotiations to bring Sweden into the war. Once again the pattern of April 1854 was repeated: the negotiations fumbled in the dark, causing much confusion, producing endless reports, settling nothing. On 21 November 1855 France and Great Britain signed a treaty of alliance with Sweden in the hope, especially on the side of the British, of extending the front of the war to the Baltic.

The hope was to be disappointed. The alliance could not operate before the spring when the Baltic would be free of ice. By then Napoleon's zest for adventure had dwindled and he was busy trying to conciliate the Russians over the peace treaty that he had just made with them. As a matter of fact, the Swedish project had on Napoleon III an effect that was the reverse of what the British had intended: it strengthened his conviction that the war must be ended, "liberal alliance" or no. As Cowley wrote: "His Majesty is fast coming to the conclusion that public opinion in France will not much longer support him in this war." [29]

There were two ways out: direct appeal to Russia on the one side; renewed approach to Austria on the other. Napoleon III's first thought was to acquiesce in the promptings of the pro-Russian members of his court, of whom Morny, his half-brother, was most conspicuous. Morny was very much a man "on the make," determined to plunder France while the opportunity lasted. He wished to fertilize Russia with French capital; and he supposed that he could change the history of the Second Empire by overthrowing "the liberal alliance" and putting a Franco-Russian combine in its place. For Morny in a sense the triumph of 1807 was as living as the triumph of 1855. He believed that Russia was crying out to join France and that all she needed was a little encouragement. This belief was totally mistaken.

Morny pushed ahead all the same. He conscripted Beust, prime minister of Saxony, and Seebach, the Saxon minister in Paris, to act as intermediaries between himself and Gorchakov. The essence of his proposal was that the Russians should swallow neutralization of the Black Sea and swallow it lock, stock, and barrel. This had, after all, been a French proposal from the start— indeed Drouyn de Lhuys's finest hour had been in March 1855 when he breathed resolution into the deadlocked negotiations at Vienna by winning the British government for neutralization. Morny proposed to play the same tune with a few enrichments. He wrote: "The Power who imposes the terms of peace is often the first to stand aside and let these terms go by the boards." As to the "liberal alliance," it was really of little moment: "France and England will in no time be astonished how little they care for each other." [30] Sooner or later, Napoleon III would get back to themes that really interested him—the overthrow of the settlement of 1815, the condition of the nationalities, the security of his frontiers. His enemies would multiply, with the British at their head. In the long run therefore he had no alternative but to seek a continental ally.

The man of most persistence listened. Gorchakov pressed for agreement with France. There can be no doubt as to the prime motive of his behavior. It was a desire to end the isolation of Russia. He was conscious of Russia's weakness; he feared a hostile coalition of Europe; and he was anxious to press on with economic development. He agreed with Morny and Napoleon III in wanting peace. He did not believe that the British could be made pacific by concession; he held that they could be deterred only by detaching France from them.

At home he encountered resistance. Though like Napoleon III, Alexander II had neither affection nor enthusiasm for the status quo; he had no burning desire to overthrow it; and the invitation to act against it first brought home to him the danger that any association with "the revolution" must involve. He liked France as he had never liked Great Britain and had considerable sympathy for the proposal that Morny had offered to Gorchakov. At heart he could not agree with it. Disagreement over which partner to choose and which enemy was going on among the diplomatic experts of Russia as never before. Alexander II had no use for it. He believed that the right course was to stand aloof. This belief was strengthened by the circumstances of the moment. Alexander II was in the Crimea, surrounded by military advisers and relations and far away from the European atmosphere of St. Petersburg. He was, in the words of the official history, "impregnated with the spirit of proud military honor while in the presence of his army." [31] A firm show of united opposition to the enemies of Russia seemed to him more important than any diplomatic undertaking. The negotiations broke down.

VI

Only the Austrians remained. The fall of Sebastopol had seen a sudden rush of activity in Paris. Walewski drew the deduction that peace could now best be achieved through the intervention of Austria. His real cause for anxiety still lay in the determination of the British government to pursue the war *va banque*. He continued to think that this would be folly. He said to Napoleon III: "We are masters of Sebastopol. We shall soon be masters of all of the Crimea . . . . These gains offer real guarantees against the aggressiveness of Russia in the Near East. Who can deny that France is strong and that Russia is weak? France has stature. She alone has gained in this war. She alone holds today a position of preeminence in Europe. We have nothing to gain by prolonging the war . . . we cannot deny that its continuation will cost us dearly." [32]

Others shared this fear, Bourqueney most of all. As ambassador to Vienna, he had set out with high boasts of achieving Franco-Austrian reconciliation; and he determined that where Drouyn de Lhuys had failed he should succeed. Bourqueney never wearied of telling Walewski that Buol would yield only to conciliation not to threats, and it suited Walewski to believe him. So convinced was Walewski that the moment was favorable for peace that on 25 September he took a very unusual step. He wrote to Bourqueney suggesting that propositions should be made to Buol. At the same time Hübner warned Buol that negotiations with France would take some time to get going: "I have reminded Buol to be under no illusions as to the nature of our relations, satisfactory only in appearance, though not in reality. . . ." [33]

Buol, on his side, was receptive to hints about better relations with France and was ready to drop such hints himself. It is unlikely that he waited for news of Morny's failure, and the casual utterances of Pfordten and the lesser German ministers tell little about his policy. Events perhaps reveal more. The allied victory at Sebastopol weighed heavily with Buol, though curiously enough he did not allow its impact to break into the calm of his holiday; and he put off sending congratulations to Paris and London until the end of September. Still, the conciliatory gestures of Walewski defined the French position clearly enough: there would, Buol supposed, be little difficulty in meeting Walewski's terms once Napoleon III showed his readiness for peace afterwards. Of course Buol may have arranged everything already in private conversations with Bourqueney which have escaped detection. But if evidence means anything the reconciliation between Austria and France, far from being planned by Buol, was very much an improvisation on his side, though not so much so on the French.

A spirit of conciliation was displayed on both sides. Goodwill was expected to triumph. And so it did. On 14 November 1855 Bourqueney and Buol put the finishing touches to the process by which the Four Points, based on a confused attitude on the Austrian side and outright duplicity on the side of the allies, were transformed into a concrete instrument of specific objects to be presented to Russia in the form of an Austrian ultimatum. Point 3 became neutralization of the Black Sea—the old formula of Drouyn's devising. Since the Russian fleet there had sunk beneath the waves, this was, or so Buol imagined, "a concession to Russia implying as it did that the Turkish fleet would cease to exist also." [34]

It was not so easy to see the advantages to Russia over point 1. The Russian protectorate over the principalities was a dead dog; the Russians had said as much at Vienna earlier in the year and even before in August 1854 when they withdrew. Now, in order to satisfy the Austrians, they were to be stripped of Bessarabia and thus cut off from the Danube. In all probability this was not Buol's idea, though he made out that it was. His critics in the army judged, as was their duty, the international situation solely in terms of military strength. They wanted an impregnable frontier; and Buol wanted to give them one. As well there remained the old Austrian object of acquiring prestige in Germany at Prussia's expense. Austria could not maintain supremacy in Germany if she appeared to have come away empty-handed from her efforts in the war.

The Bessarabian cession was to cause Buol considerable trouble later on. At the time he thought little of it. His aim was to launch a peace movement that would sweep across Europe and he made clear his own apprehensions to Bourqueney should the allies follow the opposite course. For this reason he determined to stress the dangers facing the Russians if they delayed. He dangled before Bourqueney's entranced eyes the promise to break off diplomatic relations if the Russians rejected the Austrian terms. That was all. Buol determined to walk warily and to avoid promising to go to war. He noted: "Austria does not seek to gather laurels. She will draw the sword only to defend her vital interests . . . . She will resort to force only when all else has failed." [35] From Buol there could be no truer statement.

On 18 November 1855 the text of the Austrian ultimatum was presented to the British government by Persigny, the French minister. The British did not like it. The ultimatum said nothing of the Baltic, of the Sea of Azov, of means by which neutralization was to be enforced. Palmerston snapped: "We stick to the Principles of settlement which are required for the future security of Europe . . . . If the French Government cannot change their opinion responsibility will rest with them and the People of the two countries will be told of it." [36]

There were other areas of divergence. The British were impatient with Buol's inaction. He could do nothing for them. Of the British ambassadors,

Cowley took up the case against the utlimatum with the narrow moralism of a reformed drunkard. The result was disappointing. Walewski, who did not share the British belief in Austria's weakness, pushed the British ministers to negotiate. French opinion pushed also. On 15 December the two governments reached agreement: neutralization to be part of the general treaty of peace; a fifth point to be in the Austrian ultimatum reserving to the allies the right to demand any "particular conditions" that they might deem essential to their security. Despite its vague phraseology, this point was in fact aimed at the various territories that Palmerston hoped to pry away from Russia—the Åland Islands, Circassia, Georgia. The Austrians were, however, insistent that the Russians not be told that the terms of point 5 had been laid down beforehand. They appealed to the French, and they were not disappointed. Walewski had wearied of British carping, and the British demands were pushed aside with the pious assurance that they could be aired at the peace congress.

The Austrian ultimatum, revised and sharpened, was presented to the Russian government by Esterházy on 28 December. The Russians tergiversated; and did not reply until 5 January 1856. The tsar readily agreed to neutralization; on the other hand he rejected the unconditional acceptance demanded by Buol. Point 5 stood in the way. This point was, Gorchakov told Buol, too vague; everything about it baffled inquiry. Point 1 was equally unacceptable, though for a very different reason. On 28 November 1855 the Russian army had captured the Turkish fortress of Kars; and the Russians were now able to argue plausibly, even convincingly, that their surrender of Kars to Turkey would take place only when the proposed cession of Bessarabia had been struck out of the Austrian ultimatum. This was much more than a practical calculation. The Russians, or at any rate the tsar and the more ambitious of his military advisers, were still confident that sooner or later the two western Powers, Great Britain and France, and Austria, the eastern Power, would quarrel. They would quarrel territorially because they had different outlooks. They would quarrel politically because one side was liberal and nationalist, the other side conservative and monarchical. And at a certain moment, the two extremes, instead of battering away against Russia, would fall out among themselves. This calculation almost proved correct.

It had little immediate effect. By now Buol had come to believe and wanted others to believe that peace, so urgently desired by Austria, was obstructed solely by Russian intransigence. In reality, as he recognized at the time, the Austrian ultimatum had less support in Great Britain than in Russia. Still, the Russian answer was not "the pure and simple" reply that his ultimatum of 28 December had called for. For this reason, he determined to screw up the tension. He said to Gorchakov: "Your passports will be given to you if, by 18 January 1856, a satisfactory reply has not been given."[37]

Gorchakov did not yet despair. He was in constant contact with the pro-Russian groups in Paris; and he still believed that France could be swung away from Austria if Russian diplomacy were astute enough. There was some ground for this belief. On 12 January Napoleon III wrote to Queen Victoria urging that the Bessarabian cession be dropped and that the offer of 5 January 1856 be accepted as the basis of negotiation with Russia. The British government, or most of them, would have liked to accept this offer. Clarendon was not sure whether or no Napoleon III really intended to desert Austria; he warmed to the project all the same. He said to Cowley: "I heartily wish we could wash our hands of Austria and have only to do with Russia . . . . I believe it would facilitate every arrangement, . . . Russia must hate the idea of concessions that Austria will benefit from more than the true belligerents."[38] According to Cowley, Walewski was positively insistent on the ultimatum as the only means through which the Austrian government wished to make peace. The purpose of Napoleon III's letter remains unknown. Perhaps it was mere talkativeness on his part; perhaps it was a deliberate attempt to wreck the negotiations between Austria and Russia—and there were many in London and Paris who wished to do so. This is a point that is so overlaid with controversy that it is impossible to arrive at a detached verdict.

In any case, Gorchakov was convinced that he could win Napoleon for a deal. He proposed to use the breathing space provided by Buol to launch an idea that had been in the back of Napoleon III's mind ever since he came to power—the idea, that is, of a general European congress to discuss every question under the sun and to revise the map of Europe. There were, of course, other, deeper motives behind this suggestion. Gorchakov had been instructed by Nesselrode to parade a conciliatory demeanor at Vienna. The Russians claimed to be acting out of a firm desire for peace and wished to persuade their former enemy, Napoleon III, of their sincerity. Yet the suggestion was peculiarly Gorchakov's. He was second only to Nesselrode in the eyes of the tsar. He approached foreign affairs with suspicion, but with that pedantic concern for verbal accuracy which distinguished the Russians in their internal wranglings. He regarded his proposal as the first step towards entente with France which he viewed as Russia's escape hatch from isolation. Such were at any rate the ideas that Gorchakov presented to Nesselrode in his telegram of 30 December 1855.

He was too late. Nesselrode did not share Gorchakov's outlook. Entente with France was, he believed, too brazen, would provoke an outcry against "the revolution." He therefore suppressed the telegram of 30 December "and won the council for unconditional acceptance of the Austrian terms." [39] In the words of the official history: "He was so struck with the necessity of peace, so impressed by the numerous opportunities which we had missed by our too tardy concessions, that he did not wish to run any fresh risks. It was, so to say, with closed hands that he decided to sign." [40]

He was not alone. On 15 January 1856 the decisive crown council took place at St. Petersburg. The tsar and his advisers did not underestimate the gravity of the peril that menaced Russia. The ultimatum of 28 December was not their only cause for alarm. There was, as well, ominous news from Berlin. Prussia's attitude had gradually grown more resolute. The Prussian liberals— Bernstorff, for instance, most strongly—had always been more uncompromising towards Russia than the generals, and some of them were now tempted to think that an aggressive attitude would wring from the allies an invitation to the impending peace congress—a symbol of prestige that Frederick William IV prized, in the immediate sense at any rate, above all else.

Frederick William IV was on the spot. His mind was still choked with romantic attachment to Russia; he still shrank from opening another chink in her armor. Even so, he was becoming increasingly alarmed over his estrangement from the western Powers. Rumors of a Franco-Russian combine had reached his ears; and these rumors seemed to bear witness to the suspicion, fed by Bernstorff's reports from London, that Napoleon III was bent on a revision of Europe which could only be executed at Prussia's expense. This was an alarm that Frederick William IV had been sounding since the beginning of the war and Morny's feelers to Gorchakov were a startling echo of this old theme.

Manteuffel, the prime minister, duly faced and conquered the contradictory impulses of his master. On 30 December 1855 Frederick William IV at last bestirred himself. He wrote to the tsar about the "terrible responsibility" faced by Russia. On 6 January 1856 he took a further step. He warned Alexander II that, though he still wished to remain on good terms with Russia, the rising tide of sentiment against her in Germany might make it impossible for him to do so.

Frederick William's appeals had an immediate effect. The Russians had already found themselves in a position of extreme anxiety and now had it increased by Prussia's intervention. There was a renewed stir of urgent diplomatic activity. Nesselrode could now argue persuasively, indeed irrefutably, that Prussia had slipped over to the allied side, served as a brake on Austria no longer. He expostulated that a full scale defeat of Russia lay perilously on the horizon and, more remarkable still, pointed to the specter of an anti-Russian coalition of Europe. The other ministers seconded Nesselrode's promptings. Meyendorff, Buol's brother-in-law, had never shared the confidence of the tsar. The Russian economy was, he said, being bled white, nearing collapse. Kiselev argued more sweepingly that the fabric of Russian civilization could not survive more years of war. These themes, only lightly sketched a year before, now, like the lines of the trenches that had for so long stood in front of Sebastopol, took on a new thickness.

The ministers might argue. Only the tsar could decide. Alexander II stood alone, puzzled, suspicious, with nobody whom he trusted, nobody whose opinions he accepted, and still unable to grasp the significance of the alarms that his ministers were sounding. All the same he had a profound anxiety: that if there were a great European war in which the third force, central Europe, was involved Russian society would be stood on its head, would not survive. For this reason, he gave way; and swallowed the arguments of his ministers. Also he misjudged: he believed that Great Britain and France would fall out after the war and that Napoleon III would allow Russia to alter the peace settlement in the Near East.

This was not the end of the affair. The British still determined to make victory sure. An article in the *Morning Sun* put it: "Peace will only be good when the Russians are made to demand it." Palmerston personified this attitude. He demanded that the Russians accept the "particular conditions" as a necessary condition of peace. Walewski ruled this out as a "second ultimatum." He had long believed that the British were spinning things out; and was anxious to close with Russia without delay. He said to Napoleon III: "The interests of France and Great Britain have diverged to the point where they are now positively contradictory . . . . The real goal of the war has been attained; we have nothing to gain by further delay. . . . "[41]

Walewski had an additional motive for moving against Palmerston. On 18 January 1856 he received a letter from Drouyn de Lhuys. Here, in a way that brought home memories of the past, he learnt how deeply the intransigence of the British was offending conservative opinion in France. Reverting to his old role as the man of tradition, Drouyn de Lhuys took the line that the preliminaries of peace were indispensable if good relations with Austria were to continue.

Drouyn de Lhuys had preached alliance with Austria since the beginning of the war when he was a good deal more stalwart for it than either Walewski or Napoleon III. It did not trouble him that he was nominally still a servant of a Bonaparte or that his rigidity over Austrian alliance had led to his downfall and, as the sentiment for peace mounted, he imposed his outlook on Walewski also. Walewski continued to shower rebukes on the British government. Each day he called for concessions from Palmerston; each day Palmerston formulated new negatives. Prolonged bickering arranged a compromise: the French agreed to spell out to the Russians the "particular conditions" that the British had demanded and—a more significant concession from Walewski's point of view—promised not to make peace until the conditions had been accepted. In return the British agreed to drop the "particular conditions" from the preliminary peace. Moreover, they insisted on an early meeting of the peace congress "so as to be free to threaten renewal of war in the spring."[42] Thereafter the pace quickened, culminating in the signing on 1 February 1856 of the preliminary peace. The statesmen who had won the war now had to make the peace final.

Chapter 10

THE CONGRESS AND TREATY OF PARIS

The congress of Paris represented a settlement of Europe as the congress of Vienna did before it; and both settlements were designed to promote peace by removing the dangers which had, it was supposed, produced war—a Russian advance in the Near East on the one hand, a French attempt at European hegemony on the other. The congress of Paris aimed to substitute diplomacy by general agreement for the arrangement of affairs at the direction of a single Power. At any rate this is what the statesmen of the two victorious Powers tried to do after the Russians had agreed to make peace; they were at a loss how to do it. Whatever plans, projects or ambitions they might have had before the war, the British and, to a lesser extent, the French fought simply for victory rather than for the prizes that it might bring. They sought to impose their will on the enemy—in a military sense—without any clear idea what that will would be. Two ways of life, both genuine and fundamental, were said to have been at war. This was, at any rate, what the peoples of the two western Powers had been told and had, with few exceptions, passionately believed. The peoples could not be expected to forget their crusading beliefs merely because the war was over. The statesmen who had won the war had to make peace with the same emotions and the same weapons. Behind these lay pressing immediate problems on which men now fixed their attention. These problems provided a last test of diplomatic skill of the two sides.

The Russians displayed characteristic ingenuity from the outset of the congress. They tried to evade the Austrian ultimatum that they had accepted unconditionally on 16 January 1856—tried, that is, to get round point 1, or rather to dodge yielding territory in Bessarabia. They had committed themselves to this point only when the Austrians were on the point of breaking off diplomatic relations. Afterwards they cast about for some device that would untie their hands. Such a device seemed to offer itself when the

Russian army in the Caucasus seized the Turkish fortress of Kars on 28 November 1855. Now the Russians tried to keep the future open by insisting that they should keep Bessarabia as compensation for Kars. British policy turned sour at this prospect, and drew from it the moral that all Russian gestures of compromise were devices to buy time until the victorious Powers had fallen out. Parading their own loyalty to treaty obligations the leading figures of the British government were inclined to run down the Russian success at Kars. Palmerston minuted: "It fell into their hands merely by the accident of the garrison not having enough to eat."[1]

The Bessarabian affair raised a further menace. Attempts in Austria at a consensus on the issue had been sharply arrested. None of Buol's conservative critics had any sympathy with his plan for Bessarabia and some indeed great hostility to it. They dreaded the prospect of a great national state on the lower Danube, feared—justly or not—that this was just what Buol's plan—the surrender by Russia of roughly half of Bessarabia to Moldavia—would invite. Bruck was projecting fortresses on the Danube and Prut and these plans assumed a Bessarabian cession much smaller than the one envisaged by Buol's ultimatum. The military chiefs—Hess and Coronini, for instance, most strongly—still belonged mentally to an age in which neither nationalities nor liberal institutions counted for anything. In their view, ingenious lines of geographical division drawn across the lower Danube would strengthen Austria's military position, would enable her to throw her economic net over Moldavia. Buol opposed this policy: he hoped to break Bruck and Hess in the interest of harmony with the western Powers, as he had broken them over the treaty of 2 December 1854 and on several later occasions. Francis Joseph overruled him. Buol went sulkily to Paris and the program for Bessarabia that was put forward by Austria at the congress was one in which Buol had, deep down, little faith. By underwriting the position of Hess and Bruck, Francis Joseph exposed himself to a diplomatic coalition. It was clear to Buol and to Prokesch von Osten, the Austrian minister at Constantinople, that the Russians would use Bessarabia to drive a wedge between Austria and the western Powers.

This was shown at once. On 19 February 1856 the Russians made known to the French government their intention to exchange Kars for Bessarabia. The French ought to have met the Russian demand. They now wanted to be friendly to Russia, if Russia would give France a free hand in Europe. They welcomed Orlov (the chief Russian delegate) in order to give a sporting victor's cheer, in their usual way, for a gallant loser. Palmerston stepped in to bridle their enthusiasm. Through Clarendon, the British plenipotentiary, he warned Napoleon III that, though the British had infinite confidence in him, "if that confidence should come to be shaken, it is in vain to disguise from ourselves that the strength of the Alliance would be very materially shaken."[2]

Buol, on his side, was ready to listen to the British and they were ready to listen to him. Leading members of the British government were already assuring Buol of close cooperation. Not only did Palmerston and Clarendon expect the Russians to make concessions, they also urged Buol to make demands. But the British did not really mean to bind themselves to Austria. Not yet reconciled to peace with Russia, they meant to push Buol into an unyielding position in the hope that they would then have a free hand to resume the war.

Thus by the end of February, the Bessarabian question ceased to be a dispute between Buol and his opposition at home. It even ceased to be, or rather never became, a dispute between Russia and Turkey. In the end the decision rested with the French, or rather it was dictated to them, as it often was on future occasions, by the choice of allies. Once Napoleon III saw that the "liberal alliance" lay in the balance, his object, thinly disguised, was to extract concessions from the Russians more than to aid the Austrians or, for that matter, the Turks. Together with Walewski (president of the congress) he chipped away Russian resistance; and Orlov finally gave in. On 1 March Orlov admitted the principle that Kars should be restored without compensation. In return for this concession, the Russians, aided by Napoleon, were permitted to retain a large chunk of Bessarabia—about 10,000 square miles or one-third of the territory which they originally were required to cede. This troubled no one, the British least of all. Their aim, shared by Austria, had been to cut the Russians off from the whole course and delta of the Danube and from the lower course of the Prut. The aim succeeded. The line drawn gave, or was supposed to give, the lower Prut to Moldavia. The Russian frontier was thus pushed back from the Danube by about twenty miles. The Russians attempted a counterstroke. Orlov proposed to bar the right bank of the Prut to Turkish fortresses and to bar fortification of Ismail on the left bank. British objections killed this proposal. Orlov acknowledged defeat. At his insistence all mention of the discussion was struck off the protocol. Here was a demonstration, appreciated by Orlov himself, that Napoleon III, "though anxious to win Russia, would not do so at the expense of the British alliance."[3]

II

Another, more decisive demonstration followed. The principalities had long been the focus of passionate French interest, and of passionate British and Austrian interest as well. Napoleon III effervesced with desire to liberate a nationality, particularly of Latin stock; and he would have liked the congress of Paris to liberate them without fuss and for good. As Cowley said: "The agglomeration of people of the same race under one rule is a theme so consonant to the Emperor's ears that His Majesty would be likely to listen with complacency to any scheme the basis of which is the restoration of nationality."[4] This idea was less attractive to the bulk of the British government who were puzzled and irritated over a French satellite on the lower Danube. On the other hand they did not wish to stop the clock and were—for a while at any rate—inclined to stress the advantages that the immediate resolution of the status of the principalities would have for British policy in the Near East. In Clarendon's words: "By quickly solving this problem we can avoid a guarantee *a cinq* which would give the Russians and the Austrians a pretext for interfering in the affairs of the Ottoman empire."[5] The prospect of a Rumanian national state frightened the Austrians out of their senses, Buol most of all. A united Rumania would, he objected, excite the Rumanians within the boundaries of the Hapsburg empire and so destroy the existing order in central Europe. The Turks agreed. In their view, a united Rumania would snap the link of continuity that had for centuries bound Constantinople to Bucharest and Jassy. The Russians had at first hung back and not surprisingly: if the allies could not impose a solution on Russia before the threat of discord raised its head, why should she impose one for them?

There was suspicion and coldness on all sides. Bourqueney stepped into the breach, his first assignment as secretary of the congress and his most notable achievement during it. He proposed to call the discussion off until the question of union had been put to the inhabitants of the principalities. They, not the plenipotentiaries at Paris, would decide their fate and would, in cooperation with the congress, lead both the friends of union and opponents of it to the compromise that the Powers could not arrange of themselves. The circumstances of the time made it impossible for the French to do otherwise. In February 1856 there had taken place in the principalities an underground explosion of opinion such as the historian cannot trace in precise terms. The Rumanians asserted their existence. The assertions took many forms. In essence they were spontaneous appeals to the congress, without parallel in recent memory. Petitions poured in from all segments of opinion. Such demonstrations deserved, or seemed to deserve, more than a passing tribute.

The appeals carried the day. The Austrians had occupied Moldavia and Wallachia since 1854. Now they had to promise to get out: the promise gave a formal registration to the defeat of Hess's plans for an Austrian Danube. By 1859 the fate of the principalities fell to the inhabitants themselves and they decided lopsidedly in favor of union—the first triumph of liberalism and nationalism in international affairs and, incidentally, the first time that the Powers of Europe deferred to popular sovereignty, national self-determination, government by consent of the governed. As well, the outcome of the elections was a score for Napoleon III. It marked him—quite rightly—as the strongest champion of nationalism in Europe and stiffened his determination to overthrow the settlement of Vienna. After all, the destruction of French influence in central Europe had been the decisive feature of the treaties of 1815; and the election results seemed proof of his conviction that the treaties would crumble once the issue of nationality was raised.

III

Point 4 provided a further lesson in the merits of Anglo-French cooperation and also in its limitations. From the earliest days of the war—from August 1854, as a matter of fact—the two western Powers were resolved to win the Turks for political reform. With high-minded motives, they hoped that Turkey would purge herself of centuries of religious discrimination and step forward unchallenged into the ranks of the European community of nations. This strategy ought to have made sense as the culminating point in a war for civilized virtues. Yet the British and French had different ideas how to realize their ultimate object: though they wished to ensure that the Orthodox subjects of Turkey were not ravaged by future violence, they did not wish to infringe Turkish sovereignty by dictating, or even appearing to dictate, to the sultan. Their original intention had been that they should settle among themselves what reforms they wanted and then should negotiate with the Turkish ministers to see how far they could get them.

This scheme did not work out. The French envisaged the reform project as an instrument of conciliation softening, or rather obscuring, all religious antagonisms. The British, however, wished to achieve a settlement more in accordance with the great liberal principles of religious equality than those made hitherto. Their belief in the tonic of reform, though belied by events, was intensely held at the time and explains why they worked so assiduously to promote a policy based on the principles of enlightened Whiggish liberalism. Perhaps there is a deeper explanation. Many people in Great

Britain—Whigs, radicals, as well as the revolutionary exiles from central
Europe—had regarded the war as a crusade for great ideals, not as a mere
struggle of force against Russia.

Stratford de Redcliff personified this attitude. In his view the Ottoman
empire could survive only if it reformed in a hurry. The Turks, on their side,
were ready to hold out promise, though not performance. They knew that
Turkey had made gains in the past by balancing between the two sides, not
by committing herself to either. But they were wrong on one essential point.
They thought that Stratford de Redcliff would be content with the prestige
of victory over Russia; he wanted to be won over by hard concessions from
Turkey that would again establish his claim to preeminence at
Constantinople.

Signs of strain soon showed. On 29 January 1856 a conference of
ambassadors at Constantinople considered the question of religious reform.
Stratford answered: Turkish behavior towards Moslem converts to Christianity was a canker at Turkey's heart; there could be no better time for the
sultan to abolish once and for all the death penalty for such conversions. Ali
pasha, the Turkish representative, at once objected that the war would have
been fought in vain and victory would be a mockery if the sultan came out
of the war with less authority than when he went in. He said to Stratford:
"What do you want, the death of Turkey?" Stratford replied: "Certainly not.
Otherwise my colleagues would not agree with me."[6] Thouvenel and
Prokesch, the Austrian minister at Constantinople, duly supported Stratford.
Underneath there was, to be sure, a profound divergence. Thouvenel, in
particular, was disturbed. Stratford's scheme threatened just what he wished
to avoid: a revival of religious antagonism in the Ottoman empire. Of course
this did not mean that Thouvenel meant to acquiesce in Turkish attempts to
evade reform. It meant only that he would defend western interests by
negotiation, not by dictation. He hoped to carry through great changes
without violent resistance, going far enough (just) to satisfy the aggrieved
Christian subjects of the Porte without driving the Moslems into open
rebellion. In particular, he saw no reason why the safety of the bulk of the
Christians should now be jeopardized in order to protect a few converts.

Stratford swept aside Thouvenel's reserve. Impatient with drift in Turkish
affairs and certain that he alone could stop it, he determined once more to
play the role of strong man. With his massive self-confidence, he held that
any peace that satisfied him must be beyond criticism, and that there was no
need to listen to arguments from the Turks. He would know what was best
for them and for everyone else. He said to Ali: "I have proof that the other
Powers agree with me."[7]

The discussion rambled on till after midnight with a long break for dinner. Then Thouvenel broke the deadlock by suggesting an approach of his own: a peaceful resolution of the differences at the price of considerable concessions by the Turks now became the avowed aim of his policy. Shortly before one o'clock in the morning Thouvenel finally wheedled out of the Turks a grudging formula. The sultan might say to his subjects that "because all religions are and will be freely practiced in the Ottoman empire no subject of His Majesty the Sultan will be constrained from practicing the religion of his choice. No one will be forced to change his religion."

Thouvenel's contribution was a stroke of enlightenment—a skilled blend of firmness and conciliation in his best negotiating vein. It was also quite effective, as even Stratford appreciated on reflection. All mention of the death penalty fell out of the new draft; at the same time, as Thouvenel saw it, the Turks backed down over a more important question: no Moslem who became a Christian would have to change back. In this way, religious conflict would be softened and Moslem converts preserved from the barbarities of coercion. Thouvenel was not thinking, as his critics were, in terms of an inevitable clash of wills. On the contrary, he held that the fate of the Moslem converts would be absorbed into the fabric of Ottoman society, and Ali did not disagree with him. He accepted Thouvenel's compromise. Article 5 of the firman was thus made.

There was a last kick of compromise in the cursory article 15 on the question of capitulations. This was the system under which, as a memo to Palmerston once put it: "The Porte leaves to the agents of each European Power in Turkey the right to hear and decide all cases of criminal and civil jurisdiction over the subjects of each state respectively . . . . One of the great objects of the capitulation which the European Powers have wrung from the Porte has been that their subjects being Christians should not be tried and punished by Mahommedans."[8] This practice had, over the years, gradually been extended to give foreigners similar protection in commercial affairs. It had long been vociferously denounced by the Turks as unjust, punitive, and unworkable. There was now, as there was in the case of article 5, a singular appropriateness in this argument. Turkey was the profiteer of the extraordinary circumstances in which the war ended with her antagonist Russia defeated. She owed to these circumstances her illusory independence—there could be no denying this. The complaints of the Turks no doubt pushed the allies into contemplating a thorough reform the system; at the same time it made some of them hesitate. Men who had not scrupled to browbeat the sultan did not wish to create the impression that they were now bound to obey his every whim. The result was compromise: right of nationals to buy and sell property acknowledged by the sultan; jurisdiction over these nationals to be arranged in agreements between Turkey and the respective Powers.

Other articles of a lesser nature had been taked on as the negotiations proceeded. In content they reflected Thouvenel's thinking pretty closely. Three promised freedom of worship in the Ottoman empire; article 1 recited the guarantees of previous firmans. Two guaranteed the Christian clergy against government harassment. One set up tribunals to settle religious disputes. One promised a career open to talent. One promised municipal reform. One barred discrimination against Christians in the military. One barred abusive language in government decrees. One promised a public budget. One promised uniform duties and tariffs. One promised schools for non-Moslems. One promised credits for communication. One codified criminal law. One codified civil law. The last promised banking reform.

This was a bewildering variety. But the twenty-one articles in the firman of 18 February 1856 had this much in common: they made a watershed in the history of Turkey; they brought in their train a wholesale Europeanization of the Ottoman empire. Thus a sponge was passed over the record of Turkish duplicity. This is, at any rate, what the allies confidently asserted. The firman of 18 February 1856 seemed to them a monumental achievement: undeniably hard-won, enormously promising, a triumph of the liberal causes they had been clamoring for. In this happy atmosphere, they supposed that the Eastern question would lose its sting: a reformed Ottoman empire would be able to to hold its own against a weakened Russia; Turkey would treat her Christian subjects in a civilized mannner; universal prosperity would follow and men would forget their old antagonisms. It never occurred to them—especially to the British—that the reforming zest of the Turks would soon flag and that before a generation had gone by a national revival of the Slav subjects of the Ottoman empire would thrust the Eastern question back to the center of the stage in a more menacing form than ever.

IV

A greater achievement than political reform by the Turks was secured by the allies at the congress of Paris, and concession on a greater scale followed the Turkish example—or so it seemed. The Russians formally agreed to neutralize the Black Sea. The concession was an unmistakable demonstration that they had lost the superiority there that they had maintained before 1853; to be sure, the same restrictions were imposed upon the Turks, but, because the Turks were permitted to maintain warships in the Sea of Marmora, they could now completely control the Black Sea in time of war. A punitive sanction no doubt, but an understandable one. If the allies had been fighting for high ideals and the Russians for wicked ones, then surely it was right that the Russians should be punished. A peace of reconciliation could be preached only by those who held that there was nothing to choose between Russia and Turkey and that the only fault of the Russians was to have lost. Who dared say that at the time? How many in England would say it in 1870? Besides, it seemed necessary as a security that Russia should be disarmed in the Black Sea; her navy had been used to threaten Turkey in 1853; now it was only logical that this threat be removed.

The neutralization clauses of the treaty of Paris profoundly affected Russia's interests both at home and elsewhere. Determination not to be ignored in Europe, not to be treated as a merely Asiatic Power, was always a deep motive in Russian policy; and the Russians swallowed neutralization with deep emotional resentment since it was next door to abdicating in the Near East (or so they thought); worse, it cut clean across their right as a Great Power to defend their borders. Though the Russians accepted the neutralization clauses of the treaty in the formal sense of agreeing to sign them, none of them took the signature seriously. All Russians intended to repudiate the treaty, and the neutralization clauses especially, at some time in the future, if it did not first fall to pieces of its own absurdity. This intention became on 30 March 1856 and for the next fifteen years remained the overriding consideration of Russian foreign policy.

V

The Eastern question was settled. Other questions remained. Napoleon III had hoped for a congress of all the Great Powers to settle every grievance that existed. This happy prospect was disturbed by the shadow of Prussian neutrality during the war. Here was a problem that defied ready-made answers. A German historian has written: "The attempt to draw Prussia into the peace negotiations must be considered from the standpoint of European politics as a whole as well as from the special rights and duties that devolved upon a European power. Up to now nothing had happened: the participants interpreted their own rights and their own duties in very different ways; and the process that led Prussia to join the deliberations at Paris was therefore delayed."[9]

In the eventful period of anxiety following the Austrian ultimatum to St. Petersburg, Buol had tried to commit Prussia to the treaty of 2 December

1854; this failed, like all previous attempts, and Manteuffel, the foreign minister, even hinted of direct alliance with France and Russia. He said to Malaret, the French chargé: "We have 500,000 bayonets on which to base our policy. No one has ever been isolated with such an imposing array of force."[10] Once Russia had accepted the Austrian ultimatum there was no further need of the treaty of 2 December 1854. Yet the political reasons for supporting Prussia remained. In return for securing her admission to the congress Austria could, Buol hoped, gain the whip hand in German affairs. He now took up the Prussian case with Napoleon III: he argued that, because she had supported the Austrian ultimatum at St. Petersburg, Prussia was entitled to a seat at the congress. Napoleon III, though rather indifferent to Prussia, valued German friendship and, to please the lesser states of Germany more than Austria, reached agreement with Buol at the end of February. He would support Prussia's admission to the congress; in return, Buol would demand that Prussia support a resolution at Frankfurt endorsing the terms that Austria had put up in her ultimatum.

This was window-dressing. The Russians had already accepted the Austrian ultimatum on 16 January 1856 and the preliminaries of peace had been signed on 1 February. Still, many Prussians resented the arrangement, Bismarck most of all. At Frankfurt he used the proposed resolution as his lightning conductor to work off the bitter resentment that he had accumulated against Austria during the war. The final resolution, passed on 21 February 1856, was a far cry from the unequivocal endorsement of Austrian policy that Buol had hoped for, containing as it did the telling reservation that the Confederation "preserves a free judgment regarding the special conditions that are to be brought forward by the belligerent Powers."[11] The "special conditions" were, of course, the demands that the allies, and particularly the British, intended to bring in under point 5. Thus the resolution of 21 February was emptied of meaning before it had passed.

In another, related aspect of the Prussian question Buol was equally unsuccessful. During the debate over the resolution at Frankfurt he inspired a second proposal by which Prussia was to take the same line as Austria should the negotiations break off. This scheme too was rejected. It implied, said Bismarck, that the Prussian government were to threaten that their troops would be used against Russia and to concede beforehand that the guilt and burden of wrong lay entirely on the Russian side.

Such equivocation did nothing to earn the gratitude of the western Powers. The British, in particular, were estranged and high-handedly demanded that Prussia be barred from the congress. Buol could not yet bring himself to admit defeat. At Paris he sought a way out and thought he had found one. He calculated that, by appealing to the Straits convention of 1841, he would break the existing deadlock. This device had the great practical advantage that, since the Prussians had helped to make the treaty of 1841, they had to agree to its revision. The British were still insistent that the essential work of the congress be completed before the Prussians got in. The Prussians therefore entered the congress only on 10 March. They did so with the other Powers, and especially the British, breathing an air of intellectual and moral condescension. Hübner noted: "The Prussian delegates, Manteuffel and Hatzfeldt, were introduced in a milieu of stony silence and without their appearance provoking any demonstration." [12]

The outcry over Prussian admission had serious meaning behind the exaggeration. It raised the question: was Prussia to participate, even possibly retrospectively, in the deliberations despite her neutrality? The question was raised still more sharply just after the session of 18 March got underway when Bourqueney read to the Prussians the invitation that Walewski had written them. This implied, or appeared to imply, that they had participated from the start. The British meant to lay down the law to Prussia. Clarendon, insistent as ever that the Prussians be regarded as outcasts, demanded that the invitation be at once revoked. Manteuffel expostulated that Prussia's honor was being offended and threatened to storm out. Then he reflected that such behavior would not become a Great Power. In any case the British got their way. A new, more condescending invitation, affirming the "special position" of Prussia, was drawn up by Walewski on 24 March and slapped in the preamble to the general treaty. The humiliation of Prussia appeared complete. This was a deception. The directors of Prussian policy had, in fact, squared the circle, achieved a remarkable success. Prussia had managed to scrape through the war without offending either side. Nesselrode defined the new situation when he said: "In the end we cannot forget that Prussia, and Prussia alone, harbored against us no hostile feelings. Direct interests bind Russia and Prussia and our behavior towards France and indeed towards Europe should reflect this simple fact." [13] Anyone who wishes to understand the history of Europe in the next fifteen years should study Nesselrode's statement to Orlov of 17 April 1856.

VI

There was another, deeper question that raised its head at the congress of Paris—a question that provided a topic of fierce dispute and influenced the motives and principal figures on each side. Cavour had long hoped to goad

Napoleon III into doing something for Italy; he now had the chance to show what he could do. Sardinia had made a contribution of sorts to the allied war effort, despite the deprecatory remarks made about her later. Her enemy had been Austria, not Russia; and Cavour now determined to turn allied resentment over Austria's neutrality into a device by which Sardinia could acquire a screen of small neighbors in the north of Italy. This was, as he himself recognized, no easy assignment. He was genuinely disappointed by the Austrian intervention against Russia in December 1855. This disappointment deepened when the Russians decided to lay down their arms in January 1856. He said to La Marmora, commander of the expeditionary force in the Crimea: "The cessation of war is deplorable from our point of view. I regret it bitterly . . . We must accept the inevitable and make all we can out of the unfortunate position in which that old artful woman Austria has placed us." [14]

A second calculation pulled Cavour the other way. Napoleon III could never support Austria when it came to the point. France had largely fought the Crimean war to reverse the verdict of Waterloo and to destroy the settlement of Vienna. Now, after the Russian defeat, this object seemed achieved. French prestige soared. The principles of Metternich lost their bearings. France seemed again supreme in Europe from the Bay of Biscay to the frontiers of Russia; and Cavour meant to associate himself with this success. Still, "We need to handle things tactfully so as not to shock the Emperor who sees peace as the triumph of his policy." [15]

Napoleon III, on his side, was alert to the Italian problem from the very moment of the Austrian peace feelers, even before Cavour had formulated his intentions. On 7 December 1855, when Victor Emmanuel visited to Paris to discuss the Italian question, Napoleon III replied: "Write confidentially to Walewski what I might do for Italy." [16] Nine weeks later, just three days before the congress opened, Napoleon III provided his own answer—or lack of it. In a meeting with Cavour he stressed his desire to enlarge Sardinia but added that there could be no thought of diminishing Austria's Italian possessions: "The only feasible thing would be to send the Duke of Modena and the Duchess of Parma to Moldavia and to give Parma and Modena to your King." [17]

No doubt Napoleon III appreciated fully the danger from unchecked Italian nationalism and would have liked to acquiesce in Cavour's grievances against Austria; no doubt he passionately believed that his position would remain tenuous "until the Empire has had its original, hereditary, and predestined illness, the reaction against the treaties of 1815." [18] Two calculations pulled him the other way, and these were the calculations that affected Sardinia throughout the congress of Paris and for several years thereafter. His first calculation was that in order to increase Sardinian power, not to mention the power of France, he must unite the Danubian principalities—and that could not be achieved during the negotiations: neither the Turks nor the Austrians would agree to it. The second calculation he made was of a far graver nature. If he adhered too openly to Sardinia, clerical opinion in France would explode and he would estrange the French clergy. His first action in foreign affairs had, after all, been to restore the temporal power of the pope against which he had himself conspired in 1831, and despite his desire to disassociate himself from the papal reaction, he was, for the sake of French opinion, as much committed to Rome now as in 1849.

This second calculation was clear to Cavour. He was not, however, content to sit idly by. He drummed around for friends to open the Italian question. First he tried the Turks. Ali pasha, the Turkish representative, though generous of phrases, showed himself to be stalwart against any plan to aggrandize Sardinia at the expense of Turkey in the principalities. Cavour tried the Russians. They had once tried to start the partition of Turkey; they were anxious to see Austria weakened and humiliated. The Russian representatives at Paris were, however, not bemused by former boasts of Russian strength. Orlov, in particular, believed that Cavour's schemes threatened just what the Russians should avoid: a general upheaval of Europe. He wanted the opposite: a revision of the verdict of 1856 without the destruction of the treaties of 1815. He therefore met Cavour's entreaties with cold indifference. Even the French disappointed him. The hesitation in Napoleon's mind was reflected in the conduct of Walewski, the defender of conservative policy who determined to prevent Napoleon III from going over to a policy of adventure. Cavour grew despondent. He had tried to move closer to the allied position. The allied position moved further away. He said on 31 March: "The peace treaty is signed. The drama is over. The veil falls . . . The result is sad." [19]

This was perhaps an exaggeration. Though Cavour's efforts were without immediate practical result, he had managed to accomplish this much: he had created an impression of power. At the same time he played his role as a European statesman. He was accepted by others. The British, most of all Clarendon, not only talked with Cavour, but actually grew to respect him as the man who had come to power as the friend of the allies, a man of wisdom: "I like him. He is a most respectable fellow." [20]

Perhaps this judgment was not merely an expression of personal affinity. The British had come to the congress breathing fire: at all events they meant to put the Italian question before the congress in the hope of satisfying the Protestant feeling against Austria that had accumulated in Great Britain over the preceding sixteen years. Consciences that had been stirred by the experiences of 1848 had grown more indignant at the outrages of Austrian domination of Italy. Clarendon viewed himself as the instrument of this resentment. He meant to drive Austria into humiliation, answering every concession with the phrase, "and then?" For instance, he regarded Buol's offer to end the sequestrations in Lombardy as little more than a pious pretense designed to give tyrannical Austrian rule a spurious liberal air. His own plan, as he explained it to Cavour, was much more ambitious. The congress would declare that "for the complete restoration of the political balance of power in Europe and the preservation of peace before every danger, it is necessary that the occupation of the Roman State by the troops of His Majesty the Emperor of the French and the troops of His Majesty the Emperor of Austria leave as soon as possible, before year's end."[21]

We now know that Cavour did not relish this project, and indeed contrived to have it withdrawn. Nor is this surprising. Ever since taking office in 1852, Cavour had determined to save the cause of moderate liberalism and monarchy by uniting Italy in alliance with France; he could not now risk a breach with Napoleon III and with Sardinian opinion that any discussion of Clarendon's project was bound to provoke. A myth became established in later years that Cavour seized the moment of Italian destiny when the congress addressed the Italian question on 8 April. This has no foundation. The eighth of April 1856 saw merely an impatient demand by Clarendon for the secularization of the Papal states—a demand regarded by Clarendon himself as nothing more than a point of departure for future remonstrations over the Italian question. This denunciation of the state of affairs in Italy could be turned to practical advantage only had Cavour been able to win over Napoleon III. By an ironical twist, Napoleon III was at this time courting the favor of Pius IX whom he asked to stand as the godfather of his newly born heir. The Italian question was thus temporarily removed from his consideration; and Cavour was, after much equivocation, fobbed off with a vague promise that French troops stood ready to leave Rome "when circumstances warranted."

This is not to say that Cavour's efforts at the session of 8 April 1856 were for nothing. For him, as for Bismarck later, the important thing was to get things moving, not to settle the future. He was, after all, able to air Sardinia's grievances before the highest assemblage of European diplomacy. Moreover, he was able to get a blow of sorts in against Austria. Behind the cloud of benevolent phrases two concessions had been secured that were, in Cavour's own words, "not without some importance. First, the stigma branded on the conduct of the King of Naples by France and England in the face of a united

Europe; and, second, the condemnation aimed by England at the clerical government in terms as precise and as energetic as the most zealous Italian patriot could have desired." [22]

Cavour, in his patient way, believed that the habit of concession would grow on the French with practice. This could only be achieved at Austria's expense. The Austrians were the Powers most directly connected with the Italian question; they had the most to lose from any discussion of it. Hence the "rude jolt" of Buol to the speeches of 8 April 1856. For these speeches, though devoid of practical content, amounted to a tacit recognition of Italian nationalism—a movement that represented an idea totally subversive of the Hapsburg monarchy, and with which it could never compromise. "The Powers generally, and not merely Lamartine, transient foreign minister of a provisional government, had ceased to believe in the moral validity of the treaties of 1815 and hence in Austria's European mission." [23] Before 1849, the Hapsburg position in Italy rested on tradition, on legitimacy, on international treaties. Now the Powers recognized that it rested only on force. As Cavour said: "The Italian question admits but one efficacious solution— the cannon." [24]

VII

Buol did not give up altogether. He still hoped to win Napoleon III for alliance with Austria and Turkey—a project that had been in the foreground of his calculations since the days of August 1854 when the Four Points had been drafted. On 15 April 1856 he at last got his way. On that day, Great Britain, France and Austria concluded an alliance to uphold the independence of the Ottoman empire. The three of them promised, or so they thought, to arrange among themselves for combined action that any infraction of the peace might involve. The British wished to add a secret article making any notable increase of the Russian fleet in the Black Sea a cause for deliberation among the allies. This was cut out on the insistence of Napoleon III. All discussions for putting teeth in the treaty, however prolonged, were academic. For, though no teeth were put in, there was also no one whom it was necessary to bite. The Russians, of course, wished to break off the shackles of neutralization, but only symbolically. Securing the international annulment of the Black Sea clauses was their sole concern and they pushed for this not at all with a vision of an active future; as a matter of fact the war with Turkey in 1877 found them still without a Black Sea fleet—had it been otherwise the Russians would have won the war in a hurry, with catastrophic consequences for the history of Europe.

Yet it would be wrong to say that western fears over the Black Sea were groundless, even if they turned out to be exaggerated. Given the Russian attack on Sinope in 1853, given too the claim by the western Powers that the war had been fought to secure the independence of Turkey, a clause of the kind Clarendon sought, whether part of the actual treaty or no, was a logical concern of British policy even if it could not be translated into reality. The treaty of 15 April 1856 was, in the eyes of the British government, a device to appease a substantial segment of British opinion which thought that the allies had let Russia off too easily. A few English radicals, the writer G. J. Holyoake, for example, believed that the tsar should be hanged—mainly for the crime of having lost. The treaty was designed to show this segment that the allies would take up arms the minute that Russia fired a shot against Turkey.

The Austrians regarded the treaty of 15 April with lyric enthusiasm, Buol most of all. He said to Prokesch von Osten, his ambassador to the Porte: "The treaty creates the foundation for *a new European order* and it will save Austria from the danger of isolation."[25] The Austrian success seemed complete: the triumph of a policy of careful diplomatic execution. Russia had been defeated; France won as an ally; Turkey restored and guaranteed. Yet this was a misleading success. Austria had won a Pyrrhic victory with a series of decisions that had alienated both sides. Moreover, she won without a reliable continental ally; only airy phrases from France and the impractical project of defending the settlement in the Near East with an outmoded army that was concentrated in Italy. All the traditions of Italian nationalism were bound up against Austria with the revolutionary wars of 1848–9; and Buol's hope that he could swing Napoleon III away from these traditions by pinning him to a conservative policy in the Near East were to come to nothing.

After the signing of the treaty of 15 April, the congress broke up, its work completed. The congress preserved and consolidated the position of Turkey in Europe; it pushed up the prestige of Napoleon III and pulled down the prestige of Russia; it undercut the international position of Austria; it disappointed and disillusioned the British and led them, or so they supposed in retrospect, to wash their hands of European affairs. In the realm of international law the congress had more modest results: the condemnation of privateering and a polite nod of approval for the principle of arbitration. As well, it established an international commission to oversee the work required to clear the mouth of the Danube. One looks in vain in the treaty of Paris for any satisfactory explanation of the causes of the Crimean war. The treaty followed on the defeat of Russia; its justification was that Russia had been solely responsible for the outbreak of war; and the allies were therefore concerned to pin all the blame for the outbreak on the Russian government, though here even they—particularly the French—trimmed their sails to political convenience. This is not to say that the treaty of Paris was unimportant. The treaty set in motion the forces that would, in the next fifteen years, force the states system of Europe to political and social reconstruction. This was unexpected. Sardinia had a place at the congress that seemed humiliating in view of what she expected; the Prussians got in almost as an afterthought and when the important questions had been settled. Yet by 1859 Sardinia was the acknowledged mainspring of the kingdom of Italy; by 1866 Austria had been tamed; by 1870 the Second Empire, having slithered into decay, was swept away and a year later Prussia had emerged as the heavyweight of the continent of Europe, her king crowned German emperor in the hall of Versailles.

All this flowed from the Crimean war, and particularly from the change in the international position of Russia. As Taylor says: "The war shattered both the myth and the reality of Russian Power. Whatever its origin the war was in essence an invasion of Russia by the west; of the five invasions of Russia in modern times it was by far the most successful. After 1856 Russia carried less weight in European affairs than at any time since the end of the Great Northern war in 1721; and the influence which she had commanded at Berlin and Vienna before 1854, she was never to wield again until 1945." [26] Russia was down and out; her defeat condemned her to weakness for a generation. The scars truly attributable to the war proved less deep than most Russians feared at the time. But they counted as a symbol. They created resentment, suspicion, and international hostility. The Russians had not only lost the war; they had lost territory; they had been compelled to disarm in the Black Sea; they had been saddled with terms which they regarded as incompatible with their position as a Great Power. Every touch of resentment stirred the Russians to shake off the humiliation of the treaty of Paris. More than anything else, this determination cleared the ground for the reconstruction of Europe in the following decade—that is, for the unification of Italy and Germany.

The unification of Italy and Germany completed what the Crimean war had begun: the destruction of the European order. Without realizing it, the statesmen who fought the Crimean war fired the starting-pistol in the race for the making of Italy and Germany; it remained for Cavour and Bismarck to run it. Certainly neither Clarendon nor Drouyn nor Buol was a match for Cavour or for Bismarck in diplomatic skill, in high-minded aspiration, or in romantic utterance. On the contrary, they seemed unimaginative, wooden characters—funny little men, as H. G. Wells later depicted them, who made irrelevant comments on the margin of events. Still it is not extravagant to suggest that, in turning Russia out of the Near East and—a more decisive contribution—in destroying Russian influence in central Europe, this humdrum generation of diplomats pulled off a stroke of policy which changed the face of European history. They destroyed the existing order of Europe, the old order of the Holy Alliance, without putting a new order in its place. This was the necessary condition for the rise of Italy and Germany.

VIII

Gorchakov, who became foreign minister in the spring of 1856, seemed to personify the new Russian condition. He said to Kiselev, his minister at Paris: "I am looking for a man who will annul the clauses of the treaty of Paris concerning the Black Sea question and the Bessarabian frontier. I am looking for him and I shall find him." [27] Gorchakov's policy was clear and simple: Russia must swing France away from Austria as she had tried to do during his days as ambassador at Vienna. He was knocking at an open door. Napoleon III was, as always, ready to brush aside the Austrian alliance which he regarded as a nuisance and a distraction, ready too to assure Gorchakov that the political interests of France and Russia were similar. That was all. As long as Napoleon III was bent on a political reconstruction of Europe according to the principle of nationality, he dared to estrange British opinion: "Gorchakov failed to understand that Napoleon III would not be so easily parted from the British; the Napoleonic dream was of a reconstruction of Europe *a trois*—a new Tilsit indeed, but with a British representative on the raft and not (as legend has it) hiding underneath it." [28] Still Napoleon III determined to move along the path towards agreement with Russia. His advisers shared this belief, Morny, his half-brother, most of all. Morny had long paraded himself as the friend of Russia. With financial resources and diplomatic experience, he believed that Russian resentment over the treaty of Paris would drive her into the arms of France; and this belief did not diminish when Morny was named ambassador to Russia on 24 April 1856.

Morny's calculation was on solid ground. The temptation to repudiate the treaty of Paris made the Russians almost uncontrollable. A small incident showed it. The Russians put forward a claim on Bolgrad, the frontier city of Bessarabia, which they had made at the congress of Paris and they were unmoved by British accusations that they were deliberately ignoring their obligations under the peace settlement. They made the plausible argument that the Powers had already conceded their right to keep Bolgrad even though the city they were now claiming was on the mouth of the Danube and different from another, unimportant Bolgrad that had appeared on the map used by the congress. The Russians thought they could get their way by a fait accompli. In the middle of June their troops tiptoed across Bessarabia and seized the Bolgrad that lay on the Danube. The act caught the Powers unawares. Napoleon III was pulled two ways. On the one hand he wished to conciliate the Russians. He wanted to get rid of the treaty of 15 April 1856; yet nothing the Russians offered (and they offered little) could shake Napoleon III's determination to remain on good terms with the British. It was the old stumbling block all over again. An international conference convened at Paris in November 1856 to answer the question: which Bolgrad did the congress intend to give Russia? The Crimean coalition was now ostensibly in being; and from this moment all the confusions of the Crimean war were repeated or rather outdone. There was this difference. Morny insisted that Russian pride would be broken unless Napoleon III did something to show that he took the Russian gestures seriously. Napoleon III did so. He voted on the Russian side. This amounted to little. Napoleon III had imposed himself on Sardinia; had, before the conference met, secretly instructed Cavour that Sardinia should vote with the British and against the Russians. Its outcome was therefore never in doubt. Napoleon III's gesture, though empty, allowed the Russians to come away with the feeling that they could count on French goodwill. As Morny said: "It is an alliance to which they have pinned their hopes if they can get it in a sincere and honorable way." [29]

In the uneasy sequel to the conference of Paris, Napoleon III made a feeble attempt to take the Russians at their word. He tried to recall the Italian question to life. Cavour was at this time hamstrung by domestic difficulties; and the Austrians still gave no indication that they meant to pull out of the Papal states. It therefore troubled Napoleon little, and the British government even less, to complain of political corruption at Naples. Here indeed was a fertile cause of political grievance. Bomba, the king of Naples, was a scoundrel; his government one of obscurantist tyranny. In the middle of October 1856 the British and French withdrew their diplomatic representatives from Naples hoping that this would stir up enough popular agitation to chase Bomba off his throne. Their next impulse was to threaten a naval demonstration.

Both strokes failed. The British, for all their high-minded indignation, soon came to realize that their long-term ambition in Italy—getting the Austrians out without letting the French in—was verging on collapse. Napoleon III meant, or so they feared, to replace Bomba with his half-brother Murat. They therefore called their demonstration off almost as quickly as they had announced it. Napoleon III followed suit. He shrank from any action to which the British were not a party. Nor was this his only consideration. No sooner had the western ambassadors left Naples than Alexander II warned Morny: "This is an act of interference in the domestic affairs of a free and sovereign king—a disturbance of principles which all governments ought to preserve and in the absence of which there can be no security." [30] Napoloen III backed off at this rebuff to his policy of intimidation. As always, the Italian project outstripped his resources: he needed British backing and, to a lesser extent, Russian goodwill, and neither the British nor the Russians were willing to let Napoleon III engineer a revolt in Italy even if it were done, as it must be, at Austria's expense. The Naples crisis therefore died away.

IX

The reserves and evasions of both France and Russia were repeated in September 1857 when Alexander II met Napoleon III at Stuttgart. Italy, Poland, the Near East were all discussed; agreement on none was secured. Napoleon III tried to extract from Alexander II a pledge not to aid Austria in Italy. Alexander refused; instead he insisted that Napoleon III renew diplomatic relations with Naples. When asked by Napoleon whether he meant to relax his grip on Poland, Alexander replied: "Poland will prosper under the scepter of the Emperor of Russia" [31]—a pledge that gave Napoleon III some encouragement, though not much: a far cry from the grandiose reform of the kind he was to envisage six years later. The two emperors ought to have had an easier time devising a common program in the Near East: here too expectations were disappointed. Napoleon III had just met Queen Victoria at Osborne; and the two liberal Powers had made up their differences over the principalities. This agreement took the Russians by surprise, and for the moment they were unwilling to strike out on a new course.

The Stuttgart meeting therefore ended tamely. It had, however, profound immediate effects. The Austrians watched the meeting with sharp eyes. Dark hints of a Franco-Russian combine against Austria in Italy swelled the volumes of the foreign ministry. The Austrian rulers insisted, as Metternich had before them, that the threat to their existence came from without, not from within, and they were right, without realizing how right they were. France and Russia made the pretentious claim that they were "natural allies"; and, though this was certainly an exaggeration, it had at least some practical meaning because of common hostility to Austria. This was the new element in European diplomacy—the cement that held France and Russia together; and it was the element that gave the death blow to the European order which had been created by the congress of Vienna, and so in particular to the German confederation.

This was a change heavy with consequences for the future of central Europe, and—even more important—a change that gave the Crimean war its unique quality of importance in the history of European international relations. Preservation of German disunity had, before 1856, been the guiding thread in the policies of France and Russia, France since the time of the Thirty Years war; Russia since the time of the "punctuation of Olmütz" of 1850, and even perhaps since the abortive Austro-Prussian war and the peace of Teschen of 1778. Now France and Russia ceased to be the guardians of German disunity and instead set their feet upon the course of change and adventure. This set in motion the earthquakes of the next decade: the great upheavals of 1859, of 1866, and their decisive result—the destruction of Austria's primacy in Germany and Italy. In the twenty years after 1856 Austria was indeed isolated, could count on Russian friendship no longer; no longer would the tsar respond to challenges to Austria's existence as he, with conspicuous success, had as recently as 1849. Quite the reverse. Resentful, suspicious, he sat back, vowing not to repeat the blunders of John Sobieski and Nicholas I—the two kings of Poland who had saved Vienna from destruction and had come away empty-handed. In the international history of Europe, 1856 was indeed the end of an era and the dawn of a new, more troubled, age.

LIST OF ABBREVIATIONS
(used in footnotes)

Ab. Corr.	Aberdeen Correspondence (1846-1862). Privately printed by Lord Stanmore. State Papers Room. London.
AMAE-CP	Archives du Ministère des Affaires étrangères, Correspondance politique. Paris.
AMAE-MD	Archives du Ministère des Affaires étrangères, Mémoires et Documents. Paris.
AMAE-MD-PT	Archives du Ministère des Affaires étrangères, Mémoires et Documents, Thouvenel Papers. Paris.
AMAE-MD-PW	Archives du Ministère des Affaires étrangères, Mémoires et Documents, Waleski Papers. Paris.
AN 192MI-PT	Archives Nationales, Archives privées en microfilm, reel 192, Thouvenel Papers. Paris.
Clar. dep.	Clarendon deposit. Bodleian Library. Oxford.
HHSA-PA	Haus-, Hof- und Staatsarchiv, Politische Akten. Vienna.
HHSA-KA	Feldakten. Kriegsarchiv, Vienna.
Palm. papers	Palmerston Papers. National Registry of Archives. London.
PRO-FO	Public Record Office, Foreign Office. London.
RA	Royal Archives. Windsor.
SP	Stratford Papers. Public Record Office. London.

NOTES

Chapter 1

1. Nesselrode to Meyendorff (Berlin), 27 April 1848. Anatole Nesselrode, ed., *Lettres et papiers du Chancelier comte de Nesselrode,* 11 vols. (Paris, 1904–12), 9:87.

2. Lewis Namier, *1848: The Revolution of the Intellectuals,* (London, 1944), p. 40.

3. Kolowrat, 70, replaced Metternich; Ficquelmont, 71, replaced Metternich at the foreign office; Pillersdorf, at 62, became prime minister in May, but was replaced the next month by Wessenberg, 75, until the October revolution brought Bach, 35, to power.

Chapter 2

1. A. J. P. Taylor, *The Stuggle for Mastery in Europe* (Oxford, 1954), p. 46.

2. Quoted in Asa Briggs, *The Age of Improvement* (New York, 1959), p. 427.

3. A. J. P. Taylor, "The Man of December," *Rumors of War* (London, 1952), p. 26.

4. Quoted in Pierre Renouvin, *Histoire de relations internationales,* vol. 5, *Le XIXe Siècle: De 1815 à 1871* (Paris, 1954), p. 270.

5. Taylor, "The Man of December," p. 27.

6. Napoleon III to Walewski (later foreign minister), 28 May 1852, AMAE-MD—PW.

7. Quoted in Renouvin, *Histoire de relations internationales,* 5:271.

8. Constantin Grunwald, quoted in Nicholas V. Riasanovsky, *Nicholas I and Official Nationality in Russia* (Berkeley, 1959), pp. 1-2.

9. Astolphe de Custine, *La Russie en 1839,* 4 vols. (Brussels, 1843), 1:319.

10. Constantin Grunwald, *Tsar Nicholas I,* Eng. trans. (New York, 1955), p. 156.

11. Ibid., p. 157.

12. *Nicholas I and Official Nationality in Russia,* p. 15.

13. Ibid., pp. 13-14.

14. Ibid., p. 264.

15. Quoted in Patricia Kennedy Grimsted, *The Foreign Ministers of Alexander I* (Berkeley and Los Angeles, 1969), p. 199.

16. Quoted in Riasanovsky, *Nicholas I and Official Nationality in Russia,* p. 239.

17. H. W. V. Temperley, *England and the Near East: The Crimea* (London, 1936), p. 267.

18. Quoted in Ibid., p. 269.

19. La Hitte (foreign minister) to Drouyn de Lhuys, 14 May 1850, AMAE-CP *Angleterre,* vol. 678; Thouvenel to La Hitte, 28 June 1850, AMAE-CP *Grèce,* vol. 54; Wyse to Thouvenel 18 July 1850, 192 MI, PT, reel 15.

20. Alan Palmer, *The Chancelleries of Europe* (London, 1980), p. 95.

Chapter 3

1. Taylor, *The Struggle for Mastery in Europe,* p. 49.

2. Ibid.

3. Ibid., p. 50.

4. Seymour to Aberdeen, 22 Jan. 1853, no. 73, PRO-FO 65/424.

5. Seymour to Russell, 12 Jan. 1853. G. P. Gooch, ed., *Later Correspondence of Lord John Russell,* 2 vols. (London, 1925), 2:145.

6. Seymour to Russell, 22 Jan. 1853, no. 26, PRO-FO 65/424.

7. A. M. Zaionchkovskii, *Vostochnaya Voyna, 1853-1856: Prilozheniya,* 2 vols. (St. Petersburg, 1908-13), 1:359-62.

8. Ibid., p. 362.

9. Quoted in Temperley, *The Crimea,* p. 276.

10. Taylor, *The Struggle for Mastery in Europe,* p. 52.

11. Temperley, *The Crimea,* p. 304.

12. Nesselrode to Menshikov, 28 Jan. 1853, Zaionchkovskii, *Vostochnaya Voyna,* 1:371.

13. Nicholas I to the Sultan, 24 Jan. 1853, Ibid., 1:386-87.

14. Taylor, *The Struggle for Mastery in Europe,* p. 52.

15. Quoted in Temperley, *The Crimea,* p. 310.

16. E. Llewellyn Woodward, *The Age of Reform,* 2nd ed. (Oxford, 1962), p. 165.

Chapter 4

1. A. J. P. Taylor, "Lord John Russell," *Essays in English History* (Harmondsworth, Middlesex, England, 1976), p. 67.

2. Spencer Walpole, *The Life of Lord John Russell,* 2 vols. (London, 1891), 2:480, n. 1.

3. Taylor, "Lord John Russell," p. 69.

4. Ibid., pp. 72-73.

5. Ibid., p. 73.

6. John Prest, *Lord John Russell* (Columbia, 1972), pp. 81 and 73.

7. Aberdeen to the Queen, undated, but sometime in Dec. 1852. A. J. Benson, ed., *Letters of Queen Victoria,* 1st series (London, 1907), 2:505.

8. Taylor, "Lord John Russell," pp. 67-68.

9. Kenneth Bourne, *Palmerston: The Early Years* (London, 1982), p. 212.

10. Grey to Russell, 19 Dec. 1845. Walpole, *Russell,* 1:415.

11. A. J. P. Taylor, "Palmerston," *Essays in English History,* p. 108.

12. 3 *Hansard* 97 (1850): 122.

13. Bourne, *Palmerston,* p. 622.

14. Ibid., p. 621.

15. A. J. P. Taylor, Introduction to *Palmerston* by Denis Judd (London, 1975), p. viii.

16. Taylor, "Palmerston," p. 115.

17. A. Argyll, *Autobiography and Memoirs,* 2 vols. (London, 1906), 1:451.

18. M. E. Chamberlain, *Lord Aberdeen* (London, 1983), p. 531.

19. Temperley, *The Crimea,* p. 385.

20. Aberdeen to the Queen, 23 March 1853. *Letters of Queen Victoria,* 1st series, 2:537-38.

21. Quoted in John Morley, *The Life of William Ewart Gladstone* (London, 1903), 1:428.

Chapter 5

1. Quoted in Taylor, *Struggle for Mastery in Europe,* p. 24.

2. Cowley to Clarendon, 20 March 1853, no. 161, PRO-FO 27/964.

3. Quoted in Temperley, *The Crimea,* p. 312.

4. Taylor *Struggle for Mastery in Europe,* p. 53.

5. Most recently by John Shelton Curtis, *Russia's Crimean War,* (Durham, 1979), pp. 107-9.

6. Gabriel Noradounghian, ed., *Recueil d'actes internationaux de l'Empire Ottoman,* 4 vols. (Paris, 1897–1903), 1:326-28.

7. F. F. Martens, *Recueil des traités et conventions conclus par la Russie avec les puissances étrangères,* 15 vols. (St. Petersburg, 1874-1906), 12:311-12; Taylor, *Struggle for Mastery in Europe,* p. 52.

8. Menshikov to Nesselrode, 26 April 1853, Zaionchkovskii, *Vostochnaya voina,* 1:405-7.

9. Stratford to Clarendon, 6 May 1853, no. 43, PRO-FO 78/932.

10. Taylor, *Struggle for Mastery in Europe,* p. 54.

11. *Ab. Corr.,* vol. 1852-55, pp. 109-10.

12. Bunsen (St. Petersburg) to Manteuffel (prime minister), 29 June 1853. Heinrich Ritter von Poschinger, ed., *Prussens auswärtige Politik, 1850–1858,* 3 vols. (Berlin, 1902), 2:110; Taylor, *Struggle for Mastery in Europe,* p. 54.

13. Aberdeen to Graham (first lord of the admiralty), 31 May 1853. *Ab. Corr.,* vol. 1854-55, pp. 125-26.

14. Taylor, *Struggle for Mastery in Europe,* p. 54.

15. Quoted in Temperley, *The Crimea,* p. 298.

16. Taylor, *Struggle for Mastery in Europe,* p. 54.

17. Paul W. Schroeder, *Austria, Great Britain, and the Crimean War,* (Ithaca, 1972), p. 19.

18. A. J. P. Taylor, "Francis Joseph: The Last of the Hapsburgs," *From Napoleon to Stalin* (London, 1950), p. 67.

19. Stratford to Clarendon, 27 July 1853, no. 61, PRO-FO 78/932.

20. Bourqueney to Drouyn de Lhuys, 23 July 1853, nos. 61-61, AMAE-CP *Autriche,* vol. 451.

21. Taylor, *Struggle for Mastery in Europe,* p. 57.

22. Clarendon to Loftus (Berlin), 5 Oct. 1853, Clar. dep. c. 126.

23. Russell to Clarendon, 5 Oct. 1853, ibid., c. 3.

24. Taylor, *Struggle for Mastery in Europe,* p. 57.

25. Colloredo to Buol, 8 Oct. 1853, no. 1020, HHSA-PA VII/38.

26. Quoted in Temperley, *The Crimea,* p. 357.

27. Herbert to Clarendon, 8 Oct. 1853, Clar. dep. c. 41.

28. Taylor, *Struggle for Mastery in Europe,* p. 58.

29. Aberdeen to Clarendon, 23 Oct. 1853, Add. ms. 43188.

30. Clarendon to Aberdeen, 4 Nov. 1853, ibid.

31. Adolphus Slade, *Turkey and the Crimean War,* (London, 1867), p. 152.

32. R. C. Anderson, *Naval Wars in the Levant* (Princeton, 1952), p. 582.

33. Taylor, *Struggle for Mastery in Europe,* p. 58.

34. Drouyn de Lhuys to Walewski, 19 Dec. 1853, AMAE-CP *Angleterre,* vol. 692.

35. Cowley to Clarendon, 21 Dec. 1853, no. 95, PRO-FO 27/978.

36. Aberdeen to Russell, 20 Dec. 1853, PRO 30/22/11B.

37. Aberdeen to the Queen, 22 Dec. 1853, RA G9.

38. Taylor, *Struggle for Mastery of Europe,* p. 59.

39. Ibid.

40. Castelbajac (St. Petersburg) to Drouyn de Luhys, 13 Jan. 1854, AMAE-CP *Russie,* vol. 211; Taylor, *Struggle for Mastery in Europe,* p. 60.

41. Ibid.

Chapter 6

1. Taylor, *Struggle for Mastery in Europe,* p. 54.

2. Proposal of 21 March 1854, HHSA-PA XL/48.

3. Hess's *Denkschrift,* 25 March 1854, KA-FA 1854/13/181.

4. Quoted in Otto Pflanze, *Bismarck and the Development of Germany* (Princeton, 1963), pp. 92-93.

5. Quoted in ibid., p. 97.

6. Taylor, *Struggle for Mastery in Europe,* pp. 73-74.

7. Quoted in Schroeder, *Austria, Great Britain, and the Crimean War,* p. 199.

8. Text of ultimatum of 3 June 1854 in HHSA-PA XL/48.

9. Taylor, *Struggle for Mastery in Europe,* p. 64.

10. 16 June 1854. Evelyn Ashley, *The Life of John Henry Temple, Viscount Palmerston,* 2 vols. (London, 1876), 2:67.

11. Clarendon to Aberdeen, 13 July 1854, *Ab. Corr,* vol. 1854-55, p. 169.

12. Hübner to Buol, 9 July 1854, Joseph Alexander von Hübner. *Neuf ans de souvenirs d'un ambassadeur d'Autriche à Paris,* 2 vols. (Paris, 1904), 1:253.

13. Colloredo to Buol, 28 July 1854, no. 81, HHSA-PA VII/40.

14. Westmorland to Lady Westmorland, 1 Aug. 1854. Lady Rose Weigall, ed., *The Correspondence of Priscilla, Countess of Westmorland* (London, 1909), p. 234.

15. Hübner, *Neuf ans de souvenirs,* 1:261.

16. Bourqueney to Drouyn de Lhuys, 5 and 7 Aug. 1854, AMAE-CP *Autriche,* vol. 455.

17. Gavin B. Henderson, *Crimean War Diplomacy* (Glasgow, 1947), p. 167.

18. Taylor, *Struggle for Mastery in Europe,* p. 66.

Chapter 7

1. Esterházy to Buol, 21 Aug. 1854, no. 70 A-E, HHSA-PA X/35.

2. Same to same, 30 Aug. 1854, no. 71 A-E, ibid.

3. Clarendon to Westmorland, 15 Aug. 1854, no. 262, PRO-FO 71/429.

4. Golo Mann *Secretary of Europe: The Life of Friedrich Gentz, Enemy of Napoleon* (New Haven, 1946), p. 277.

5. Buol to Francis Joseph, 26 Sept. 1854. Henderson, *Crimean War Diplomacy,* pp. 173-74.

6. Clarendon to the Queen, 3 Oct. 1854, RA G17.

7. Buol to Hübner, 23 Sept. 1854, HHSA-PA IX/46.

8. Drouyn de Lhuys to Walewski, 2 Nov. 1854, AMAE-CP *Angleterre,* vol. 698.

9. Clarendon to Aberdeen, 2 Nov. 1854 *Ab. Corr.,* vol. 1854-55, p. 266.

10. Taylor, *Struggle for Mastery in Europe,* p. 69.

11. Ibid., p. 70.

12. Hübner to Buol, 3 Nov. 1854, no. 140, HHSA-PA IX/46.

13. Quoted in Charles W. Hallberg, *Franz Joseph and Napoleon III* (New York, 1955), p. 82.

14. Taylor, *Struggle for Mastery in Europe,* p. 70.

15. V. Esterházy to Buol, 8 Dec. 1854, HHSA-PA X/35.

16. Quoted in Henderson, *Crimean War Diplomacy*, pp. 187-88.

17. Hübner, *Neuf ans de souvenirs*, 1:284; Taylor, *Struggle for Mastery in Europe*, p. 70.

18. Ibid.

19. Ibid.

20. Westmorland to Clarendon, 18 Oct. 1854, Clar. dep. c. 12.

21. Drouyn de Lhuys to Guiche (Turin), 11 March 1854. William Roscoe Thayer, *The Life and Times of Cavour*, 2 vols. (Boston, 1912), 1:322.

22. Hudson to Clarendon, 24 Oct. 1854, Clar. dep. c. 21.

23. Taylor, *Struggle for Mastery in Europe*, p. 71.

24. Ibid., p. 72.

25. Giuseppe Massari, *La vita ed il regno di Vittorio Emanuele II di Savoia*, 2 vols. (Milan, 1878), 1:258.

26. PRO-FO 67/198.

27. Guiche to Drouyn de Lhuys, 9 Jan. 1855. Paul Matter, *Cavour et l'unité italienne*, 3 vols. (Paris, 1927), 2:307.

28. Massari, *Vittorio Emanuele II*, 1:262-63.

29. Luigi Chiala, ed., *Lettere edite ed inedite di Camillo Cavour*, 6 vols. (Turin, 1883–87), 2:66-67.

30. Quoted in Thayer, *Life and Times of Cavour*, 1:327.

31. Ibid., pp. 327-28.

32. Taylor, *Struggle for Mastery in Europe*, p. 72.

33. Ibid.

34. Frederick William IV to Gerlach, 5 Dec. 1854. Kurt Borries, *Preussen im Krimkrieg* (Stuttgart, 1930), p. 251.

35. Ibid., p. 266; Taylor, *Struggle for Mastery in Europe*, p. 73.

36. Ibid.

37. Quoted in Leopold von Gerlach, *Denkwürdigkeiten*, 2 vols. (Berlin, 1891), 2:266.

38. Quoted in Borries, *Preussen im Krimkrieg*, p. 268; Taylor, *Struggle for Mastery in Europe*, p. 73.

Chapter 8

1. Clarendon to Westmorland, 20 Jan. 1855, no. 2, PRO-FO 7/446; Taylor, *Struggle for Mastery in Europe*, p. 74.

2. Thouvenel to Benedetti, 6 Oct. 1854, AN 192MI, reel 21, no. 36.

3. Borries, *Preussen im Krimkrieg*, p. 266

4. Procureur report (Aix), 7 Jan. 1855. Lynn M. Case, *French Opinion on War and Diplomacy during the Second Empire* (Philadelphia, 1954), p. 32.

5. Quoted in Hallberg, *Franz Joseph and Napoleon III*, p. 124.

6. Cowley to Clarendon, 21 Jan. 1855, no. 56, PRO-FO 519/4.

7. *History of the Times,* vol. 2, *The Tradition Established* (London, 1939), p. 166.

8. Richard Cobden, *Political Writings,* 4th ed., 2 vols. (London, 1903), 1:142.

9. Administrative Reform Association, *Official Papers,* no. 1, May 1855, p. 7.

10. Henderson, *Crimean War Diplomacy,* p. 35.

11. Palmerston to Clarendon, 10 Feb. 1855, Clar. dep. c. 31.

12. Hugh Seton-Watson, *The Russian Empire 1801–1917* (London, 1967), p. 327.

13. Taylor, *Struggle for Mastery in Europe,* p. 75.

14. Pierre de la Gorce, *Histoire du Second Empire,* 7 vols. (Paris, 1894–1905), 1:364.

15. Taylor, *Struggle for Mastery in Europe,* p. 75.

16. Cowley to Clarendon, 18 March 1855, no. 330, PRO-FO 27/1065.

17. Russell to Clarendon, 26 March 1855, Clar. dep. c. 30.

18. Benedetti to Thouvenel, n.d. [but probably 27 or 28 March 1855]. Louis Thouvenel, ed., *Pages de l'histoire du Second Empire* (Paris, 1903), pp. 47-48.

19. Cowley to Clarendon, 27 March 1855, no. 79, RA G29.

20. Taylor, *Struggle for Mastery in Europe,* p. 76.

21. Russell to Clarendon, 10 April 1855, no. 66, PRO-FO 7/464.

22. PRO 30/22/12B, n.d. [probably early March 1855].

23. S. M. Goriainov, *Le Bosphore et les Dardanelles* (Paris, 1910), p. 109.

24. Schroeder, *Austria, Great Britain and the Crimean War,* p. 270.

25. Taylor, *Struggle for Mastery of Europe,* p. 76.

26. Clarendon to the Queen, 30 April 1855, no. 67, RA G29; Henderson, *Crimean War Diplomacy,* p. 57.

27. Ibid., p. 58.

28. Aberdeen to Clarendon, 3 May 1855, ibid., p. 59.

29. Taylor, *Struggle for Mastery in Europe,* p.

30. Cowley to Clarendon, 4 May 1855, Clar. dep. c. 33.

31. Ibid.

32. Clarendon to Cowley, 5 May 1855, PRO-FO 419/71.

33. Drouyn de Lhuys to Napoleon III, 7 May 1855. Thouvenel, *Pages de l'histoire du Second Empire,* pp. 81-82.

34. Schroeder, *Austria, Great Britain and the Crimean War,* p. 283.

35. Palmerston to Newcastle, 16 June 1854. Ashley, *Life of Palmerston,* 2:67.

36. A. F. Tiutcheva, *Pri dvore drukh imperatorov Vospominaniia, Dneviki* (Moscow, 1928), 1:124.

Chapter 9

1. Cowley to Clarendon, 4 May 1855, no. 584, PRO-FO 519/4; Taylor, *Struggle for Mastery of Europe,* p. 77.

2. Same to same, 18 May 1855, Clar. dep. c. 31.

3. Report of 16 July 1855. Case, *French Opinion on War and Diplomacy during the Second Empire*, p. 37.

4. *3 Hansard*, 138 (1855): 18-24.

5. R. T. Shannon, *Gladstone*, 2 vols. (Chapel Hill, 1984), 1:315.

6. Gladstone to Aberdeen, 26 June 1855, Add. ms. 43071.

7. *Hospital Report* (London, 1855), p. 339.

8. E. V. E. Boniface de Castellane, *Campagnes de Crimée, d'Italie, d'Afrique, de Chine et de Syrie, 1849-1862* (Paris, 1898), p. 136.

9. Queen Victoria to Baron Stockmar, 1 Sept. 1855. A. C. Benson, ed., *The Letters of Queen Victoria*, 1st series, 3 vols. (London, 1907), 3:177.

10. Report of 11 July 1855. Case, *French Opinion on War and Diplomacy during the Second Empire*, p. 38.

11. Cowley to Clarendon, 31 May 1855, PRO-FO 27/1069/646.

12. Clarendon to Palmerston, 2 July 1855, Palm. Papers, GC/CL/64.

13. Stratford to Clarendon, 23 Aug. 1855, Stratford Papers, 352/42(2).

14. Ibid.

15. Ibid.

16. Clarendon to Stratford, 3 Sept. 1855, ibid.

17. Thouvenel to Walewski, 2 Sept. 1855, AMAE-CP *Turquie*, vol. 322.

18. Ibid.

19. Pisani to Stratford, 4 Sept. 1855, PRO-FO 78/1086/656.

20. Thouvenel to Walewski, 2 Sept. 1855, AMAE-CP *Turquie*, vol. 322.

21. Walewski to Thouvenel, 15 Sept. 1855, no. 17, AN 192 MI, PT, reel 15.

22. Clarendon to Stratford, 10 Sept. 1855, PRO-FO 352/42.

23. Clarendon to Cowley, 15 Sept. 1855, PRO-FO 519/172.

24. Thouvenel to Walewski, 30 Sept. 1855, AMAE-CP *Angleterre*, vol. 322.

25. Same to same, 1 Oct. 1855, ibid.

26. Stratford to Clarendon, 18 Oct. 1855, PRO-FO 78/1089/833.

27. Quoted in Vulliamy, *Crimea*, p. 319.

28. Taylor, *Struggle for Mastery in Europe*, pp. 77-78.

29. Cowley to Clarendon, 24 Oct. 1855. Victor Wellesley and Robert Sencourt, eds., *Conversations with Napoleon III* (London, 1934), p. 94.

30. Morny to Gorchakov, n.d. [probably in the middle of November 1855]. Charles Joseph de Morny, *Extrait des Mémoirs de duc de Morny: Une ambassade en Russie, 1856* (Paris, 1892), p. 20; Taylor, *Struggle for Mastery in Europe*, p. 78.

31. Alexander Jomini, *Diplomatic Study of the Crimean War*, 2 vols. (London, 1882), 2:347.

32. Walewski to Napoleon III, 14 Sept. 1855, AMAE-MD-PW.

33. Hübner to Buol, 20 Sept. 1855. Hübner, *Neuf ans de souvenirs*, 1:341.

34. Taylor, *Struggle for Mastery in Europe*, p. 79.

35. Buol to Hübner, 19 Nov. 1855, HHSA-PA IX/5.

36. Palmerston to Clarendon, 1 Dec. 1855, Clar. dep. c. 31; Taylor, *Struggle for Mastery in Europe*, pp. 79-80.

37. Gorchakov to Nesselrode, 5 Jan. 1856. Francois Charles-Roux, *Alexandre II, Gortchakoff et Napoléon III* (Paris, 1913), p. 76.

38. Clarendon to Cowley, 15 Jan. 1856, PRO-FO 519/173.

39. Taylor, *Struggle for Mastery in Europe,* p. 80.

40. Jomini, *Diplomatic Study of the Crimean War,* 2:361.

41. Walewski to Napoleon III. Gaston Raindre, ed., "Les papiers inédits du Comte Walewski," 18 Jan. 1856. *Revue de France* 5 (1925): 92-93.

42. Taylor, *Struggle for Mastery in Europe,* p. 83.

Chapter 10

1. Palmerston to Clarendon, 21 Jan. 1856, Clar. dep. c. 49.

2. Buol to Hübner, 18 Jan. 1856, HHSA-PA IX/54.

3. Taylor, *Struggle for Mastery in Europe,* p. 83.

4. Cowley to Clarendon, 11 May 1857, no. 753, PRO-FO 27/1196.

5. Clarendon to Stratford, 15 Sept. 1856, no. 720, PRO-FO 78/1066.

6. Thouvenel to Walewski, 31 Jan. 1856, AMAE-CP *Turquie,* vol. 324.

7. Ibid.

8. Memorandum by J. B. Bidwell, endorsed by Palmerston, 20 June 1851. Temperley, *The Crimea,* pp. 232-33.

9. Winfried Baumgart, *Der Friede von Paris, 1856* (Munich and Vienna, 1972), p. 205.

10. De Launay (Berlin) to Cibrario (f.m. Turin). *Cavour e l'Inghilterra,* 2 vols. (Bologna, 1933), 1:182-83.

11. Julius Jasmund, ed., *Aktenstücke zur orientalischen Frage,* 3 vols. (Berlin, 1855, 59), 2:328-29.

12. Hübner to Buol and Francis Joseph, 19 March 1856, no. 149, HHSA-PA XII/219.

13. *Krasny Archiv* 75 (1936): 52.

14. Cavour to La Marmora, 21 Jan. 1856. *Cavour e l'Inghilterra,* 1:154-57.

15. Ibid.

16. Cavour to D'Azeglio, 8 Dec. 1855. Chiala, *Lettere edite ed inedite di Camillo Cavour,* vol. 2., no. 390.

17. Cavour to Victor Emmanuel II, 22 Feb. 1856. *Cavour e l'Inghilterra,* 1:193-95.

18. Napoleon III to Walewski, 24 Dec. 1858, AMAE-MD-PW.

19. Cavour to d'Azeglio, 31 March 1856. *Cavour e l'Inghilterra,* 1:400.

20. Clarendon to Palmerston, 15 April 1856. Ennio di Nolfo, *Europa e Italia nel 1855-1856* (Rome, 1967), p. 509.

21. Nigra (Cavour's right-hand man) to d'Azeglio, 3 April 1856. *Cavour e l'Inghilterra,* 1:418-19.

22. Quoted in Thayer, *Life and Times of Cavour,* 1:386.

23. Taylor, *Struggle for Mastery in Europe,* p. 91.

24. Quoted in Thayer, *Life and Times of Cavour,* 1:386.

25. Buol to Prokesch, 21 April 1856, HHSA-PA XII/56.

26. Taylor, *Struggle for Mastery in Europe,* p. 88.

27. A. P. Zablotsky-Desyatovsky, *Graf. P. D. Kiselev,* 4 vols. (Berlin, 1923), 3:37; Taylor, *Struggle for Mastery in Europe,* p. 91.

28. Ibid.

29. Morny to Walewski, 25 Oct. 1856, AMAE-CP *Russie,* vol. 213.

30. Quoted in Charles-Roux, *Alexandre II, Gortchakoff et Napoléon III,* p. 176.

31. Ibid.

BIBLIOGRAPHY

It would be absurd to pretend that this bibliography on the Crimean war contains everything on the subject—equally absurd to pretend that I have read everything that the bibliography contains. I have, however, made a serious effort to list all the sources and most outstanding secondary literature in the five European languages. I have listed no book or article that I have not at least turned the pages of.

Part I of my bibliography lists manuscript sources—that is, the various documents, public and private, to be found in the archives of the Great Powers. This is a routine arrangement. Part II is more elaborate. It is arranged in five sections and there is an extended commentary on the works listed in each. The first three sections list secondary works on (1) general diplomatic history; (2) the revolutions of 1848 and their sequel; (3) the setting. The fourth section deals strictly with the literature on the Crimean war and is itself arranged in two categories: raw material and secondary works. The former falls into (a) official publications; (b) published papers of individuals, themselves given as rulers, prime and foreign ministers, ambassadors and diplomats, and others. Each of these is listed by country: in alphabetical order, Austria, France, Great Britain, Prussia (as well as the smaller German states), Russia, and Sardinia (as well as the smaller Italian states). The list of secondary works divides into three categories. The first gives books which pertain mainly to one country or one statesman. The second is confined strictly to general diplomatic histories of the Crimean war. Having now produced a book on this subject, I believe that I can evaluate the ones I list with experience, though I hope without jealousy, by comparing their respective viewpoints with those I have advanced in the preceding pages. The third category lists a few works on the military side of the war. The final section gives the periodical literature on the war. Where a work has been translated into English I usually give only the English version.

I. MANUSCRIPT SOURCES

Official Archives

Austria. Haus-, Hof- und Staatsarchiv. Politische Akten.
  Correspondence with England, Frankreich, Preussen, Russland, Türkei.
France. Archives du Ministère des Affaires étrangères. Correspondance politique.
  Correspondence with l'Angleterre, l'Autriche, la Prussie, la Russie, la Sardaigne,
    la Turquie.
  ——— . Mémoires et Documents Séries.
Great Britain. Public Record Office. Foreign Office.
  Correspondence with Austria, France, Prussia, Russia, Sardinia, Turkey.
  ——— . Royal Archives.

Private Papers

France. Archives du Ministère des Affaires étrangères.
  Bourqueney Papers.
  ——— . Archives nationales. Persigny Papers.
  ——— . Archives du Ministère des Affaires étrangères. Mémoires et Documents.
    Thouvenel Papers.
  ——— . Archives nationales. Archives privées en microfilm. Thouvenel Papers.
  ——— . Archives du Ministère des Affaires étrangères. Mémoires et Documents.
    Walewski Papers.
Great Britain. British Museum. Aberdeen Correspondence.
  Privately printed by Lord Stanmore.
  ——— . Bodleian Library. Clarendon deposit.
  ——— . Public Record Office. Foreign Office. Cowley Papers.
  ——— . National Registry of Archives. Palmerston Papers.
  ——— . Public Record Office. Russell Papers.
Great Britain. Public Record Office. Foreign Office. Stratford Papers.

II. PRINTED SOURCES

General Diplomatic Histories

The French produce the most detailed accounts, one of them magisterial. This is
the *Histoire des relations internationales* by Pierre Renouvin, vol. 5 (Paris, 1954),

which covers the years 1815–70 and is much more than a diplomatic history. Another indispensable work is *The Struggle for Mastery in Europe, 1848–1918* by A.J.P. Taylor (Oxford, 1954). It is stamped with the willful personality of its author; all the same it remains one of the finest studies of its kind, unmatched in its range and power of analysis, to say nothing of its whiplash wit and the dazzling brilliance of its language. There are a number of good, shorter accounts. *From Vienna to Versailles* by L.C.B. Seaman (London, 1955), though slight, is a brilliant book. The author, like Taylor, is inclined to hurry events along the way he wants them to go, and I have not escaped his influence. The character of international relations is studied by W. E. Mosse, *Liberal Europe* (London, 1974), and E. J. Hobsbawm, *The Age of Revolution* (London, 1972). *The Great Powers and the European States System, 1815–1914* by F. R. Bridge and Roger Bullen (London, 1980) ranges effectively over the period in a small compass. *The Chancelleries of Europe* by Alan Palmer (London, 1980) is an accomplished literary picture—at times overdrawn. *The Diplomatic History of Europe since the Congress of Vienna* by René Albrecht Carrié (New York, 1958) is singularly conventional; it means no offense and gives none. Among the more specialized works, Gordon A. Craig, "The System of Alliances and the Balance of Power," in the *New Cambridge Modern History,* vol. 10, ed. J.P.T. Bury (Cambridge, 1960), covers the period from 1830 to 1854 in a masterly fashion. The volume edited by Alan Sked, *Europe's Balance of Power* (London, 1979), has crisp pieces on the foreign policies of the Great Powers and on overriding diplomatic themes. There are two good books on the relations of Turkey and the Powers—the Eastern Question as we like to call it. The one by J.A.R. Marriott, 4th ed. (Oxford, 1940) has long enjoyed a great reputation; but it was first published in 1917 and is now superseded by the book by M.S. Anderson (London, 1966) with the same title. There is an excellent textbook on *The Balkans since 1453* by Leften Stavrianos (New York, 1958). It has an outstanding bibliography and is certainly the best general book on the history of the area.

The Revolutionary Year and Its Sequel

Most important of the attempts to deal with the revolutions is the symposium, *The Opening of an Era: 1848,* edited by *europäischen Grossmachte und die deutsche Revolution* (Leipzig, 1942), is not much better. Italy is better provided for: A.J.P. Taylor, *The Italian Problem in European Diplomacy* (Manchester, 1934), and Cesare Spellanzon, *Storia del Risorgimento e dell'unità d'Italia* (Milan, 1936), both derive from the Italian archives, the former from the Austrian archives as well. Émile Bourgeois and Émile Clermont, *Rome et Napoléon III* (Paris, 1907), covers the period from 1849 to 1870. The reaction in Italy is described by Ruggero Moscati, *Austria, Napoli, e gli stati conservatori italiani, 1849–1852* (Naples, 1942). On Hungary: Istvan Deak, *The Lawful Revolution: Louis Kossuth and the Hungarians 1848–1849* (New York, 1979), scholarly and readable; Revekka Averbukh, *Tsarskaya intervent-*

siya v borbe s vengerskoi revolyutsiei (Moscow, 1935); Eugene Horvath, *Origins of the Crimean War* (Budapest, 1937); and Charles Sproxton, *Palmerston and the Hungarian Revolution* (Cambridge, England, 1919), rather slight.

The Setting

General Accounts

A complete bibliography would need a list of all the works on general history during the period. There is a short list in W. L. Langer, *Political and Social Upheaval, 1832-1852* (New York, 1969). Here I stick to books on nationalism and its implications for the Powers. There are some inevitable exceptions. It cannot be said, for example, that *The Historical Evolution of Modern Nationalism* by Carlton J. H. Hayes (New York, 1931) provides much information on international politics even though it is an indispensable work, the most satisfactory survey of its kind. The same is true of Eugen Lemberg, *Geschichte des Nationalismus in Europa* (Stuttgart, 1950), which stretches back to the Renaissance. Robert Schnerb, *Le XIX siècle: L'apogée de l'expansion européenne, 1815-1914* (Paris, 1955), is more pertinent. So, in a different way, is Feliks Gross, *The Seizure of Political Power in a Century of Revolutions* (New York, 1958), a novel and most useful book. Charles Morazé, *The Triumph of the Middle Classes: A Study of European Values in the Nineteenth Century* (London, 1966), discusses the impact of nationalism on the bourgeois world, with special reference to France. Boyd C. Shafer, *Nationalism: Myth and Reality* (New York, 1955), is aloof, urbane, and uninformative.

During the nineteenth century, the state came to play a greater part in economic affairs, and economics inevitably strays into politics. There is one very good recent survey: *The Birth of a New Europe: State and Society in the Nineteenth Century,* by Theodore S. Hamerow (Chapel Hill, N.C., 1983); it is really a collection of essays on independent themes; all the same it is a most illuminating book, combining sound grasp and lucid organization. There are many books on the industrialization of Europe. The one by Clive Trebilcock (London, 1981), is an indispensable account, with much raw material. *The Age of Capital* by E. J. Hobsbawm (New York 1975) has the defect of being marred by erratic Marxism. *Peaceful Conquest* by Sidney Pollard (Oxford, 1981) is a remarkable exercise in creative understanding. *Industrialization in the Nineteenth Century* by Tom Kemp (London, 1969) is a quick and efficient, though less recent, survey. *Economic Backwardness in Historical Perspective* by Alexander Gerschenkron (Cambridge, Mass., 1962) is a collection of most perceptive essays; the first, from which the title of the book derives, effervesces with stimulating speculations. No doubt this is a random, highly selective list.

Austria

The best general accounts are A.J.P. Taylor, *The Hapsburg Monarchy* (New York, 1948), and Hugo Hantsch, *Die Geschichte Österreichs,* vol. 1 (Graz, 1969). Both abound in refreshing and independent judgments. C. A. Macartney, *The Hapsburg Empire, 1790–1918* (London, 1968), and Victor L. Tapié, *Monarchie et peuples du Danube* (Paris, 1969), rank among the more useful, up-to-date approaches. Robert A. Kahn, *The Multinational Empire: Nationalism and National Reform in the Hapsburg Monarchy,* 2 vols (New York, 1950), still has value—and controversy. Its solemn tone is suited to the subject. Barbara Jelavich, *The Hapsburg Monarchy in European Affairs* (Chicago, 1969), is a highly competent survey by a highly competent historian. Edward Crankshaw, *The Fall of the House of Hapsburg* (New York, 1963), is a good, popular account. The period before 1848 is exhaustively covered in Heinrich von Srbik, *Metternich, der Staatsmann und der Mensch,* 2 vols. (Munich, 1925); not unduly laudatory, it is shapeless, weighed down with undigested material. Friedrich Walter, *Die österreichische Zentralverwaltung, 1848–1852* (Vienna, 1964), covers the period immediately afterwards and, unlike Srbik, is a volume of reasonable size that can be held in the hand without muscular exhaustion. Josef Redlich, *Das österreichische staats und reichsproblem* (Berlin, 1920), is rather out of date. *Mitteleuropas Vorkämpfer: Fürst Felix zu Schwarzenberg* by Eduard Heller (Vienna, 1933) is a political analysis of the first order. *Fürst Felix zu Schwarzenberg* by Rudolf Kiszling (Graz, 1952) discovers, regretfully, that Schwarzenberg did not singlehandedly restore absolutism to the empire. *Versäumte gelegenheiten: Die oktroyierte Verfassung von 4. März 1849* by Hanns Schlitter (Vienna, 1920) is rather overdrawn. John Komlos, *The Hapsburg Monarchy as a Customs Union* (Princeton, 1983), is a fine, recent work that perhaps belongs in the last section. Though a little too confident in its judgments, it contains much raw material and is certainly a great improvement on the treatment in previous histories.

France

The classic history, *Histoire du Second Empire* by Pierre de La Gorce, 4th ed., 7 vols. (Paris, 1894–1905), is still helpful. The most comprehensive recent account is Theodore Zeldin, *France, 1848–1945,* vol. 1, *Ambition, Love and Politics* (Oxford, 1973), original and entertaining; vol. 2 *Intellect, Taste and Anxiety* (Oxford, 1977), highly revealing for the subjects it covers, though it does not think highly of diplomacy. There is no adequate biography of Napoleon III. We must make do with F. A. Simpson, *The Rise of Louis Napoleon,* 3rd ed. (London, 1950), and *Louis Napoleon and the Recovery of France,* 3rd ed. (London, 1951), both pioneer works. Heinrich Euler, *Napoleon III in seiner Zeit* (Würzburg, 1961), is an indispensable original study. E. A. Babeau, *Louis-Napoléon Bonaparte avant l'Empire* (Paris, 1951), plays old tunes with few enrichments and is surpassed by Adrien Dansette, *Louis Napoléon à la conquête du pouvoir, 1808–1851,* 2 vols. (Paris, 1961). Albert Guérard, *Napoleon III: A Great Life in Brief* (New York, 1969), is an interpretation of Napoleon's political philosophy, rather than a life. John Patrick Tuer Bury, *Napoleon III and the Second Empire* (London, 1964), is an agreeable account with a good bibliography. Henri Guillemin, *Le coup du 2 décembre* (Paris, 1951) is too hostile;

Earl of Kerry (Henry William E. P. F. Lansdowne), ed., *The Secret of the Coup d'Etat* (London, 1924), a bit better. Theodore Zeldin, *The Political System of Napoleon III* (London, 1958), has much information on parties and electoral management, and surpasses Paul Bastid, *Doctrines et institutions politiques de la Seconde République,* 2 vols. (Paris, 1945). Lynn M. Case, *French Opinion on War and Diplomacy during the Second Empire* (Philadelphia, 1954), breaks fresh ground in a short space. William E. Echard, *Napoleon III and the Concert of Europe* (Baton Rouge, 1983) is an impressive achievement, though it misses a few points. Nancy Nicholas Barker, *Distaff Diplomacy: Empress Eugenie and the Foreign Policy of the Second Empire* (Austin, 1967) describes brilliantly the influence of Napoleon III's wife on his policy, as does Jasper Ridley, *Napoleon III and Eugenie* (New York, 1979). On economics and demography: Hendrik N. Boon, *Rêve et réalité dans l'oeuvre économique et sociale de Napoléon III* (The Hague, 1936), rather dull; Claude Fohlen, *L'industrie textile française au temps de Second Empire* (Paris, 1954), a wonderful book; Rondo Cameron, *France and the Economic Development of Europe, 1800–1914* (Princeton, 1961), a good summary; Charles H. Pouthas, *La population française pendant la première moitié du XIX siècle* (Paris, 1956), thin, but important.

Great Britain

There are two good general histories: Ernest Llewellyn Woodward, *The Age of Reform, 1815–1870,* 2d ed. (Oxford, 1962), with an extensive bibliography; Asa Briggs, *The Age of Improvement, 1784–1874* (New York, 1959), a fine achievement. There are several good studies dealing with movements and particular aspects of politics: high on any list must be Kenneth Bourne, *Palmerston: The Early Years* (London, 1982), an outstanding contribution that has permanently stamped the literature on its subject; J. H. Gleason, *The Genesis of Russphobia in Great Britain* (Cambridge, Mass, 1950), a creditable undertaking centered perhaps too much on *The Times;* unfortunately, it goes up to only 1840; David Hempton, *Methodism and Politics in British Society, 1750–1850* (Stanford, 1985) covers a long period and is particularly useful for its last two chapters; Bernard Porter, *The Refugee Question in mid-Victorian Politics* (Cambridge, England, 1979), a detailed analysis, rich in documentation; Stephen Koss, *The Rise and Fall of the Political Press in Britain,* vol. 1, *The Nineteenth Century* (Chapel Hill, N.C., 1981), an engaging accomplishment, particularly strong on economic and social themes; H. W. C. Davis, *The Age of Peel and Gray* (London, 1929), now rather out of date; Norman McCord, *The Anti-Corn Law League* (London, 1958), somewhat lopsided. *Britain in Europe* by R. W. Seton-Watson (London, 1937) is still of value and has many quotations from the diplomatic correspondence, but it has been overtaken by *The Foreign Policy of Victorian England* by Kenneth Bourne (Oxford, 1970), a brilliant survey of general policy. *The Victorian City,* edited by Harold J. Dyos and Michael Wolff (London, 1973), has a mine of information on urban development, as does the older work on *The Growth of Cities in the Nineteenth Century* by A. F. Weber (New York, 1899).

J. H. Clapham, *An Economic History of Modern Britain,* vol. l, *The Early Railway Age, 1820–1850,* 2d ed. (Cambridge, England, 1939), and vol. 2, *Free Trade and Steel, 1850–1866* (Cambridge, England, 1932), is indispensable and gives references to most of the material up to the date of publication. L. H. Jenks, *The Migration of British Capital to 1875,* 2d ed. (New York, 1938), studies the relations between finance and policy, but is surpassed by Brinley Thomas, *Migration and Economic Growth: A Study of Great Britain and the Atlantic Economy* (London, 1954), and Desmond C. St. Martin Platt, *Finance, Trade, and Politics in British Foreign Policy, 1815–1915* (Oxford, 1968).

Prussia

Theodore Hamerow, *Restoration, Revolution, Reaction* (Princeton, 1961), surveys the period 1815–70. *Social Foundations of German Unification* by the same author (Princeton, 1969) is a more detailed account, focusing on the fifties and sixties. Both are good. *Der Aufsteig des Reiches* by Erich Marcks (Stuttgart, 1936) adds little. *History of Germany in the 19th Century* by Heinrich von Treitschke, 7 vols. (London, 1915-19), is primarily a work of polemics, forcefully written. Vol. 2 of *A History of Modern Germany* by Hajo Holborn (New York, 1967) covers our period and is the most distinguished account of the subject in English. *Die deutsche Einheitsbewegung* by Egmont Zechlin (Frankfurt, 1967) combines some analysis, much polemic, and some passages from the Prussian archives. Maurice Baumont, *La grosse industrie allemande et le charbon* (Paris, 1928), is a competent survey, though less judicious than Pierre Benaerts, *Les origines de la grande industrie allemande* (Paris, 1933). W. O. Henderson, *The Zollverein* (Cambridge, England, 1939), is the essential work on the subject. On demography there is Mack Walker, *Germany and Emigration, 1816–1865* (Cambridge, Mass, 1964), balanced and authoritative.

Russia

Background in *Endurance and Endeavor* by J. N. Westwood, 2d ed. (Oxford, 1981), an excellent account that describes the years from 1812 to 1980; *Russia: A Short History* by Michael T. Florinsky, 2d ed. (New York, 1969), an older and less detailed work that lacks the balance of *A History of Russia* by Nicholas V. Riasanovsky, 4th ed. (Oxford, 1984); and *The Russian Empire, 1801–1917* by Hugh Seton-Watson (Oxford, 1967), the fullest account in English of the years it covers. On more specialized themes: Hugh Seton-Watson, *The Decline of Imperial Russia* (New York, 1952), nothing before 1855, though the first chapter has some good points; Barbara Jelavich, *A Century of Russian Foreign Policy* (Philadelphia, 1963), a complete picture of the period; and N. V. Riasanovsky, *Nicholas I and Official Nationality in Russia* (Berkeley, 1959), a classic work that will be read as long as anyone cares about Russian history or, for that matter, about history at all. The basic source for the period is still Theodor Schiemann, *Geschichte Russlands unter kaiser Nikolaus I,* 4 vols (Berlin, 1904–1919); it has valuable documentary appendixes. Constantin Grunwald, *Tsar Nicholas I* (London, 1954), though slight, brings out the importance of his early years—an altogether attractive portrait; no doubt the way Nicholas I would prefer to be remembered. *Nicholas I: Emperor and Autocrat of All the Russians* by W. Bruce Lincoln (Bloomington, 1978) is a felicitous addition to the literature available in English. The life of *Imperator Aleksandr II* by S. S. Tatishchev, 2 vols. (St. Petersburg, 1903), is less useful; nevertheless, it is important, though often evasive, for the peace congress. There are several fine books on the particular wrinkles of Russian history: J. S. Curtis, *The Russian Army under Nicholas I* (Durham, N. C., 1965), a definitive study; Martin Malia, *Alexander Herzen and the Birth of Russian Socialism* (Cambridge, Mass, 1962), a brilliant work, much broader than its title suggests; Philip Squire, *The Third Department: The Establishment and Practices of the Political Police in Russia of Nicholas I* (Cambridge, England, 1968), a model of brief exposition; N. V. Riasanovsky, *A Parting of Ways: Government and the Educated Public in the Russia of Nicholas I* (Oxford, 1976), an accomplished and elegant work from which all later work will derive; Jerome Blum, *Lord and Peasant in Russia, from the Ninth to the Nineteenth Century* (Princeton, 1961), and W. L. Blackwell, *The Beginnings of Russian Industrialization, 1800–1960* (Princeton, 1968), both good for economic affairs.

The Crimean War

Sources—Official Publications

Great Britain

Foundations of British Foreign Policy from Pitt (1792) to Salisbury (1902), edited by H. W. V. Temperley and L. M. Penson (London, 1938), gives a random selection of documents from 1792 to 1902. Those on the Crimean war include a few documents erratically chosen from the Austrian archives. The *Sessional Papers, Eastern Papers,* vol. 61 (London, 1854), contain protocols of the conferences as well as a few important diplomatic dispatches. *Hansard's Parliamentary Debates,* 3d series, vols. 124-62 (London, 1853–56), give the proceedings in Parliament.

Prussia

Prussian foreign policy can be followed from the time of the agreement of Olmütz. *Preussens auswärtige Politik, 1850–1858,* edited by Heinrich Poschinger, 2 vols. (Berlin, 1902), reproduces Manteuffel's dispatches. Poschinger also published Bismarck's reports from Frankfurt as *Preussen in Bundestag, 1851 bis 1859,* 4 vols. (Leipzig, 1882–84); this collection has largely been superseded by the relevant volume in Bismarck's collected works. *Akenstücke zur orientalischen Frage,* edited by Julius von Jasmund, 3 vols. (Berlin, 1855–59), gives mainly the correspondence between Prussia and Austria during the war.

Russia

A. M. Zaionchkovskii, *Vostochnaya voyna, 1853–1856: Prilozheniya,* 2 vols. (St. Petersburg, 1908–13), has an indispensable collection of documents on the origins of the war. Apart from this the Russian material is a muddle, thanks to the Bolshevik practice of leaking segments in a polemical way. The 1936 issue of their magazine *Krasny Archiv* published a collection of documents on the congress of Paris.

Sardinia (and the Secondary Italian States)

The role played by Sardinia in the Crimean war spearheaded the unification of Italy, at any rate in the eyes of Italian historians. There is therefore an enormous amount of material on the subject, as well as on the relations among the Italian states during the war. Here come *Le relazioni diplomatiche fra l'Austria e il Regno di Sardegna,* edited by Franco Valsecchi, vols. 3-4 (Rome, 1963), on the period from 1849 to 1857; *Le relazioni diplomatiche tra la Gran Bretagna e il Regno di Sardegna,* edited by Federico Curato, vols. 4-5 (Rome, 1968), 1848–56; *Le relazioni diplomatiche fra l'Austria e il Granducato di Toscana,* edited by Angelo Filipuzzi, vol. 4 (Rome, 1968), 1853–56; *Le relazioni diplomatiche fra la Francia e il Granducato di Toscana,* edited by Armando Saitta, vol. 2 (Rome, 1959), 1851–57. All these have been published by the Instituto Storico Italiano per l'Età moderna e contemporanea. In addition, Curato has edited *Il carteggio diplomatico di Sir James Hudson,* 2 vols. (Turin, 1956), which gives the reports of the British ambassador (translated into Italian) between 1852 and 1856.

Others

Acte și documente relative la istoria renașterii Romîniei . . ., 10 vols. (Bucharest, 1889–1909), published by the Academia Româna, of little value for the period before 1857.

Sources—Private Papers

Rulers

Austria.—The letters of Francis Joseph contain little of either personal or political interest. *Briefe kaiser Franz Josephs I an seine Mutter, 1838–1872,* edited by Franz Schnürer (Munich, 1930), has a few important points. His correspondence with Nicholas I before the Crimean war is reproduced by Hanns Schlitter, *Aus der Regierungszeit Franz Joseph I* (Vienna, 1919), and in Joseph Redlich, *Kaiser Franz Joseph von Österreich* (Berlin, 1928). *Erinnerungen an Franz Joseph I,* edited by Eduard Steinitz (Berlin, 1931), adds nothing.

France.—No historical figure is more cryptic than Napoleon III. He wrote few letters; fewer survived. The only published fragments are in *Napoléon III et le prince Napoléon: Correspondance inédite publiée,* edited by Ernest d'Hauterive (Paris, 1925). One or two pertain to the Crimean war.

Great Britain.—The papers of Prince Albert at Windsor are supposed to contain much data, but it is not revealed in the official life by Theodore Martin, 5 vols. (London, 1876–80). *Letters of the Prince Consort, 1831–1861,* edited by Kurt von Jagow (New York, 1938), gives a smattering of his correspondence with his German relatives, little of value. *The Prince Consort and His Brother,* edited by Hector Bolitho (New York, 1934), reproduces 200 letters between the two, most of them trivial. On the other hand, *The Letters of Queen Victoria* are very important. They are in three series of three volumes each. The first series edited by A. C. Benson (London, 1907), covers the period of the Crimean war.

Prussia.—Frederick William IV liked to write letters. The most useful collection is the oldest: *Aus dem Briefwechsel Friedrich Wilhelms IV. mit Bunsen,* edited by Leopold von Ranke (Leipzig, 1873). There is also *König Friedrich Wilhelm IV. Briefwechsel mit Rudolf Camphausen,* edited by Erich Brandenburg (Berlin, 1906): *Briefwechsel zwischen König Johann von Sachsen und Friedrich Wilhelm IV. und Wilhelm I. von Preussen,* edited by Johann Georg, Duke of Saxony (Leipzig, 1911); and *Revolutions-briefe, 1848: Ungedrucktes aus dem Nachlass König Friedrich Wilhelms IV. von Preussen,* edited by Karl Haenchen (Leipzig, 1930).

Russia.—There is some original correspondence in the last volume of the book on Nicholas I by Schiemann and in both volumes of the life of Alexander II by Tatishchev, cited respectively in the second section above. S. W. Jackman *Romanov Relations* (London, 1969), gives the correspondence between Nicholas I and his sister; there is not much after 1849.

Sardinia.—The official life of *Vittorio Emanuele II di Savoia* by Giuseppe Massari (Rome, 1878) has some original material.

Others.—*Aus meinem Leben und aus meiner Zeit* by Ernst II, Duke of Saxe-Coburg, 3 vols. (Berlin, 1887–88), though mainly devoted to German affairs has some curious data on Napoleon III. *Grossherzog Friedrich I. von Baden und die deutsche Politik von 1854 bis 1871,* edited by Hermann von Oncken, 2 vols. (Stuttgart, 1927), also has scattered bits of original information.

Prime and Foreign Ministers

Austria.—*Briefe des Staatskanzlers fürsten Metternich-Winneburg . . . und des Aussern, grafen Buol-Schauenstein, 1852–1859,* edited by Carlo J. Burckhardt (Munich, 1934), reproduces Metternich's complaints against the policy of his successor.

France.—The most pro-Austrian foreign minister of the Second Empire is the focus of Bernard H. M. d'Harcourt, *Diplomatie et diplomates: Les quatres ministères de M. Drouyn de Lhuys* (Paris, 1882), still useful for the period 1852–55. Also: P. L. E.

Pradier Fodere, *M. Drouyn de Lhuys* (Paris, 1881) and Warren F. Spencer, "Eduard Drouyn de Lhuys and the Foreign Policy of the Second French Empire" (Ph.D. thesis, University of Pennsylvania, 1955). The latter has much detailed information. On Walewski: two doctoral theses, Francoise Chalamon de Bernardy, "Un fils de Napoleon I" (Sorbonne, 1951); James Bloomfield, "Count Walewski's Foreign Ministry" (University of Pennsylvania, 1971); an inadequate life by Philippe Poirson (Paris, 1943).

Great Britain.—Lord Aberdeen by Muriel E. Chamberlain (London, 1983), is the best recent account. It supersedes the earlier biographies by Lady Francis Balfour, 2 vols. (London, 1922) and A. C. Stanmore (London, 1893). The private papers of Palmerston have recently been moved from the British Museum to the National Registry of Archives. There are a few fragments in *The Life of Henry John Temple, Viscount Palmerston, 1846-1865* by Evelyn Ashley, 2 vols. (London, 1876). Malmesbury (f.s. 1852) wrote *Memoirs of an Ex-Minister,* 2 vols. (London, 1884); they are dreary and inaccurate. Clarendon has a superficial life by Herbert Maxwell, 2 vols. (London, 1884); his private papers at the Bodleian Library are indispensable. *Lord John Russell* by John Prest (Columbia, S. C., 1972), is an almost impeccable work of political biography, far surpassing the earlier official life by Spencer Walpole, 2 vols. (London, 1889); his *Later Correspondence,* edited by G. P. Gooch, 2 vols. (London, 1925), includes everything of value from his papers (in the Record Office) on foreign affairs.

*Prussia.—*On Radowitz (f.m. 1850), a full collection of *Nachgelassene Briefe und Aufzeichnungen zur Geschichte der Jahre 1848-1853,* edited by Walter Möring Stuttgart, 1922). Poschinger edited the *Denkwürdigkeiten* of Manteuffel, 3 vols. (Berlin, 1901), as well as the correspondence mentioned earlier.

*Russia.—*The last two volumes of the *Lettres et papiers* of Nesselrode (Paris, 1911-12) have a good deal of material. There is nothing on Gorchakov.

*Sardinia.—*The diary of Dabormida (f.m. 1850-55) is used by Luigi Chiala, *L'Alleanza di Crimea* (Turin, 1879). The correspondence of Cavour is the single most important source in any language for Sardinian diplomacy in the Crimean war. The *Lettere edite ed inedite di Camillo Cavour,* edited by Chiala, 6 vols. (Turin, 1883–87), have much material on Cavour's dealings with Napoleon III; *Cavour e l'Inghilterra,* 2 vols. (Bologna, 1933), gives his correspondence with V. E. d'Azeglio (amb. to Great Britain).

*Others.—*Friedrich Beust (f.m. Saxony) wrote his memoirs as *Aus drei Viertel-Jahrhunderten,* 2 vols. (Stuttgart, 1887)—interesting though unreliable.

Ambassadors

*Austria.—*The two volumes of diary by Joseph Alexander von Hübner (amb. at Paris, 1849–59), *Neuf ans de souvenirs* (Paris, 1904), are very important. There is a hole between March 1849 and January 1850. *Aus den Briefen des Grafen Prokesch von Osten* (Vienna, 1896) has a little about Frankfurt in the early fifties.

France.—Louis Thouvenel published selections from the papers of his father, Edouard Thouvenel. Some of them cover the period when he was French ambassador at Constantinople: *Nicholas Ier et Napoléon III, 1852–1854* (Paris, 1891), on the outbreak of the war; *Trois années de la question d'Orient, 1856–1859* (Paris, 1897), on its sequel; *Le secret de l'empereur,* 2 vols. (Paris, 1889), and *Pages de l'histoire du Second Empire* (Paris, 1903), the most helpful. Maurice Parturier, *Morny et son temps* (Paris, 1969), has some information. Gerda Grothe, *Der Herzog von Morny* (Berlin, 1966), is a crude summary. In 1870 the Germans looted the French foreign office and stole the main body of Thouvenel's private ministerial correspondence. These so-called Cerçay Papers were held, unused, by the Germans until the treaty of Versailles compelled their restitution. They are now in the Archives du Ministère des Affaires éstrangëres in twenty-one volumes. A large body of Thouvenel's private correspondence has recently been discovered by Lynn M. Case and is now in the Archives Nationales on twenty-five rolls of microfilm. Case brings together the results of his twenty years' researches in *Edouard Thouvenel et la diplomatie du Second Empire* (Paris, 1976).

Great Britain.—Many British ambassadors received biographies, most of little value. The best is still the *Life of the Right Honourable Stratford Canning* by Stanley Lane-Poole, 2 vols. (London, 1888). The private papers of Stratford are in the Record Office. The trenchant spirit that marches through his official dispatches is captured there as well. The *Diplomatic Reminiscences* of Lord Augustus Loftus (British amb. at Berlin), 4 vols. (London, 1892–94), are silly. The papers of Cowley are used unsuccessfully by F. A. Wellesley in *The Paris Embassy during the Second Empire* (London, 1928).

Prussia (and the Smaller German States).—The essential source for Bismarck is the collection of *Politische Schrifte* in his *Gesammelten Werke.* Vol. 1, edited by Hermann von Petersdorff (Berlin, 1924), and vol. 2, edited by Friedrich von Thimme (Berlin, 1925), give virtually all his correspondence during his years at Frankfurt. These and the other volumes in the *Gesammelten Werke* (15 vols. bound in 19) are perhaps the only collection of diplomatic documents which can be recommended as bedside reading to the layman. Bismarck recounted his experiences at Frankfurt in *Gedanken und Erinnerungen,* 3 vols. (Stuttgart, 1898–1922), which ranks with the most remarkable political memoirs ever written, not least for its inaccuracy of detail. His judgments lack any sense of historic truth or philosophic detachment; they seek merely to discredit those who ran Prussia at the time—jibes against the military chiefs; attacks on Manteuffel; hits at Frederick William IV. Reviewing Bismarck's arguments, it is difficult to resist the impression that Prussian policy in the Crimean war had one overriding fault in his eyes: it was being conducted by men other than Bismarck. Of the other ambassadors, *Russland, 1851–1871: Aus den Berichten der bayerischen Gesandtschaft in St. Petersburg,* edited by Barbara Jelavich (Wiesbaden, 1963), has some interesting sidelights on Russia during the war.

Russia.—There are only two sets of private papers, but both are important. The *Politischer und privater Briefwechsel* of Peter von Meyendorff (amb. to Berlin), edited by Otto Hoetzsch, 3 vols. (Berlin, 1923), is essential for the origins of the war. A. P. Zablotsky-Desyatovsky, *Graf P. D. Kiselev,* 3 vols. (Berlin, 1883), has a good bit on Franco-Russian relations after the war.

Other Witnesses

To be complete this would include almost every public figure of the war years. I have tried to cut it down to those who were primarily concerned with foreign affairs.

Austria.—The *Tagebuch des Polizeiministers Kempen von 1848 bis 1859,* edited by Josef Karl Mayr (Vienna, 1931), has some interesting points.

France.—Napoléon Eugène Beyens, *Le second empire vu par un diplomate belge,* 2 vols. (Paris, 1924–26), is more interesting for atmosphere than for facts.

Great Britain.—The various volumes of Nassau Senior's conversations, too numerous to list, have scraps of information. A particularly important fragment on the "Cowley interview" is preserved by his daughter, Mary Charlott Mair Simpson, in *Many Memories of Many People* (London, 1898). *The Greville Memoirs,* edited by Lytton Strachey and Roger Fulford, 8 vols. (London, 1938), are very important. Greville was clerk to the Privy Council from 1821 to 1859 and therefore in a position to know a good deal about the details of party politics and the methods and personal qualities of the leading men of the country. The *Autobiography and Memoirs of Argyll,* 2 vols. (London, 1906), has some points of value. So does *The Correspondence of Lord Aberdeen and Princess Lieven, 1832–1854,* edited by E. J. Parry, 2 vols. (London, 1938–39). The third and fourth volumes of the *Life of Benjamin Disraeli* by W. F. Monypenny and George E. Buckle (London, 1913) have some material, though somewhat tendentious in arrangement. The first volume of *Gladstone* by Richard Shannon (Chapel Hill, N. C., 1982) is of interest for the parliamentary debates during the war. David Urquhart is still in need of a biographer; the life by Gertrude Robinson (London, 1920) does not go deep. The second volume of the classic *History of the Times* has the subtitle *The Tradition Established* (London, 1939). It has an enormous stock of material, especially on Delane, and a valuable appendix as an added bonus.

Prussia (and the Smaller German States).—The Saxon diplomat, Karl Friedrich Vitzthum von Eckstädt, ranks as an independent observer for the period: *St. Petersburg und London in den Jahren 1852–1864,* 2 vols. (Stuttgart, 1886); *Berlin und Wien in den Jahren 1845–1852* (Stuttgart, 1886). *Briefe des Generals Leopold von Gerlach an Otto von Bismarck,* edited by Horst Kohl (Stuttgart, 1912), has some material of value; Gerlach's *Denkwürdigkeiten,* edited by his daughter, 2 vols. (Berlin, 1891–92), is less useful.

Russia.—A. F. Tiutcheva, *Pri dvore drukh imperatorov Vospominaniia, Dneviki,* vol. 1 (Moscow, 1928), is an unusually perceptive diary by a young maid of honor at the court of Nicholas I.

Secondary Works

Countries

Austria.—*Die orientalische Politik Oesterreichs seit 1774* by Adolph Beer (Prague, 1883), despite its age, is a work of great penetration. *Die deutsche Frage und der Krimkrieg* by Franz Eckhart (Berlin, 1931) is excellent and supersedes *Der Krimkrieg und die österreichische Politik* by Heinrich Friedjung (Stuttgart, 1907). There are some good books on the Austrian ambassadors: *Die Berliner Mission des grafen Prokesch-Osten, 1849-1852* by Joachim Hoffmann (Berlin, 1959), essential for Austro-Prussian relations before the war; *Der freiherr von Hübner, 1811-1892* by Friedrich Engel-Janosi (Innsbruck, 1933), also good, though not a replacement for Hübner's diary; *Graf Buol-Schauenstein in St. Petersburg und London* by Waltraud Heindl (Vienna, 1970), equally instructive. Charles W. Hallberg, *Franz Joseph and Napoleon III* (New York, 1955), laments the lost alliance. Bernard Unckel, *Österreich und der Krimkrieg* (Lübeck, 1969), implies that it was not there to lose.

France.—A modern treatment is still to seek. The best account is the book by Simpson, referred to above, on *Louis Napoleon and the Recovery of France.* Edmond Bapst, *Les origines de la guerre de Crimée* (Paris, 1912), does not go very deep, though it contains a number of documents that are otherwise hard to come by. Alyce E. Mange, *The Near Eastern Policy of the Emperor Napoleon III* (Urbana, 1940), is a crude summary. Franklin C. Palm, *England and Napoleon III* (Durham, N. C., 1948), has some good points.

Great Britain.—The outstanding, though somewhat dated, work is H. W. V. Temperley, *England and the Near East: The Crimea* (London, 1936). There is an odd study of public opinion in Kingsley Martin, *The Triumph of Lord Palmerston* (London, 1924). Both give out in 1854. The essential work for political and economic history is Olive Anderson, *A Liberal State at War* (London, 1967), with which J. B. Conacher, *The Aberdeen Coalition* (Cambridge, England, 1968), compares favorably. H. C. F. Bell, *Lord Palmerston,* 2 vols. (London, 1936), is probably the best biography, though by no means definitive. The life of Jasper Ridley (London, 1970) is lively and entertaining, but sloppy on details. Phillip Guedalla, ed., *Gladstone and Palmerston* (London, 1928), gives the correspondence of the two men from 1851 to 1865. Donald Southgate, *'The Most English Minister. . . ': The Policies and Politics of Lord Palmerston* (London, 1966), has some points of value.

Prussia.—Some good books here: Kurt Borries, *Preussen im Krimkrieg* (Stuttgart, 1930), authoritative and well documented; Helmut Böhme, *Deutschlands Weg zur Grossmacht, 1848-1881* (Cologne, 1966), good on Frederick William IV; Arnold Oskar Meyer, *Bismarcks Kampf mit Österreich im Bundestag zu Frankfurt* (Berlin, 1927), also instructive, though it judges too narrowly from the Prussian side. Walther Fuchs, *Die deutschen Mittelstaaten und die Bundesreform, 1853-1860* (Berlin, 1934), is the best book on the subject. Peter Hoffman, *Die diplomatischen Beziehungen zwischen Württemberg und Bayern in Krimkrieg . . .* (Stuttgart, 1963); Reinhold Müller, *Die Partei Bethmann-Hollweg und die orientalische Krise, 1853-1856* (Halle,

1926); and Peter Rassow, *Der Konflikt König Friedrich Wilhelms IV mit dem Prinzen von Preussen im Jahre 1854* (Wiesbaden, 1960), all split hairs and lack substance and shape.

Russia.—A. M. Zaionchkovskii, *Vostochnaya voyna,* 2 vols. with supplements (St. Petersburg, 1908–13), very good; S. M. Goriainov, *Le Bosphore et les Dardanelles* (Paris, 1910), with an important collection of documents covering the entire nineteenth century; Marceli Handelsman, *Czartoryski, Nicholas Ier, et la question du Proche Orient* (Paris, 1934), a wonderful book; Andrei N. Shebunin, *Rossiya na Blizhnem Vostoke* (St. Petersburg, 1926), rather slight.

Sardinia.—Franco Valsecchi, L'alleanza di Crimea (Milan, 1948), is excellent, especially for the alliance of January 1855. Ennio di Nolfo, *Europa e Italia nel 1855–1856* (Rome, 1967), is a more detailed account, careful and persuasive. William Roscoe Thayer, *The Life and Times of Cavour,* 2 vols. (Boston, 1912), is still the standard biography. Paul Matter, *Cavour et l'unité italienne,* 3 vols. (Paris, 1922–27), is also useful.

Turkey.—Derek Hopwood, *The Russian Presence in Syria and Palestine, 1843–1914* (Oxford, 1969), has some information on the Holy Places. Moshe Ma'oz, *Ottoman Reform in Syria and Palestine, 1840–1861* (Oxford, 1968), is a better, more detailed account. There are some penetrating essays on Stratford and the Tanzimat in *Beginnings of Modernization in the Middle East,* edited by William R. Polk and Richard L. Chambers (Chicago, 1968). Niyazi Berkes, *The Development of Secularism in Turkey* (Montreal, 1964), is bland.

Others.—Alan Dowty, *The Limits of Isolation: The United States and the Crimean War* (New York, 1971) is occasionally useful. Albin Cullberg, *La politique du roi Oscar I pendant la guerre de Crimee* (Stockholm, 1912), has quotations from the Swedish archives. Peter Gugolz, *Die Schweiz und der Krimkrieg, 1853–1856* (Basel, 1965), is interesting on this side issue. Also on side issues: Emanuel Halicz, *Danish Neutrality during the Crimean War (1853–1856): Denmark between the Hammer and the Anvil* (Odense, 1977); Jon V. Kofas, *International and Domestic Politics in Greece during the Crimean War* (Boulder, 1980).

Diplomatic Histories

Many of the earlier works were written by writers who had some political or personal axe to grind. *The Invasion of the Crimea* by Arthur W. Kinglake, 8 vols. (London, 1883–87) blames the war on Napoleon III; *Diplomatic Study on the Crimean War* by Aleksandr G. Jomini, 2 vols. (London, 1882), gives the official Russian version. Both have a propagandist character, the more dangerous because it is concealed by an air of scholarly impartiality. *La guerre de Crimee* by Eugene Guichen (Paris, 1936) is another anthology of archival quotations, heavy in style, atrocious in organization. V. J. Puryear, *England, Russia and the Straits Question, 1844–56* (Berkeley, 1931), and *International Economics and Diplomacy in the Near East, 1834–52* (Berkeley, 1935), have novel, if untenable ideas. Many of them are repeated in *Krymskaya voyna* by E. V. Tarle (Moscow, 1950) which gives only a smattering of the Russian archives. Ann Pottinger Saab, *The Origins of the Crimean Alliance* (Charlottesville, 1977), sees the war as a struggle over influence in the Near East; it is written with a rather trenchant pen. *Étude sur les origines de la guerre de Crimée* by Luc Monnier (Geneva, 1977) is a lively posthumous narrative with material from the archives of Prince Napoleon I and Napoleon III. There is a collection of most valuable essays in *Crimean War Diplomacy* by Gavin B. Henderson (Glasgow, 1947). Unfortunately, they are not arranged in chronological order. The most extensive account of the diplomacy of the war is Paul Schroeder, *Austria, Great Britain and the Crimean War* (Ithaca, 1972). It picks on Palmerston and Clarendon and cheers for Buol, more convincingly in some places than in others, but still it is, on the whole, a most impressive achievement. *The Peace of Paris, 1856* by Winfried Baumgart (Santa Barbara, 1981) is the best history of the congress, though it is based only on the Austrian archives. Ennio di Nolfo, *Adam J. Czartoryski e il congresso di Parigi* (Padua, 1964), is a most illuminating book which derives from Czartoryski's private papers (Warsaw) as well as from the British and French archives. The immediate aftermath of the war is in W. G. East, *The Union of Moldavia and Wallachia* (Cambridge, England, 1929), and T. W. Riker, *The Making of Roumania* (London, 1931); the latter is the better of the two. There are some excellent books on the postwar period. François Charles-Roux, *Alexandre II, Gortchakoff et Napoléon III* (Paris, 1913), covers 1856 to 1870, but is most valuable for the years before 1863; there are many quotations from the French archives. Werner Mosse, *The Rise and Fall of the Crimean System* (London and New York, 1963), covers the same period less successfully: for example, it ignores France and like many other books, arbitrarily and, I think, wrongly, equates the "Crimean system" with the terms of the treaty of Paris, neglecting other aspects, such as the Anglo-French alliance. Ernst Schule, *Russland und Frankreich vom Ausgang des Krimkrieges bis zum italienischen Krieg, 1856–59* (Berlin, 1935), is a more detailed survey. Christian Friese, *Russland und Preussen von Krimkrieg bis zum polnischen Aufstand* (Berlin, 1931), is also good.

Military Histories

Colwyn E. Vulliamy, *Crimea: The Campaign of 1854–56* (London, 1939), describes the horrors of the war. Sir William Howard Russell, *The British Expedition to the Crimea,* new and rev. ed. (London, 1977), is an account written by *The Times* correspondent at the war. General Sir Edward Bruce Hamley, *The War in the Crimea* (London, 1891), is a short but authoritative summary of the military operations. Cecil Woodham-Smith, *Florence Nightingale* (London, 1950), is good on the administrative side of the war, though John Sweetman, *War and Administration: The Significance of the Crimean War for the British Army* (Edinburgh, 1984), is better and more recent. On naval history: Bernard Brodie, *Sea Power in the Machine Age* (Princeton, 1947); C. J. Bartlett, *Great Britain and Sea Power, 1815–1852* (Oxford, 1963); and especially Wilhelm Treue, *Der Krimkrieg und die Entstehung der modernen Flotten* (Göttingen, 1954). Germain Bapst, *Le marechal Canrobert,* 6 vols. (Paris, 1898–1913); Victor Bernard Derrécagaix, *Le merechal Pellissier, duc de*

Malakoff (Paris, 1911); and Brison D. Gooch, *The New Bonapartist Generals in the Crimean War: Distrust and Decision-making in the Anglo-French Alliance* (The Hague, 1959), describe the role of the French commanders. F. E. I. de Todleben, *Défense de Sébastopol,* 2 vols. (St. Petersburg, 1863–74), traces Russian operations and strategy. There are two good, recent treatments: A. J. Barker, *The War against Russia* (New York, 1970), lucid and concise; Albert Seaton, *The Crimean War: A Russian Chronicle* (New York, 1977), somewhat more prosaic.

Periodical Literature

Introduction

There is an enormous stock of material in the periodicals, ranging from women's work in the defense of Sebastopol to the Four Points. It is scattered through the learned historical journals in five languages. It is an uncharted sea; and I have shrunk from listing all of it as a measure of economy. Generally speaking, I list only pieces of recent origin—say, of the last twenty years. This criterion is, of course, arbitrary and has inevitable exceptions. I have also tried to cut down my list to those articles which deal mainly with diplomacy with some articles on the military affairs thrown in. Essentially I keep to the same arrangement as the previous section.

General Accounts

There are several bibliographical essays which merit inclusion. Winfried Baumgart, "Probleme der Krimkriegforschung," *Jahrbücher für Geschichte Osteuropas* 19 (1971): 49-109, 243-64, 371-400, gives the literature since 1961. Though it analyzes only a handful of the works which it lists, it is indispensable for the student of the subject. I am less happy about the other pieces. Edgar Hösch, "Neuere Literatur (1940–1960) über den Krimkrieg," *Jahrbücher für Geschichte Osteuropas* 9 (1961): 399-434, leaves off where Baumgart begins. It is mainly on military history and treats diplomacy rather casually. Brison D. Gooch, "A Century of Historiography on the Origins of the Crimean War," *American Historical Review* 62 (1956/57): 33-58, though useful ignores literature in Russian. Gooch, "The Crimean War in Selected Documents and Secondary Works since 1940," *Victorian Studies* I (1958): 271-79, is rather slight.

Countries

Austria.—There is an excellent bibliography in Lajos Jordáky and Keith Hitchins, "The History of the Hapsburg Monarchy (1789–1918) in Romanian Historiography since 1945," *Austrian History Yearbook* 4-5 (1968/69): 303-34. It is particularly good on Austria's relations with the principalities. Julius Marx, "Polizei und Studenten," *Jahrbuch des Vereines für Geschichte der Stadt Wien* 19-20 (1963/64):

218-50, though mainly on Matternich, has a certain amount on general politics until his fall. Srbik, "Die Wiener Revolution des Jahres 1848 in socialgeschichtler Beleuchtung," *Schmollers Jahrbuch* 43 (1919): 829-68, though dated is important for the outbreak of the revolution, the dismissal of Metternich, and the Hammelauer mission. The sequel to the revolution is in Fritz Valjavec, "Ungarn und die Frage des österreichischen Gesamtstaates zu Beginn des Jahres 1849," *Historische Zeitschrift* 165 (1942): 81-98. Ferdinand Bilger, "'Grossdeutsche' Politik im Lager Radetzkys," *Historische Blätter,* no. 4 (1931), pp. 3-36, though pedestrian, contains some information and impressions. G. Zane, "Die österreichischen und die deutschen Wirtschaftsbeziehungen zu den rumänischen Fürstentümern 1774–1874," *Weltwirtschaftliches Archiv* 26 (1927): 30-47, 262-81, is seriously dated. Dénes Jánossy has produced two excellent pieces on a subject which needs much more investigation, "Die ungarische Emigration und der Krieg im Orient," *Archivum Europae Centro-Orientalis* 5 (1939): 113-275, and "Die Schweiz und die ungarische Emigration, 1849–1856," *Zeitschrift für schweizerische Geschichte* 18 (1938): 438-49. "Die Geheimpläne Kossuths für einen zweiten Befreiungsfeldzug in Ungarn, 1849–1854," *Jahrbuch des Graf Kuno Klebelsberg Institut für ungarische Geeschichtsforschung in Wein* (Vienna and Budapest, 1936), pp. 226-302, by Jánossy is less perceptive. Enno E. Kraehe, "Foreign Policy and the Nationality Problem in the Hapsburg Monarchy, 1800–1867," *Austrian History Yearbook* 3, part 3 (1967): 3-36, is important for the events just before and just after the outbreak of the Crimean war. Schroeder, "Bruck versus Buol: The Dispute over Austrian Eastern Policy, 1853–1856," *Journal of Modern History* 40 (1968): 193-217, and "Austria and the Danubian Principalities, 1853–1856," *Central European History* 2 (1969): 216-36, seeks to show that Austria never intended to annex the principalities. Leonid Boicu, "Les Principautés roumaines dans les projets de Karl von Bruck et Lorenz von Stein pour la constitution de la 'Mittle-europa' à l'époque de la guerre de Crimée," *Revue roumaine d'histoire* 6 (1967): 233-56, and Reinhold Lorenz, "Alexander Freiherr von Bach," Hugo Hantsch, ed., *Gestalter der Geschicke Österreichs* (Innsbruck, 1962), pp. 407-30, seek to show that she did. Schroeder, "A Turning Point in Austrian Policy in the Crimean War: The Conferences of March 1854," *Austrian History Yearbook* 4-5 (1968/69): 159-202, records the facts which tell in favor of Buol and finds many to record—a curious twist from his earlier view, "Austria as an Obstacle to Italian Unification and Freedom, 1814–1861," *Austrian History Newsletter,* no. 3 (1962), pp. 1-32, which is based solely on published sources. S. A. Kaehler, "Realpolitik zur Zeit des Krimkrieges—eine Säkularbetrachtung," *Historische Zeitschrift* 174 (1952): 417-78, is a skillful survey. Milorad Ekmechich, "Mit o revoluciji i Austrijska politika prema Bosni, Hercegovini i Crnoj Gori u Vrijeme Krimskog rata 1853–1856" [The myth about the revolution and Austrian policy towards Bosnia, Herzeogvina, and Montenegro at the time of the Crimean war, 1853–1856], *Godishnjak Istoriskog Drushtva Bosni i Hercegovini* 13 (1963): 95-165, argues, unconvincingly, that Austria's fear of "the revolution" was groundless. Ion Ciută, "Unele aspecte ale staţionării trupelor austriece în oraşul Bacău (1854–1857)," *Studii şi articole de istorie* 5 (1963): 457-

65, is a Marxist account which adds little. Nicolae Iorga, "Politica Austriei față de Unire. I: Inainte de conferințele din Paris [Ședința de la 6 aprilie 1912]," *Analele Academiei Române,*, ser. 2, 34, Memoriile secțiunii istorice (1912): 835-64, has some points of value.

France.—Background in Raymond T. McNally, "The Origins of Russophobia in France, 1812-1830," *American Slavic and East European Review* 17 (1958): 173-89. Lamartine's activities as foreign minister are treated in J. Salwyn Schapiro, "Lamartine: A Study of the Poetic Temperament in Politics," *Political Science Quarterly* 34 (1919): 632-43, a skillful survey despite its age. Gordon Wright, "A Poet in Politics: Lamartine and the Revolution of 1848," *History Today* 8 (1958): 616-27, brilliantly handles his relations with the constituent assembly. Neither, however, replaces the biography by R. H. Whitehouse, 2 vols. (Boston, 1912). Daniel H. Thomas, "The Reaction of the Great Powers to Louis Napoleon's Rise to Power in 1851," *Historical Journal* 13 (1970): 237-50, is an attractive piece based on a study of the ministerial archives. Richard Salomon, "Die Anerkennung Napoleons III: Ein Beitrag zur Geschichte der Politik Nikolaus I," *Zeitschrift für osteuropäische Geschichte* 2 (1912): 321-66, is incomparably the best account of the subject. There is, strangely enough, no general account of France in the Crimean war. Most of the pieces in the journals are distinguished by their pedestrian quality and are best avoided. Albert Pingaud, "La politique extérieure du Second Empire," *Revue historique* 156 (1927): 41-68, is hardly an exception but gives a few passages from the archives. There are some points of interest in G. Raindre, ed., "Les papiers inédits du Comte Walewski: Souvenirs et correspondance, 1855-68," *Revue de France* 5 (1925): 74-104. André Artonne, "Le comte de Bourqueney," *Revue d'histoire diplomatique* 66 (1952): 52-66, is fatuous. Maurice Parturier, "Morny, ambassadeur en Russie," *Revue de Paris* 76 (1969): 84-106, is surpassed by his biography. Adrien Dansette, "Napoléon III et le duc de Morny," *Annuaire-Bulletin de la Société de l'Histoire de France* 469 (1962/63): 31-41, is rather slight. Jacques Godechot and François Pernot, "L'action de représentants de la France à Turin et l'intervention sarde dans la guerre de Crimée," *Rassegna storica del Risorgimento* 45 (1958): 39-56, is illuminating on this side issue. Rondo E. Cameron and Jean Bouvier, "Une lettre inédite de Persigny (1855) à Napoléon III," *Revue historique* 230 (1963): 91-96, is useful mainly as a reflection of contemporary opinion. Stanislas Bóbr-Tylingo, "Napoléon III et le problème polonaise (1830-1859)," *Revue internationale d'histoire politique et constitutionelle* 5 (1955): 259-80, does not add much. G. B. Henderson, "Ein Beitrag zur Entwicklung der napoleonischen Ideen über Polen und Italien während des Krimkrieges," *Zeitschrift für osteuropäische Geschichte,* new ser., 4 (1934): 552-67, is a vigorous and independent exposition. L. M. Case, "A Duel of Giants in Old Stambul: Stratford versus Thouvenel at Constantinople," *Journal of Modern History* 35 (1963): 262-73, produces important documents from the French foreign ministry and the Public Record Office. Leonid Boicu, "Tentatives de pénétration du capital français dans l'économie de Moldavie (1853-1859)," *Revue roumaine d'histoire* 2 (1963): 287-326, is a most accomplished and refreshing account. F. de Bernady, "Le congrès de Paris (février-avril)," *Revue des Deux Mondes* 6 (1956): 207-23, is occasionally useful as is Pierre Rain, "Le centenaire du Quai d'Orsay et le congrès de Paris (1856)," *Revue d'histoire diplomatique* 70 (1956): 61-75. On public opinion: Philippe Gut, "La presse parisienne et la question italienne pendant le congrès de Paris (1856)," *Revue d'histoire diplomatique* 84 (1970): 228-66, an excellent account which distinguishes clearly between myth and reality.

Great Britain.—Background: Radu R. Florescu, "British Reactions to the Russian Regime in the Danubian Principalities, 1828-1834," *Journal of Central European Affairs,* 22 (1962): 27-42—solid and well documented; G. H. Bolsover, "David Urquhart and the Eastern Question, 1833-37: A Study in Publicity and Diplomacy," *Journal of Modern History* 8 (1936): 444-67—good, though rather out of date; Florescu, "Stratford Canning, Palmerston, and the Wallachian Revolution of 1848," *Journal of Modern History* 35 (1963): 227-44—a splendid analysis; Jánossy, "Great Britain and Kossuth," *Archivum Europae Centro-Orientalis* 3 (1937): 53-190—lucid and stimulating; Frank E. Bailey, "The Economics of British Foreign Policy, 1825-50," *Journal of Modern History* 12 (1940): 449-84—rich in the details of economic liberalism; J. Potter, "The British Timber Duties, 1815-60," *Economica* 22 (1955): 122-36—a dull summary; Desmond C. St. Martin Platt, "The Role of the British Consular Service in Overseas Trade, 1825-1915," *Economic History Review* 15 (1962/63): 494-512—rather slight. The whole period has been graced by the splendid work of Olive Anderson whose researches have exploded many assumptions which have been taken for granted: "Cabinet Government and the Crimean War," *English Historical Review* 79 (1964): 548-51; "Early Experiences of Manpower Problems in an Industrial Society at War: Great Britain, 1854-56," *Political Science Quarterly* 82 (1967): 526-45—models of brief exposition; "The Growth of Christian Militarism in Mid-Victorian Britain," *English Historical Review* 86 (1971): 46-72; "The Janus Face of Mid-Nineteenth Century English Radicals: The Administrative Reform Association of 1855," *Victorian Studies* 8 (1965): 231-42; "The Reactions of Church and Dissent towards the Crimean War," *Journal of Ecclesiastical History* 16 (1965): 209-20—lively and excitingly revisionist pieces, encyclopedic in range; "Economic Warfare in the Crimean War," *Economic History Review* 14 (1961/62): 34-47; "Loans versus Taxes: British Financial Policy in the Crimean War," *Economic History Review* 16 (1963/64): 314-27; "Wage-Earners and Income Tax: A Mid-Nineteenth Century Discussion," *Public Administration* 41 (1963): 189-92; "The Russian Loan of 1855: An Example of Economic Liberalism?" *Economica* 27 (1960): 368-71; "Great Britain and the Beginnings of Ottoman Public Debt, 1854-55," *Historical Journal* 7 (1964): 47-63—most remarkable acounts of economic policy, combining profound grasp and passionate analysis. After Anderson, England during the Crimean war is a squeezed orange; there is not much more that can be said about it. There are, however, a few other essays which merit inclusion. J. K. Herkless, "Stratford, the Cabinet, and the Outbreak of the Crimean War," *Historical Journal* 18 (1975): 497-523 is an exhaustively detailed analysis that extends Temperley's conclusions. J. H. Jenson and Gerhard Rosegger, "British Railway Builders along the

Lower Danube, 1856–69," *Slavonic and East European Review* 46 (1968): 105-28, goes gingerly round political questions. W. H. G. Armytage, "Sheffield and the Crimean War: Politics and Industry, 1852-1857," *History Today* 5 (1955): 473-82. A. J. P. Taylor, "John Bright and the Crimean War," *Bulletin of the John Rylands Library* 36 (1954): 501-22, combines arresting style and incorrigible subtlety. Asa Briggs, "David Urquhart and the West Riding Foreign Affairs Committees," *Bradford Antiquary*, new ser., part 39 (1958), pp. 165-81, ranges effectively over the map of Europe. His "Crimean Centenary," *Virginia Quarterly Review* 30 (1954): 542-55, though slight, is also instructive. F. de J. (Fritz de Jong), "Ernest Jones and Chartism c. 1856: Some Remarks in Connection with a Letter of That Year by Jones to Holyoake," *Bulletin of the International Institute of Social History* (Amsterdam) 5 (1950): 99-104, is surpassed by Anderson's work. The same is true of W. L. Burn, "The Age of Equipoise: England, 1848–1868," *Nineteenth Century* 146 (1949): 38-69. Temperley and Henderson, "Disraeli and Palmerston in 1857, or, the Dangers of Explanations in Parliament," *Cambridge Historical Journal* 7 (1942): 115-26, gives a good account of its subject. H. P. Collins, "Aberdeen, the Pacifist at War," *Contemporary Review* 187 (1955): 187-203, reveals only what is known already. J. R. Vincent, "The Parliamentary Dimension of the Crimean War," *Transactions of the Royal Historical Society* (1981), pp. 37-49 has a few points of interest. Rudolph Craemer, "Der Krimkrieg und die englische Politik in Südosteuropa," *Volk und Reich* 16 (1940): 636-42, is a polemic which adds nothing.

Prussia.—Not much of importance here. Francesco Cataluccio, "Brassier de Saint-Simon e la politica italiana della Prussia dal 1855 al 1861," *Achivio storico italiano* 120 (1962): 281-346, though tendentious in organization is the only work on the subject. Joachim Mai has produced several articles on economic affairs: "Das deutsche Kapital in Industrie under Handel Russlands von 1850 bis 1876," *Jahrbuch für Wirtschaftsgeschichte*. no. 2 (1968), pp. 205-36, and "Das deutsche Kapital im russischen Eisenbahnwesen 1857 bis 1876," *Jahrbuch für Geschichte der UdSSR und der volksdemokratischen Länder Europas* 12 (1968): 247-65—admirable accounts, though the earlier parts dealing with our period are rather slight. Valentin Borzunov, "Die kapitalistischen Grossmächte und der Bau der Transsibirischen Eisenbahn im den fünfziger bis achtziger Jahren des 19. Jahrhunderts," *Jahrbuch für Geschichte der UdSSR und der volksdemodratischen Länder Europas* 7 (1963): 145-71, despite its title deals mainly with Prussia.

Russia.—Background: Eugene Horvath, "Russia and the Hungarian Revolution, 1848–9," *Slavonic Review* 12 (1934): 628-45; Jánossy, "Die russische Intervention in Ungarn im Jahre 1849," *Jahrbuch des Wiener Ungarischen Historischen Instituts* I (1931): 314-35; S. Tatishchev, "Diplomatcheskii razryv Rossii s Turtsiei v 1853 g" [The diplomatic rupture between Russia and Turkey in 1853), *Istoricheskii Vestnik* 47 (1892)]: 153-76; S. Nikitin, "Russkaya politica na Balkanakh i nachalo vostochnoy voiny" [Russian policy towards the Balkans at the beginning of the eastern war], *Voprosy Istorii* 4 (1946): 3-29—all rather out of date; Charles and Barbara Jelavich, "The Danubian Principalities and Bulgaria under Russian Protection," *Jahrbücher für*

Geschichte Osteuropas 9 (1961): 349-66—somewhat better; G. H.. Bolsover, "Nicholas I and the Partition of Turkey," *Slavonic and East European Review* 27 (1948): 115-46—a sustained advocacy for the Russian government. Jacob C. Hurewitz, "Russia and the Turkish Straits: A Revaluation of the Origins of the Problem," *World Politics* 14 (1961/62): 605-32, ranges effectively over the problem. These are two good articles on historiography: V. O. Divin and N. I. Kazakov, "Ob osveshchenii nekotorykh voprosov istorii Krymskoy voyny v literature poslednikh let" [On the interpretation of certain questions concerning the history of the Crimean war in recent years], *Voprosy Istorii* 25 (1957): 141-50; I. V. Bestuzhev, "Osveshchenie Krymskoy voyny v sovetskoy istoriografii" [An interpretation of the Crimean war in Soviet historiography], *Voprosy Istorii* 39 (1964): 144-52. There are also two good articles on Russia during the war: I. N. Kovaleva, "Slavyanofily i zapadniki v period Krymskoy voyny (1853-1856 gg.)" [Slavophiles and Westerners at the time of the Crimean war (1853-1856)], *Istoricheskie Zapiski* 80 (1967): 181-206; N. M. Druzhinin, "Moskua v gody Krymskoy voyna" [Moscow at the time of the Crimean war], *Vestnik Nauk SSSR* 17 (1947): 49-63. Carl Lefevre, "Gogol and Anglo-Russian Literary Relations during the Crimean war," *American Slavic and East European Review* 8 (1949): 106-25, presumably comes in here. The aftermath of the war is in Bestuzhev, "Krymskaya voyna i revolyutzionnaya situatziya" [The Crimean war and revolutionary conditions], *Revolyutzionnaya situatziya v Rossii v 1859-1861 gg.* 3 (1963): 189-213—a most remarkable analysis of the domestic problems created by the war; Joachim Hoffmann, "Die Politik der Mächte in der Endphase der Kaukasuskriege," *Jahrbücher für Geschichte Osteuropas* 17 (1969): 215-58—an equally useful analysis of diplomatic questions.

Sardinia (and the Lesser Italian States).—André Lefèvre, "Les répercussions en Europe occidentale de l'insurrection de Milan de 1853," *Revue d'histoire diplomatique* 69 (1955): 329-46, is important for the outbreak of the war, the cabinet of Victor Emmanuel, and the impact of "the revolution" on the Austrian government. Alberto Ghisalberti, "L'alleanza di Crimea e l'opinione pubblica," *Il Risorgimento* 7 (1955): 195-222 and 8 (1956): 14-32, has some valuable material, especially during the crisis of December 1854 when it perhaps exaggerates the influence of Cavour. Paul Matter, "Cavour et la guerre de Crimée," *Revue historique* 145 (1924): 161-202, is a competent, though hurried, survey. Giuseppe Giarrizzo, "L'Inghilterra di fronte all'unificazione italiana," *Rassegna storica toscana* 6 (1960): 201-25, is often revealing, despite its cautious tone. Guido Quazza, "La politica orientale sarda nei dispacci el Tecco (1850-1856)," *Rassegna storica del Risorgimento* 48 (1961): 663-80, adds little. Carlo Baudi di Vesme, "Il Regno delle Due Sicilie durante la guerra di rimea nei documenti diplomatici francesi," *Rassegna storica del Risorgimento* 39 (1952): 395-409, and Cataluccio, "La crisi diplomatica del Regno delle Due Sicilie dopo la guerra in Crimea," *Archivio storico italiano* 109 (1951): 162-92, are interesting on this side issue. Paul Guichonnet has produced two attractive essays on the war and the congress: "l'Intervention piémontaise en Crimée et le congrès de Paris," *L'Information historique* 19 (1957): 189-97; "L'agenda di Cavour al Congresso di Parigi," *Convivium* 29 (1961): 717-21. Valsecchi, "Cavour al Congresso di Parigi," *Il Risorgimento* 8 (1956): 93-109, is useful, though by no means a replacement for his book.

Turkey.—Stanford J. Shaw, "Archival Sources for Ottoman History: The Archives of Turkey," *Journal of the American Oriental Society* 80 (1960): 1-12, is an indispensable guide for researchers. Eduard von Wertheimer, "Die Kossuth-Emigration in der Türkei," *Ungarischen Jahrbücher* 8 (1928): 377-82, is important for the crisis of 1849. On the Holy Places: Baumgart, "Politik und Religion in Syrien im 19. Jahrhundert," *Zeitschrift für Missionswissenschaft und Religionswissenschaft* 55 (1971): 104-8; Moshe Ma'oz, "Syrian Urban Politics in the Tanzimat Period between 1840 and 1861," *Bulletin of the School of Oriental and African Studies* (University of London) 29 (1966): 277-301; Bekir S. Beykal, "Die Frage der heiligen Stätten im Gelobten Lande und die Hohe Pforte," *Geschichte in Wissenschaft und Unterricht* 10 (1959): 407-16. Hurewitz, "Ottoman Diplomacy and the European State System," *Middle East Journal* 15, (1961): 141-52, is an illuminating account which draws on the Turkish archives. W. E. Mosse, "The Return of Reschid Pasha: An Incident in the Career of Lord Stratford de Redcliff," *English Historical Review* 68 (1953): 546-73, has some useful points.

Others.—Boicu, "Introducerea telegrafiei in Moldova," *Studii şi cercetări ştiinţifcei. Istorie* (Jassy) 7 (1957): 279-303, is a stimulating account of a little-known episode. N. Corivan, "Deux documents sur le choix d'un prince étranger en 1856," *Revue historique du Sud-Est européen* 7 (1930): 78-85, is rather slight. Elvire Georgescu, "Sur un projet d'organisation militaire et politique de Dobrogea en 1855, par Mehmed Sadyk-Pacha (Michel C. Czajkowski)," *Revue historique du Sud-Est européen* 8 (1931): 161-69, is not much better. Alexandru I. Gonţa, *"Firmanul pentru convocarea divanurilor ad-hoc şi problema Unirii Principatelor Române,"* Academiei Republicii Populare Romîne, Institutul de Istorie, *Studii privind Unirea Principatelor* (Bucharest, 1960), pp. 281-96, is important for the elections of 1857.

R. Gerba, "Zur Geschichte der Ereignisse in Bosnien und Montenegro 1853," *Mittheilungen des k. k. Kriegs-Archivs* 9 (1887): 83-159, despite its age, is a most illuminating essay, richly documented.

Radi Boev, "Oshte za uchastieto na Bulgari v Krimskata voyna" [More about Bulgaria in the Crimean war]. *Istoricheski Pregled* 24 (1968): 90-94, is a fly speck.

Luis Mariñas Otero, "España ante la guerra de Crimea," *Revista española de historia* 26 (1966): 410-46, exhausts the subject.

Torun Hedlund-Nyström, "The Swedish Crisis of the 1850's," *Economy and History* 6 (1963): 101-24, though somewhat tendentious in organization, is a most perceptive piece, combining knowledge and understanding.

Frank A. Golder, "Russian-American Relations during the Crimean War," *American Historical Review* 31 (1926): 462-76, is rather out of date.

Diplomatic History

There is an enormous amount of material here. I list the more general in this category and keep others under the various country-headings, no doubt an imperfect arrangement.

The articles by H. W. V. Temperley merit inclusion if only because of their effect on the historiography of the diplomacy of the war. "British Policy towards Parliamentary Rule and Constitutionalism in Turkey (1830–1914), *Cambridge Historical Journal* 4 (1933): 156-91—a sweeping survey; "Stratford de Redcliff and the Origins of the Crimean War (Part II)," *English Historical Review* 49 (1934): 265-98—a convincing defense of Stratford's policy over the Holy Places and the Menshikov mission; "The Alleged Violations of the Straits Convention by Stratford de Redcliff between June and September, 1853," *English Historical Review* 47 (1932): 216-59—an account of his duel with Thouvenel; "The Treaty of Paris of 1856 and Its Execution," *Journal of Modern History* 4 (1932): 387-414, 523-43—an agreeable summary; "The Union of Roumania in the Private Letters of Palmerston, Clarendon, and Cowley, 1855–1857," *Revue historique du Sud-Est européen* 14 (1937): 218-32—important for the crisis of 1957, as is "More Light on the Pact of Osborne, 9 August 1857," *Cambridge Historical Journal* 5 (1937): 315-23—an improvement on the article by Alice M. Carter, "New Light on the Pact of Osborne, 9 August 1857," *Cambridge Historical Journal* 5 (1937): 214-23. Franklin A. Walker, "The Rejection of Stratford by Nicholas I," *Bulletin of the Institute of Historical Research* (University of London) 40 (1967): 50-64, is a credible piece. Bernadotte E. Schmitt, "The Diplomatic Preliminaries of the Crimean War," *American Historical Review* 25 (1919): 36-67, is out of date. Johann H. Blumenthal, "Österreichische und russische Balkanpolitik, 1853–1914," *Der Donauraum* 8 (1963): 117-30, is a crude summary. Florescu, "The Rumanian Principalities and the Origin of the Crimean War," *Slavonic and East European Review* 43 (1964/65): 46-67, is not much more successful. Georg Franz, "Der Krimkrieg, ein Wendepunkt des europäischen Schicksals," *Geschichte in Wissenschaft und Unterricht* 7 (1956): 448-63, has some good points. N. Corivan, "Renseignements sur la conférence de Vienne (1855)," *Revue historique du Sud-Est européen* 8 (1931): 1-5, is bland. Handelsman, "La guerre de Crimée: La question polonaise et les origines du problème bulgare," *Revue historique* 169 (1932): 271-315, is an essay of exhaustive importance. Olive Anderson, "Some Further Light on the Inner History of the Declaration of Paris," *Law Quarterly Review* 76 (1960): 379-85, is a model of brief exposition. S. Goriainov, "Les étapes de l'alliance franco-russe (1853–1861)," *Revue de Paris* 19 (1912): 1-29, 524-43, 755-76, is still helpful. Mosse, "The Triple Treaty of 15 April 1856," *English Historical Review* 67 (1952): 203-29, is good on the relations of Austria and Great Britain, less good on the relations of these two with France. V. Boutenko, "Un projet d'alliance franco-russe en 1856 d'après des documents inédits des archives russes," *Revue historique* 155 (1927): 277-325, and F. Charles-Roux, "La Russie et l'alliance anglo-française après la guerre de Crimée," *Revue historique* 101 (1909): 272-315, exaggerate the importance of their subject. Charles-Roux, "La Russie, la France et la question d'Orient après la guerre de Crimée," *Revue historique* 109 (1912): 272-

306, is a little better. T. W. Riker, "The Concert of Europe and Moldavia in 1857," *English Historical Review* 42 (1927): 227-44, is eclipsed by his book.

Military History

The essays by generals and other military men are too numerous to list, especially as some of the most important appeared in periodicals not specifically historical—political, administrative, or general. Of the historical periodicals, the *Journal of the Society for Army Historical Research* and *History Today* are particularly useful for military history. The first gives a list of periodical articles each year in its December number, and there is more than one large-scale index of military periodicals which can be consulted in any good library. Other pieces are scattered through the learned journals in five languages. This book only touches the military side of the Crimean war; therefore, I give only preliminary indications of where they can be found.

By far the best piece on the military history of the Crimean war is Baumgart, "Der Krimkrieg in der angelsächsischen und russischen militärgeschichtlichen Literatur der seckziger Jahr," *Militärgeschichtliche Mitteilungen,* no. 2 (1970), pp. 181-94. It is rich in bibliographical references and particularly strong on technological themes. R. E. Barnsley, "The Diaries of John Hall, Principal Medical Officer in the Crimea, 1854 to 1856," *Journal of the Society for Army Historical Research* 41 (1963): 3-18, is a brief sketch of the misery of the British army in the Crimea. Hiley Addington, ed., "The Crimean and Indian Mutiny Letters of the Hon. Charles John Addington, 38th Regiment," *Journal of the Society for Army Historical Research* 46 (1968): 156-80, 206-12, is even briefer. J. S. Curtiss, "Russian Sisters of Mercy in the Crimea, 1854–1855," *Slavic Review* 25 (1966): 84-100, is admirably wise and well-informed. On battles: R. L. Blanco, "The Blundering British Army in the Crimean Campaign, 1854–1856," *Mankind* 1 (1967): 20-29, 78-81; T. F. J. Collins, "Redan Massy," *Journal of the Society of Army Historical Research* 42 (1964): 92-95; Henry G. Farmer, "Bands in the Crimean War," *Journal of the Society for Army Historical Research* 41 (1963): 19-26; N. I. Cimmer, "O sud'be Sevastopolya" [The siege of Sebastopol], *Voprosy Istorii* 45 (1970): 199-205. Abraham S. Duker, "Jewish Volunteers in the Ottoman-Polish Cossack Units during the Crimean War," *Jewish Social Studies* 16 (1954): 203-18, 351-76, is an attractive exposition. On naval history: Ernest A. Gray, "The Stone Frigates of Sebastopol," *History Today* 19 (1969): 388-96; G. A. Osbon, "The Crimean Gunboats," *Mariner's Mirror* 51 (1965): 103-16, 211-20.

INDEX

Åland Islands, neutralization of, demanded by Great Britain, 177.

Aberdeen, British prime minister: meets Nicholas I (1844), 29-30; and *Charlemagne* incident, 44; attitude of, to Russia, 48, 55; Russell and, 59; becomes prime minister, 64; rise of, 65-69; and Turkey, 70, 76, 78-81, 88, 91, 93; coalition of, shaky, 95; and revolt in Greece, 106; assumptions of, disputed, 145; coalition of, defeated, 148; still has influence, 155; legacy of, 161, 163.

Administrative Reform Association, 148.

Adrianople, treaty of, 30.

Albert, prince consort: and Prussia, 138; urges peace (1855), 155.

Alexander I, Russian tsar, 25, 27, 28, 44.

Alexander II, Russian tsar: and Louis Napoleon, 20; succeeds Nicholas I (1855), 149; in Crimea, 174; approach to, of Napoleon III, 174; holds state council, 179-81; meets Napoleon III at Stuttgart, 202.

Ali pasha, Turkish prime minister: meets Thouvenel, 171; opposes Stratford, 188; Cavour disappointed by, 195.

Alliance of the Three Kings (1850), 7.

Alma, battle of (1854), 116, 122.

Antioch, 43.

Antsey, British radical, 147.

Argyll, British lord privy seal, 64.

Athens: British fleet at (1850), 34; Anglo-French negotiations at (1850), 36-37; Kornilov in, 106.

Aupick, French ambassador: pressures Turkey, 32; and the Holy Places, 42-43.

Austria: Revolution in (1848), 2; and war in Italy, 4-6; struggle of, with Prussia (1850), 7-10; alliance of, with Prussia (1851), 11, 44; makes up differences with Russia, 13; foreign duties of, 15; recognizes Napoleon III, 22; week, 24, 31, 66; suspicions of, of Russia in Balkans, 25; importance of, to Nicholas I, 27; alliance of, with England (1829), 28; and Hungarian refugees, 32; and the Straits convention, 43; and Montenegro, 49; and Eastern crisis (1853), 50-55; Russell and, 58; importance of, to Drouyn de Lhuys, 73-74; British on bad terms with, 74; Nicholas I wishes to partition Turkey with, 77; aims of, in Crimean war, 81-84; Vienna note and, 85-87; and the Buol project, 90; British distrustful of, 91, 93; Nicholas I wrong about, 96; question of, raised by Crimean war, 100-1; alliance of, with Prussia (1854), 102-5; and the Greek revolt, 106; and Sweden, 107; ultimatum from, to Russia, 108-10; Four Points and, 111-15; makes alliance with Great Britain and France (1854), 119-27; signs convention with France over Italy, 128; and the Italian question, 130-37; and Prussian neutrality, 138-39; and the Vienna conference, 141-45, 152-54, 156, 158, 160-61; sends ultimatum to St. Petersburg, 174-81; Bessarabian cession and, 183-85; denounced at congress of Paris, 194-97; guarantees Turkey, 197-98; Crimean war, a blow to, 199-200, 202-3.

Azov, Sea of, Austrian ultimatum silent on, 176.

Bach, Austrian minister of the interior, 126.

Balaklava, battle of (1854), 116-124.

INDEX